FIRST-TIME MANAGER

FIRST-TIME MANAGER

Joan Iaconetti

Patrick O'Hara

Collier Books

Macmillan Publishing Company

New York

Collier Macmillan Publishers

London

Macmillan Publishing Company
866 Third Avenue, New York, N.Y. 10022
Collier Macmillan Canada, Inc.

Library of Congress Cataloging-in-Publication Data
Iaconetti, Joan.
    First-time manager.
    Reprint. Originally published: New York : Macmillan ; London: Collier Macmillan, c1985.
    Includes index.
    1. Executives.   2. Executives—Training of.
I. O'Hara, Patrick, 1946–   II. Title.
HD38.2.I19   1987   658.4   86-24454
ISBN 0-02-085730-6

Macmillan books are available at special discounts for bulk purchases for sales promotions, premiums, fund-raising, or educational use. For details, contact:

Special Sales Director
Macmillan Publishing Company
866 Third Avenue
New York, N.Y. 10022

First Collier Books Edition 1987

10 9 8 7 6 5 4 3 2 1

Designed by Jack Meserole

First-Time Manager is also published in a hardcover edition by Macmillan Publishing Company.

Printed in the United States of America

To MAI, RAI, and NYC

and

To Michael, Kate, and Chris

Contents

Part Three Stepping Up:
Strategies to Move You Ahead

Acknowledgments

Personal thanks go to my loving parents, Frank and Mary, for providing for my education; to my wonderful aunts, Mary and Rosie, for taking me to the World's Fair and changing my life; to Marian Faux, writer, friend, and constant source of excellent advice, whose life convinced me that I could do it too; to my friends Garrison Botts, for the idea that got me started, and Joe Rauen, for the humor that kept me going; to Gayle B. Bridger, for being the best, most supportive friend and colleague imaginable; and finally, especially, to my longtime friend Bruce Bossard, writer and critic, without whose auspicious and well-timed push I would never have thought to begin writing at all.

Thanks also go to Dominic Abel, my agent, for his professionalism and willingness to answer all my questions, sometimes twice; and to editor Alexia Dorszynski and Jill Herbers, her assistant, for patient help, suggestions, and encouragement.

Authors frequently talk in this section about how their thanks also go to individuals whose precise contributions to the book have been inseparably blended in the brain's vast historical memory bank. I now understand what they mean. Still, these people deserve recognition both for their particular contributions and as authorities in the fields of management and human relations: Dr. T. H. Holmes and Dr. R. H. Rahe, Ronald Burke and Lester Bittel, Howard I. Glazer, Dr. Marshall Duke and Dr. Steven Nowicki, Taibi Kahler, Nancy Carter Ferrantella, Dr. Ronda Motycka, and Dr. William Owen.

Finally, I want to thank the hundreds of managers I've gotten to know while conducting training seminars—women and men who have taught me at least as much as the experts have.

JOAN E. IACONETTI
New York
April, 1985

To those who honor me with their love and friendship, my thanks, especially to Kate, whose patience and understanding sustained me as this book grew from idea to manuscript to finished product.

I thank all my academic colleagues for stimulating me to thought and action. And finally I must thank all the working managers I know. You are my true teachers. This book is yours.

PATRICK O'HARA
New York
April, 1985

Finally, we'd like to thank each other for the work that became this book.

Introduction

Congratulations on Your Promotion!

"Congratulations—you're the new manager." Wherever you work—a megaconglomerate or a small nonprofit organization, producing heavy machinery or programs on transcendental meditation, in a small town, on Wall Street, or in Silicon Valley—this book is an invaluable tool that will help you survive and triumph in your first months as a newly promoted manager. *First-Time Manager* was written expressly to help you carry out your new supervisory responsibilities successfully.

You were promoted, at least in part, because of your success as a salesperson, diemaker, respiratory therapist, or butcher. Despite your competence in your field, however, you may be unsure just what it is managers are supposed to do.

First-Time Manager explains what management is all about, using plenty of real-life examples. The stories you'll read throughout the book are drawn from the experiences of thousands of managers we've met in seminars and development programs. Their problems and accomplishments are the basis—and the reason—for this book.

Training managers is our business—a frustrating business, because much of the training comes too late. The managers we teach have often muddled through the first year or two on their own, working long and hard just to keep their departments afloat. They have become locked into procedures that have little to do with effective management. The training they—and you—need should have been available before their promotion, not years later.

This book, then, is written for you: the newly promoted manager who, without benefit of formal training, wants a head start on making a success of an unfamiliar job. The techniques we teach work for bank officers, head nurses, office managers, line supervisors—in short, for *any* soon-to-be-promoted manager and for experienced managers willing to learn more about proven management skills. However, this book offers you no "one-minute" solutions to managing, because there are none. Supervising and managing your staff and their work is complicated, fascinating, sometimes time-consuming, occasionally thankless, and often very rewarding work.

First-Time Manager is designed to take you through your first year as manager, from your early weeks learning the basics to the day you're ready to pursue your next promotion. On the way, you'll learn to use the **STEP-UP** program, a down-to-earth, step-by-step guide to making sense of every task you're likely to face in your new managerial career. You'll learn about the finer points of managing through checklists, charts, self-assessments, and questionnaires. Equally important, you'll gain confidence in yourself and your supervisory abilities.

Enjoy reading this book, and enjoy using it. Best of luck in your new job, and here's to your continued success.

Part One

Stepping In:

The First Three Months

1

The **STEP-UP** Program

THE **STEP-UP** PROGRAM is a systematic guide you can put to work immediately. No matter what situations you confront as a new manager, you can use **STEP-UP** to simplify them and handle them successfully.

Whether it's learning how to motivate your staff, delegate the workload, or find your way through the maze of the company budget, the **STEP-UP** program shows you, the new manager, that dealing with unfamiliar problems and issues is easier when you:

SET YOUR GOALS
TALLY YOUR RESOURCES
ENHANCE YOUR RESOURCES
PLAN YOUR ACTION

USE AND ABUSE YOUR PLAN
PLAN AND PLAN AGAIN

Whether you wanted to be a manager or not, whether you think you know what you're doing or not, whether it all seems like a nightmare or a dream come true—the **STEP-UP** approach is a tool to help you do any job better (and if you're not sure what job you're supposed to be doing, **STEP-UP** can help you with that too).

STEP-UP SET YOUR GOALS

If you're not sure where you're going, you're unlikely to get there; if you don't know what you want, neither will anyone else. The **STEP-UP** program shows you how to set realistic, measurable, specific goals so that you (and your subordinates) can work toward a common, meaningful objective.

3

STEP-UP   TALLY YOUR RESOURCES

If you don't know what you have on hand to reach your goal, you waste precious time and energy—and increase your risk of failure. Rather than drown in oceans of paper, use **STEP-UP** to take stock of your written organizational resources (including some you may not be aware you have), and choose the information you really need. We'll tell you where to find it, how to interpret it, and what questions to ask once you've digested it.

STEP-UP   ENHANCE YOUR RESOURCES

You've studied what's on paper—now find out what people can add. **STEP-UP** shows you, step by step, how to identify the co-workers who have information you need, how to approach them for objective advice, informed opinions, and inside information—and how to present yourself as a professional and a colleague while you do it.

STEP-UP   PLAN YOUR ACTION

Without a thoughtful plan, you take the long, rocky, and frustrating road. The **STEP-UP** program shows you how to stand back, look at the larger picture in your company and department, set priorities and dead-lines, and chart the quickest, most effective path to your goals.

STEP-UP   USE AND ABUSE YOUR PLAN

Once you've planned it—do it! **STEP-UP** helps you avoid the trap of overplanning, refining and polishing for so long that you never get around to putting your plan into action.

If, once in action, your plan goes awry, no one else may be willing or able to point out the split seams and frayed edges. **STEP-UP** shows you how to control and evaluate ongoing plans so you can spot and fix flaws before they become disasters. You'll also learn when junking an unworkable plan makes sense, and how to sell your staff and superiors on necessary changes.

STEP-UP   PLAN AND PLAN AGAIN

If you have only one plan, you get only one shot at being successful. No plan is foolproof, and no one can (or should) plan for every eventuality. The **STEP-UP** program shows you what commonly goes wrong with managerial plans, gives you a running start on modifying ongoing programs, and keeps you moving toward your goals despite unforeseen snags.

And when minor snags become major obstacles, **STEP-UP**'s built-in contingency plan helps you cut your losses by rethinking your objectives, salvaging what you can, and resetting your goals with the **STEP-UP** program cycle whenever needed.

As you read, you'll learn to use the **STEP-UP** program to help you make sense of your firm's products, personnel, and procedures. Each chapter begins with a newly promoted manager's how-not-to-do-it story, followed by solid why-and-how-to-do-it-right information. You'll see managers just like you in action in offices, hospitals, banks, department stores, manufacturing companies, schools, advertising agencies, government offices, and publishing firms. Everything you'll learn will give you a head start in accomplishing your goals, week by week, in your organization, your personal life, and your career.

Welcome to your new role!

When you first step into a management role—before you even begin managing—you need to know what your unit produces, the employees who do the producing, and the bosses who look over your shoulder. The next three chapters of part 1, "Stepping In," tell you all about the basics.

Your Products and Services

CALLENDER was at his first staff meeting. He had been made manager of magazine production only the week before. Callender wanted to impress his superiors and his new peers. For a week he had been learning all about the company, its aims, and the publishing business in general.

At the beginning of the meeting he felt right at home. The general manager and the chief counsel of the organization were talking about the overall goals of the company. They made no overtures to Callender, however, and Callender, knowing his place, kept quiet, although he was a little disappointed.

Toward the end of the meeting, Callender got his first chance to speak.

"Callender," said the general manager, "how many hours does it take your unit to produce a twenty-page glossy brochure?"

Well, Callender knew about his company's market position, but he did not know how many hours it would take to produce the brochure. Every eye was on him, and Callender could hardly speak.

"Well, sir, I don't know for sure. I'll have to find out."

After a moment of deafening silence, the general manager decided not to find out more things Callender did not know, and so proceeded to other things. Callender, who had learned all about the company in his first week on the job, and little about the operational details of his unit, left the meeting a shaken and discouraged new manager.

STEP-UP   SET YOUR GOALS

Why You MUST Know What Is Being Produced

You cannot afford to start off like Callender. He knew everything that he did not need to know and nothing that he needed to know. The very first thing that will be expected of you as a new manager is that you know your operations.

6

So the very first thing you must do is learn the necessary facts about *the work your office does.*

What do we mean by necessary facts?

First, you need to know the *different kinds of products (services)* that your office (business) makes (offers) on behalf of others inside or outside the firm.

You must also know the *time it takes to produce* each thing that your office provides as a product to some customer—whether that customer is inside the firm (a boss requesting a file) or outside the firm (a buyer of books).

You must know *how many products*—approved applications, classroom teaching hours, car rentals, audits of another unit's books—are produced in a day, in a week, in a month, and in a year.

You must know *who* helps make or deliver the product(s) or service(s) and how many complaints or errors each product generates.

There are some very good reasons why the first thing that you should know is information about your products or services:

1. The first questions that your superiors ask in a staff meeting will likely concern the output of your unit. (They don't expect and probably don't want you to be familiar with matters that are *their* day-to-day concerns.)

2. In learning the answers to these questions, you'll discover all kinds of interesting things about your unit's operations. (Your superiors will only want to know, for instance, that the production time for the brochure is eight days. *You*, however, may learn [with an eye toward future action] that production could be completed in seven days were it not for McGrouch, a disaffected typesetter who works at half-speed.)

3. In learning the answers to production questions, you will get to know your workers. (If your workers first meet you as a boss who makes an effort to learn, they may be more willing to make a special effort when you require learning and extra effort from them—as will certainly be the case.)

4. In focusing on production issues, you will best use your time in those hectic first four weeks on your new job. (You will be miles ahead of the idiot who spends four weeks trying to act "managerial" and the fusspot who spends four postponable weeks trying to shave five minutes from one of the unit's ten operations.)

Setting Your Specific Goals

Now it's time to set your production learning goals for the first four weeks on your new job.

You'll remember from our discussion in chapter 1 that *structuring* your goals successfully is crucial to *accomplishing* those goals. In other words, your chances of success are highest when:

· Your goals are defined in measurable terms
· Your goals in any aspect of management and in any time period are specific and few in number
· You have a realistic, specified deadline for achieving each goal
· You have tests built into each goal so you can see if you have made the progress you want

GOAL (BAD EXAMPLE)	GOAL (GOOD EXAMPLE)
Improve brochure production as soon as possible.	Cut one day from brochure production within one month by monitoring and streamlining typesetting process.
Not to get stuck in the house again this weekend.	By Thursday night, have confirmed plans for a Saturday afternoon volleyball game with the Wilsons and the Randalls. By Friday night, have ball and net in working condition. Saturday morning, order beer and hot dogs.
Get a feel for this place.	Know each and every product this unit makes and know it by the end of the week.

You have the idea now. Whether it's personal or business, if you have no clear idea of where you're going, how to get there, and when you want to arrive, the odds are you'll end up lost and frustrated.

What you need in these first several weeks on the job is knowledge—knowledge about the operations *you* oversee. You gain this knowledge by asking questions that apply in any work situation. They are What? Who? How long? and How many? (For now, don't worry about the Why?)

Again, each of these questions refers to your unit's product and how it's created. In short, any new manager in any business setting should know:

· What (is the product)?
· Who (produces the product)?
· How long (does it take to make one unit of a product)?
· How many (products are produced in a day/week/month)?
· How many (complaints are made about the product)?

Here's an example. Consider the production learning goals of J. P. Morgan, the newly appointed manager of a medium-sized branch of a big-city bank. What J.P. needs to do is:

Learn enough about his (your) department's product so that two weeks after becoming manager, he (you) can list on paper, without using notes:

1. *All of the services or products* provided by Morgan's (your) department. (Morgan needs to know all the types of accounts serviced by his branch. You need to draw up a similar list for your job.)

2. The *job(s)* that each person in Morgan's (your) unit performs. (Morgan needs to know what the tellers, service reps, note tellers, maintenance people, etc., are supposed to be responsible for. You should know the job(s) of each of your workers and know how each worker's activity contributes to your unit's output.)

3. The *production time* required for each product or service unit. (Morgan wants to know how long it takes to process a withdrawal, a deposit, the cashing of a check, etc. You will want to know how long it takes to produce a single unit of each product or service your office produces.)

4. The *percentage of complaints or errors* noted for each product or service. (Morgan needs the number of customer contacts made, and the number of complaints about each account and service. You will want to have similar information about your unit's work.)

Remember: You must know *what* you produce because you are in charge of production.

You must know *each employee's job responsibilities* because you are in charge of the workers.

You must know *how long each product takes to produce* because you must be ready to answer the questions What is the shortest time in which we can get a widget? How much staff time goes into widget production? and Are the benefits worth the effort (that is, is it cost-effective?)?

You must know *the number of complaints* because the manager must know where the problems are. And because a year from now, these first problem reports can demonstrate that productivity, accuracy, and customer satisfaction have improved . . . thanks to you.

Another case history: Let's consider the basic production information that F. Nightingale, the new nursing supervisor in a small hospital, has to discover:

1. The types of patient care offered that require a nurse's expertise (e.g., surgical, pediatric, general medical-surgical, intensive care, detoxification, etc.)
2. The duties of the RNs, LPNs, and nursing aides assigned to each unit
3. The number of nursing hours (RNs, LPNs, aides, etc.) devoted to each unit
4. The number of incident reports involving nursing practices that were filed for each unit in the previous month

Again, the key questions are What? Who? How long? and How wrong?

If you're wondering, "How do I find all this out? I don't even know where to begin," don't worry—we get to that next. The thing to remember now is that answering these questions is *your basic goal for the next four weeks*. Don't get distracted. Pursue only that information which bears directly on what your unit does. Resist the temptation (at least in this first month) to collect information that pertains to other units or to the finer details of your job. In other words, *do not* spend your first month finding out:

· What the other bank branches are producing (if you're J. P. Morgan) or the capabilities of the hospital's radiology division (if you're F. Nightingale). *Stick to your own shop.*
· Who among your employees has the best or worst attendance record, or who's the captain of the bowling team. *Stick to what they produce.*
· How long the computer takes to respond to an account verification. *Stick to a whole unit of work* (in this case the amount of time it takes to complete a transaction on a particular account).
· New ways to do existing jobs. *First find out how they do—and do not—work.*

Let's go on now to the resources you'll use in order to achieve your information-gathering goals.

THE MANAGER WITHOUT A LEARNING GOAL   Casey had been a crack appraiser for the mortgage loan division of the Federal Savings Bank. She knew houses, she knew how to get her reports in on time, and she got along well with her co-workers in the mortgage loan division. And so Casey was promoted to loan processing manager.

The previous loan processing manager had left under fire. Casey's superiors had given her little to go on other than a handshake and "you can handle it." When Casey sat at the loan processing manager's desk for the first time, she felt like a nonswimmer thrown into fifty feet of water.

There were papers, and forms, and more papers, and letters from lawyers, and brochures, and memos announcing interest-rate changes, not to mention mortgages that were assumable, "balloonable," prepayable, and convertible.

Casey put the stuff in a pile and started reading it top to bottom in order. But it was all so new, varied, and complicated that Casey's progress after three days was minimal, painful, and exhausting.

That's when Mr. Darrow, the bank's assistant counsel, called.

"Casey, I know you probably don't know this off the top of your head, but I wonder if you could pull out the report on our adjustable-rate mortgages—it's one of the three monthly sales reports—and let me know how we've been doing on that one over the last couple of months."

Casey was as apologetic as she could be.

"Well, Mr. Darrow, I think I saw the report right here. Oh . . . no. That's not it. You know I just have so many papers on my desk and I've been working day and night to get to them all. It's got to be here someplace."

Darrow, who had better things to do with his time than to listen to a free-form apology accompanied by shuffled papers, cut Casey short.

"Casey, why don't you have your secretary call me back with the figures."

Casey did hang up, but she was not the sort of person to be deterred when challenged. She, *not the secretary*, would find the report.

The next morning, Casey finally went to the secretary.

"Oh, that report. I've got your desk copy over here. I'm updating it. You know, it's funny—Darrow, over in the counsel's office, just called me for the very same figures you're asking for."

After four days of intense work, Casey had failed to find the answer (or to identify the person with the answer—in this case, her secretary) to a crucial question about her unit's operations.

Why You Must Know where to Find Information

What had Casey done wrong? Just about everything. But at this point we are most interested in why Casey's hard work in trying to learn about production was an embarrassing failure.

In the first place, Casey searched through her resources *without referring to goals* that make for success in the first weeks on a new job. Had she decided that knowledge of her products had first priority, Casey could have quickly located and set aside the sales reports. Instead, when the secretary removed the file from Casey's desk, Casey had no way of knowing that the information she needed was somewhere else. She didn't even know yet that it existed.

In addition, Casey's search for resources was *too narrow in scope*. She looked only on her desk and was going to keep slogging through the pile—and nowhere else—until she had digested it all. Which is why Casey got indigestion, while Mr. Darrow got his tidbit of information directly from the secretary, a vital resource that Casey failed to exploit.

Paradoxically, Casey's search of her resources was also *too thorough*. The new manager who tries to read all of everything will learn much that is unimportant and will only by chance stumble upon things that are important. There are ways of separating the wheat from the chaff without fingering every kernel.

When you tally your informational resources in order to become thoroughly familiar with your unit's operations, you can profit from Casey's mistakes. If you do, you will:

- List the operations under your direction and gather information about them right away
- Talk to people as well as to papers on your desk
- Recognize and give a quick ax to uninformative reading
- Resist the temptation to do it all yourself

STEP-UP   TALLY YOUR RESOURCES

Useful and Useless Information

Casey's story notwithstanding, most new managers must at some point wade through a massive pile of unfamiliar information even to find the data that will tell them about the products and services of the unit. So, given the inevitability of the paper bog, here are a few hints about how to make the best of that pile on your desk.

- If it's on glossy paper, file it or fling it. Glossy-paper brochures are generally for public consumption. In order to get to what you want to digest—hard-and-fast figures about your operations—you have to eat syrupy advertising copy and even then may get to nothing better than "and last year was another great year for our municipal bond division." Somewhere in your office there is a report with real numbers and no crap.

· If it's the union newsletter, a health-plan bulletin, or a "limited time only" opportunity to increase your company life insurance, put it in your briefcase immediately and read it only on your own time. It isn't relevant to your managerial responsibilities, particularly in the first four weeks, when learning your operations is a top priority.

· Remember always that this first search is for data pertaining to *operations*. You will see personnel action forms, you will see memos announcing meetings, you will see memos announcing training seminars, you will see memos announcing changes in expense-account policies, budget reporting policies, and the like. These are important, but *not now*. Make neat files, set the files aside, and get to them after you have acquired a command of your production operations. The put-aside files will wait, in many cases forever.

· Remember that you have two weeks to achieve your goal of becoming thoroughly familiar with your production operations. You have a real deadline, and to help you meet it you can dispense with certain other requests on your desk that have far-off deadlines or none at all. If the deadline on some requests is four or more weeks off, and the requests take little time to fill, put the requests in dated files. The date should be five days before the items are due; don't touch these files before then.

Your Specific Resources: Reading the Right Reports

Now that you've gotten rid of most of the stuff on your desk, you should be left mainly with material that will tell you a whole lot about your operations. You should have:

Production Statistics: How much did you produce this month, last month, year to date, and last year? The printing operation of a large institution might list its monthly production of brochures, pamphlets, and company newsletters.

Service Reports: How many clients your office has seen, how many customers were in the store today, how many information requests from other units were filled last week. For J. P. Morgan, our bank manager, this report might list total number of weekly transactions, broken down by type of transaction. For F. Nightingale, this report might list the week's census of patients, broken down into the number of patients per unit.

Product Lists: Sometimes this is simply the written part of the production statistics or the service reports. Each item that you produce, or each service that you provide, is listed. Sometimes there is a memo floating around listing the products alone.

Payroll Reports: This is usually the simplest list of your employees. It tells you who they are, what their title is, and how much they make.

Staffing Reports and Assignment Schedules: These reports tell you who is working where. Of J. P. Morgan's five tellers, the staffing report will tell him who is working on the business-accounts window and who is working on the regular-accounts window. Of F. Nightingale's fifty nurses, the staffing report or assignment schedules will tell her which nurses are working on the surgical floor and which nurses are working in the intensive care unit.

Incident Reports/Customer Complaint Reports/Defective Product Reports: These are reports about how your unit has screwed up (or reports about how some customer or company official *believes* your unit has screwed up, which is much the same thing when you think about it). For J. P. Morgan, it can be a report about errors made on particular accounts or by particular tellers. For F. Nightingale, it can be a report about errors made by particular nurses or in particular units.

Reports from Quality Control: In most organizations, some unit, department, or individual reviews the quality of your group's operations on a periodic basis. Copies of their reports are almost certainly in your office. Find them and know them—it's likely your superiors already do.

You'll find a sample of this kind of report on the following page. Familiarize yourself with it; the notes following should help you along. The reports in your workplace may not look exactly like this, but the resemblance should be close enough so that what you see here should help you understand better what you see at work.

Tank Bank, Midtown East Branch
SIX-MONTH PERFORMANCE AND QUALITY REPORT
July 1, 1985–December 31, 1985

	SERVICE UNITS		
	Preferred Commercial Depositors	Regular Depositors	Deposit Certificates
SERVICE MEASURES			
Service Activity			
No. of accounts (7/1/85)	500	5,000	1,500
Value of accounts at 7/1/85	$5,000,000	$4,500,000	$2,000,000
No. of new accounts/loans	90	500	400
No. of accounts/loans closed	5	700	50
Accounts at 12/31/85	585	4,800	1,850
Value of accounts at 12/31/85	$6,500,000	$4,250,000	$2,500,000
Service Quality			
Processing errors/New accounts	9	45	25
Customer complaints	25	200	75
Disbursement errors (as a % of all transactions)	1.0%	.1%	.5%
Deposit/payment record errors (% of all transactions)	.5%	.1%	.0%
Resources Applied			
Full-time employees (weekly average)	3	8	2
Average weekly payroll	$2,000	$4,000	$1,350
No. of transactions (per employee day)	50	100	2

This report contains information about the volume and dollar value of business at the beginning and end of a six-month period (the first and last entries in the service activity section). The report tells you about three distinct areas of service to depositors: preferred business depositors, regular depositors, and certificate-of-deposit holders. By reading from top to bottom in each column, you can see which services are growing and which services are shrinking. One answer to the question Why are regular deposits shrinking? suggests itself: regular depositors are shifting some of their funds over to certificates of deposit—which is indeed the case in many banks.

The form also tells you about the quality of service. It tells you the number of processing errors for new accounts: incorrect application review, too large a credit line granted, failure to complete all the steps required to initiate an account. It also tells you about customer complaints, although you need to determine what lies behind them—many certificate-of-deposit complaints are from customers confused by the myriad of interest rates and time periods attached to certificates of deposit, not from customers who have been treated poorly by your staff. Information is included in this section about the error rate in the routine day-to-day business of the branch (deposit/payment record errors).

Finally, the form tells you about resources applied to particular functions: how many people work on each activity, how much they cost, and how many transactions they process each day. With this kind of information you can find out how much it costs to process each transaction and you can see the allocation of resources among services.

Your firm may have a composite form like this, but more likely this information is spread around in pieces on reports with titles like "Service Activity," "Error and Complaint Summary," and "Personnel Staffing." Whatever they are called, gather them together and start learning what's going on in your unit.

What to Do If You Can't Find Any Reports

Some new managers come upon a report wasteland. The unit that has almost no records is not unheard of, and some newer operations have little systematic record keeping. Other units may have falsified records; records may even have been destroyed in order to protect certain individuals or to thwart top management control. If you find yourself in a report wasteland, start developing production reports, service reports, assignment reports, and complaint reports. (Use the preceding sample to help get yourself started.) By doing this, you accomplish two things: You achieve your learning goals, and you become the darling of upper management, who are usually the greatest fans of reports from operating units.

STEP-UP   ENHANCE YOUR RESOURCES

Talking to People

For all the paper you can dredge up, *people* are your most important resource. Once you have read each relevant report, talk with every person responsible for putting those reports together (often the same people you spoke to when you first requested production reports and assignment charts). The individuals who prepare these reports have the most intimate knowledge of the operations that you want to learn about. They'll translate the abbreviations, jargon, and statistics into a language that a newcomer (you) can understand. You need to learn fast, and the subordinates, peers, and superiors who write the reports about your unit's operations are crucial sources of information.

A word of caution: You may be tempted to throw yourself on the mercy of your secretary or support staff in the hope that they can tell you all the answers, or give you only the documents you really need. After all, if *they* tell you what's happening, then you don't have to go digging through all that paper and reading all those unfamiliar reports, do you?

Resist that temptation. You do.

You are the manager. Your job is to familiarize yourself with what is going on *before* you speak to subordinates (even if, as will be the case in these first weeks, you're not really sure of what you're reading). If you take this approach, *you* are the monitor—a primary management role. Your finger is lightly on everything, and you reserve the right to ask later for more in-depth information. If you let your subordinates control the information that comes to you from the start, then *they* have decided what you will monitor and, in fact, what you will manage! This is why it's important to get information first and ask questions later.

The individuals who prepare production, assignment, and quality-control reports are invaluable resources. Whether subordinates, peers, or superiors, in nearly every case they will have a better grasp than you do of the subject at hand. Your assistant who compiles the production statistics can tell you how things were a year ago or how Beasely is the one who holds the output down. The peer who handles the payroll can tell you if any of your subordinates have cause for salary grievances. The superior in charge of quality-control audits can tell you whether this year's report is better than last year's, and can explain what recommendations have been made and followed or ignored in the past. But remember that people are unpredictable resources. Approach them in the right way and they can yield priceless information. Approach them wrong and they can make a fool of you. Consider the following (unfortunately typical) story:

The Direct Approach to Finding Out Nothing

Mark Maycie, brand-new men's better clothing manager in a large department store, had conscientiously studied the last five months' worth of sales reports and projections for his departments. He realized with sinking heart and mounting blood pressure that profits for men's accessories had steadily been dropping. (He also realized why his friend Charlie, the former manager of the department, had been let go.) Mark wasn't one to give in to depression. He decided to dive into the disagreeable task ahead of him right away and find out if salesclerk morale was, as he suspected, at the bottom of the problem. He marched right out to the floor and told each salesman that he wanted to see him on his break to talk about why profits had been slipping and what the sales team could do about it.

Mark went back to his office to wait and read more reports. Three hours and five defensive, untalkative salesmen later, Mark had collected:

15 excuses
 3 changes of subject
10 criticisms of the economy
 5 criticisms of Charlie
 0 suggestions of how the sales team could possibly do any more than
   they already were to improve the department's profitability
 1 uncomfortable feeling that the guys just weren't on his side

Talking and Listening to Your Subordinates

Mark did a poor job of approaching his employees, and got worse than nothing. He ignored a few simple communication rules and talked himself right out of both essential information and future cooperation from his staff. His mistakes:

Ordering his staff to spend their breaks in his office talking with him, rather than going to them on work time when the store wasn't busy

Zeroing in on a threatening topic right away ("Why are sales slipping?") rather than finding out what each salesclerk did and what he thought the department's problems might be

Implying that the clerks were somehow responsible for falling sales before explaining the situation more fully

Expecting them to be as concerned as he was about the problem

Using your people resources means using *communication*, the lack of which, as any business school freshman can tell you, is at the root of virtually every management blunder ever made. They're right: communicating clearly and adequately is the most important skill you can develop. Managing people becomes an impossible struggle if you can't tell them what they need to know and do in a way that they can understand and accept. Management also becomes more difficult if you can't ask and listen in a way that makes employees comfortable and willing to speak frankly.

Asking the Right Kinds of Questions

It's a mistake to assume that everyone in your employ is free from axes to grind, personal biases, misinformed opinions, fear, hostility, and the need to appear as if they know exactly what they're doing. It's also a mistake to assume that because of these things, no one will answer your questions honestly. The key is to think and plan before you question. Know what you need to find out from each person. Plan for biased and even hostile answers by considering each employee's position (relatively low paid, on probation, poor performance) before talking with him or her. Consider even a small gain in knowledge a benefit.

Mark, for example, would have done well to establish himself as an interested information-gatherer rather than an inquisitor, if for no other reason than that he lacks credibility with the staff. (*They* know that his previous position was staff assistant to the store's general manager, which involved little work on the sales floor.) Mark asked questions that put everybody on the spot, and that's exactly where he ended up. Mark needed to approach people in a way that gave them a *choice* about how to answer.

One way of giving room to people you are talking to is posing an *open-ended question*. Here are some sample open-ended questions (questions that cannot be answered with a simple yes or no) that encourage the staff to talk freely, by allowing them to choose their answers and to avoid (for now) uncomfortable subjects.

1. Tell me about what you do in the department: what you sell, what you like about your job, how our suppliers treat you.
2. Tell me about the projects (or one specific project) you've been working on.
3. What's been working out well?
4. What kind of problems have you been having?
5. What effect have these problems had on your quotas/deadlines/output?

Listen carefully to what's said, whether or not you like it, agree with it, or think it's utter bull. Pay attention to tone and what goes unsaid as well: Is the employee cooperative and thoughtful, or glib and evasive, or apathetic? You can often tell from the answers to general questions whether the employee is willing or able to answer more specific questions about operational problems. The salesman who blames everything on top management and the clerk who says "What problems?" are unlikely to respond when you ask if low morale contributes to declining sales. Other employees may have a more realistic view, but may also be hesitant about opening up to you. Be prepared, then, to have this initial meeting consist of nothing more than a general conversation. Initiate things by asking open-ended questions, and allow the talk to proceed as the employee desires.

If you have a concerned employee ready to talk specifics in response to your questions, or if you have arranged a second meeting with a more hesitant (but also concerned) employee, you can zero in on specific information by asking questions like this:

1. My main concern right now is that the department's profitability has been falling. What, in your opinion, is the most important reason for this?
2. The problems have been causing delays, according to the production reports. In your opinion, would you say it's more the faulty machinery or the assembly people's absences that contribute to the delays?
3. I'm interested in getting your point of view on customer complaints. What do you think are the main causes for them? Do you think it's possible to reduce them within two months?

Whether or not you actually get useful suggestions or clues from these meetings, other important goals are being served. You're getting to know your people and how they think. You're letting them get to know you as a manager who is interested in their opinions. You're letting them know you've "done your homework" and are serious about improving the department.

Do this, and you'll have a head start on your next major goal: getting to know your subordinates (chapter 3).

Priming a Resource: Your Peers and Colleagues

Some of the reports you read may be written by people who work on the same level you do. If you are J. P. Morgan, our new bank manager, one of the report writers may be the manager of a nearby bank branch who is trying to identify the causes of customer complaints. Another report writer may be the bank vice president's assistant whose title is the equivalent of J.P.'s. J.P. should set appointments to meet with these people. It's an appropriate way to flesh out a written report and it builds relationships with colleagues whose help and support may be useful in the future.

Incidentally, peers and superiors are not as likely as subordinates to be threatened by your questions, even direct ones. Ask them why they wrote what they did in their reports. You're likely to get a very informative picture of your operations. Be aware, however, that peers' and superiors' evaluations may be inaccurate for several reasons. They are not as close as you to the operations of your unit. Their vantage point is distant. Their information may come from unreliable messengers. Your predecessor may have exaggerated your unit's foibles, or the auditor may distort the picture or convey only part of what goes on in your office.

Peers and superiors may also be biased. A fellow manager bucking for promotion may champion greater employee discipline as the cure for performance problems simply because it worked in his unit. A superior who would like to integrate your unit with another in order to get rid of *your* boss might write reports highlighting disparaging figures that are not relevant to the effectiveness of your operation (for example, high employee turnover in a simple, minimum-wage job that is attractive to transient employees).

Because even peers and superiors may circulate reports that falsely claim to give an accurate picture of operations, it also makes sense to establish relationships with other managers on your level during your first few weeks on the job. Call three or four of the people in the company who do the same things, or have the same title, that you do. Ask them to lunch.

Tell them about the reports you've been reading. Ask them what they think about information that pertains to both your job and theirs, using open-ended questions: "You know, Mr. Legree wrote thus-and-such in the Whatever report; it sounds pretty critical of the way we do things here." Then listen carefully. Answers can range from "Hmm" to "He's right" to "Legree is an ass who would like to see us all dead." Eat more lunches with the latter two managers. They'll help you understand what's really going on, or at the very least provide you with interesting gossip.

Another benefit of early and widespread contact with your peers: You become a real person to them before office politics and rumormongering can establish a false image of you.

Talking and Listening to Your Boss

Unless your boss is a tyrant (and there are some), shuffling into her office and saying "Just tell me what you want me to do" is a mistake. You need to make use of her expertise and experience while coming across as the thorough, on-the-ball, brand-new manager that you are.

Of course, you will have a meeting with your boss before (or as soon as) you start your new job. At that point, three questions are in order:

- Any problems I should know about?
- Any ongoing projects with deadlines coming in the next two months?
- What do you see as the most important projects, products, or functions of my unit?

You want the answers to these questions because you don't want to get caught off guard, and you want help in directing your information search. Anything the boss mentions in response to these questions deserves your close attention, both in day-to-day managing and in collecting relevant operational information.

If you approach your boss in this way, you accomplish several things: You let your boss know you're a self-starter, serious about the job, and willing to learn; you compliment your boss by valuing her input without wasting her time; you recognize the boss's decision-making role; you pick up some useful hints about what's important to your boss: her priorities, pet projects, and annoying tasks that she'd rather forget about and leave to *you*. (Keeping the boss unannoyed can be just as important to your success as knowing your job duties cold. More on this in chapter 4.)

STEP-UP PLAN YOUR ACTION

Plans are ideas that are expressed as actions. Getting married is an idea. Arranging for the ceremony, reception, honeymoon, and so on, are actions that carry out the idea of getting married. These arrangements constitute the plan.

Learning about your unit is an *idea*. The idea of learning becomes a *plan* for learning when you decide how to organize, read and inquire about written reports on your unit's operations. What we outline below is one way of going about organizing, reading, and inquiring.

ORGANIZING   Time Frame: Week 1, Days 1–3. (Be prepared to stay after 5 P.M, since workday distractions may interfere with the job.) Separate all of the paper on your desk into:

READING PILE	DEFERRAL PILE (EVERYTHING ELSE, SUCH AS:)
Production reports	The organization's annual report
Sales reports	
Customer statistics	Health benefit brochures
Client statistics	Company newsletter
Patient statistics	Trade journals
Complaint reports	Picnic announcements
Error reports	Carbon copies of letters
Audit reports	Position announcements
Work schedules	Memos announcing new ideas
Payroll sheets	
Position descriptions	Memos looking for volunteers
Work flowcharts/unit organization charts	Order/requisition forms
	Advertising brochures

Remember: Your job here is merely to make piles. Go through everything on your desk. Then go through everything on your secretary's (if you have one) desk that is waiting to be filed. Ask him or her to give you any reports in column 1 that may be in the files. Call around to the appropriate departments (auditing, payroll, personnel, record keeping, systems analysis) and ask them to send you any reports with information pertaining to your department.

Keep a list of people from whom you have requested reports. If they said they would send them to you, and the reports haven't arrived in three business days after you made the request, call them. Tell them you haven't received the report yet and wondered if it was in the mail. If it's remotely feasible, tell them that you would be willing to come over and pick it up if necessary.

READING   Time Frame: Week 1, Days 4–5; Week 2, Days 1–3. (Again, be prepared to use evenings and the weekend to get this job done.) Separate your reading materials into three piles. Each pile will answer a particular question in your learning goals.

WHAT	WHO	HOW WRONG
Production reports	Payroll reports	Customer complaints
Service reports	Position descriptions	Incident reports
Customer counts	Assignment sheets	Error reports
Patient counts	Work schedules	Audit reports
Client counts	Work flowcharts	Employee grievances

The fourth question in your initial learning goals—How long?—is really derived from an analysis of the *What*s and the *Who*s. That is, if ten employees service one hundred clients per hour, each transaction takes an average of six minutes.

You've got a batch of relevant reading materials in the appropriate piles. Now read! (Yes, we know some of the stuff you requested is still on its way. *Read what you already have!* The person who waits for *everything* to come in may wait forever.)

As you read, make lists of your products or services and include any of the information below that the reports provide:

PRODUCT/SERVICE	NUMBER PRODUCED	PERCENTAGE OF TOTAL	IMPORTANCE
#1	65	32	B
#2	102	51	A
#3	33	17	C

Importance is measured different ways in different organizations. "Most important" can mean the most profitable and central product your company offers, for example, Coca-Cola for the Coca-Cola company. "Most important" can mean the service that is the subject of most complaints, for example, the police department's K-9 unit in the wake of a series of brutality charges. "Most important" can mean the product your boss is most interested in. In any case, figuring out what is more and less important can help you concentrate your limited time and energy on issues that can make you, your boss, and your organization look good.

As you read, make another list of the employees under your direction.

Note where they are and what they do as well as who they are. The list below illustrates what is being done and who's doing it:

EMPLOYEE	TITLE	ASSIGNMENT	RANK
Jane L.	Registered nurse	Intensive care	Head nurse
Harry Q.	Practical nurse	Pediatrics	Staff
Sheila V.	Nurse's aide	Floating	Staff

Getting the "how long" information is simply a matter of matching up people-hours and products. One approach is illustrated by the columns below:

SERVICE/PRODUCT	WEEKLY NO./TOTAL	WEEKLY LABOR	HOW LONG?
Certificates of deposit	120/$60,000	Joy (full time) Jay (half time) 40 + 20 = 60 hours	30 minutes per C.D./ $1,000 per hour

As you see, by knowing production totals and labor inputs, you can figure time expenditures per unit of production. With exact dollar figures you can compute how much is produced per hour in dollar terms.

The next step is to incorporate the "How wrong?" information into what you already have. This involves adding columns to the production list you've already created. Below is column 1 of our same production list with "Number of Complaints" and "Workers" columns added:

PRODUCT/ SERVICE	NUMBER AND/OR PERCENTAGE OF COMPLAINTS	WORKERS
#1	10 (17% error rate)	Harry (7), Sam (3)
#2	0 (0% error rate)	
#3	3 (10% error rate)	Leslie (3)

Remember, just because Harry, Sam, and Leslie are involved in the errors does not mean that the errors are their fault. The machinery or the materials may be at fault. You list their names simply because they are people you will need to talk to in order to find out what the problem might be, which leads us to our next order of business.

INQUIRING   Time Frame: Week 2, Days 3–5 (and earlier). Decide whom you need to talk to, and talk to them.

When we say "and earlier," we want you to be aware that you may come across reports during the reading phase that will not be understandable unless you talk to someone. For instance, personnel and production reports may show an employee performance as a percentage of a "standard." Even if the employee is listed as performing at 100 percent of standard, you may not know from the report that seventy-five widgets a day is considered standard. In order to find this out (and in order to make your reading meaningful), you need to talk to the employee, the shop floor supervisor, or the author of the report. This discussion should take place during the reading phase, not during the inquiry phase.

The inquiry phase is designed to test the knowledge you gained from reading. Reports can be misleading, so proceed cautiously. Again, use open-ended questions: "You know, Smedley, the way I read this production report, it appears that product servicing is sort of a stepchild around here. I wonder if I'm reading it correctly, since this is my first time around with this report." This approach not only gives your colleague room to breathe; it prevents you from making authoritative statements that may be entirely wrong.

In any event, you can't see people unless you know who they are, where they work, how they can be reached, and when you can see them. To do this systematically, you need a list. As you read your reports and complaints, fill out the first column below with the names of the report writers, employees singled out by complaints, and people who are in key positions above or below you. Then fill out the rest.

NAME	FUNCTION	RANK	PHONE NO.	APPOINTMENT MADE
Jones	Auditor	Superior	5026	Thursday, 4:00
_____	_____	_____	_____	_____
_____	_____	_____	_____	_____

Be sure to complete this list. These are the people who can verify, correct, or expand your knowledge about the operations of your unit. It's useful to review the communications section above before you meet with each of the individuals.

Unless you are dealing with a subordinate who is a known disciplinary problem, see people where *they* work, rather than having them come to you. You'll learn more about them and what it takes to do their jobs;

your subordinates, pleased that you respect their time, are likely to be less defensive.

STEP-⑪P   ⑪SE AND ABUSE YOUR PLAN

Get the Law on Your Side

> The amount of work expands to fill the time allotted to complete it.
> —PARKINSON'S LAW

It would seem ridiculously obvious that if you've gone to the trouble of making a good plan, you will of course put it into action. But we all know better: call it inertia, human perversity, procrastination, whatever—what we set out to do in two weeks takes longer and longer as we contemplate it, replan it, resize it, and, soon, despise it.

Do not overplan and *do not* modify your deadline. You have enough time to do everything you've set out to do as long as you realize that your learning is a top priority. Other things can wait.

Your plan, even if it is not perfect, is *good enough* if it follows the outlines given above and gathers 75 percent of the information being sought.

Kick yourself, and kick yourself hard, if you hear a voice inside your head saying any of the following:

- I haven't planned enough/well enough
- It's safer/easier to plan than to act
- I have too many other things to attend to
- My people won't like it if I bother them
- I already know most of that stuff; I've worked here for years
- I'm scared it won't work, and then what will I do?
- I probably haven't set the right priorities . . . I'll give it some more thought
- Just making these plans has given me a better understanding of the department . . . so I'll just wing it from here
- My superior and the auditor who examined our operation are too busy and important to be bothered by me

Remember you must learn in order to know whether (and how) you need to change things, and you must get going because people's schedules, including your own, change unpredictably. Don't let your whole plan derail by starting it too late. Pretty soon you *will* be expected to manage the department, and then you *won't* have time to research the basics. If you're running only a bit behind your learning schedule, remember always that the world of management is a world of options. Are you doing other things that you needn't be doing? Are you only a day behind? Don't panic. You'll survive.

If time is running seriously short, however, your priority list is a must. Don't pore over every word of every report (no matter how useful) only to find you have no time to talk with your staff. Read only enough to get a basic idea of what the report tells you, note the questions you need to ask to flesh out the information, and talk to the people who know. You can read the rest of the report on your own time, if need be.

STEP-UP PLAN AND PLAN AGAIN

Did you get the most out of your time and plan? If you learned all you needed to know by your deadline, congratulations! Nothing succeeds like success, except writing down how you succeeded so you can use the information again. (Please don't trust your memory here—you have too much else to think about.) Learn from your mistakes, too: Note what reports and people *weren't* useful, and write down why. Do it right now and right here.

These reports supplied me with information I'll need regularly:

_____   _____   _____   _____

These reports are best read as received/best read all at the end of the month before the regular staff meeting/best read once a year/etc.:

AS RECEIVED   AS NEEDED   MONTHLY   NEVER

_____   _____   _____   _____

_____   _____   _____   _____

_____   _____   _____   _____

These times of day were relatively useful for reading, talking to people, and planning

READING TIME   MEETING TIME   PLANNING TIME   WRITING TIME

____ ____ ____ ____

____ minutes is generally sufficient time to get information from subordinates about one issue or problem without disturbing either of our schedules.

I need to meet with the following people on a regular basis:

____ ____ ____ ____

Now get out your appointment book and calendar and continue making plans and noting regular meetings. If you're the type who chafes at so much structure, take heart: it won't be forever. After a few months this will all be second nature, and you won't need to write everything down. But *now you do*, so don't set yourself up to reinvent the wheel. You've used these first two weeks to learn. Make sure the learning sticks.

Your Subordinates

PEGGY SANGER had just been appointed director of the hematology lab in Euphoria General Hospital. Peggy had eight years' experience as a blood technician in the lab, the first six years as a part-timer while she raised three small children. Although she was skilled in only one of the several functions performed by the hematology lab, Peggy was a favorite of the hospital's administrators. Some knew her socially, others had worked closely with her, and all valued her level-headedness, her ability to communicate clearly, and her popularity with her co-workers. When Mrs. Downey, long-time head of the lab, retired, Peggy was the unanimous choice of the hospital's administrators.

On the first day of her new job, Peggy met with the two assistants whom she had inherited from Mrs. Downey (and who, the week before, had been Peggy's superiors). One was Lester O'Toole. Lester had worked side by side with Peggy on blood typing until he became Mrs. Downey's assistant just two months before Mrs. D. retired. Peggy's other assistant was Janice Bowie, a woman who was both the most abrasive and, after eight years as Mrs. Downey's assistant, the most technically accomplished member of the hematology lab.

Their first meeting was pleasant enough. Peggy told Lester and Janice that she was slowly feeling her way into the new job and would rely on them for advice. When she asked about problems in the lab, Lester mentioned a few personnel issues but Janice said that everything was under control. When Peggy asked about upcoming issues, Janice mentioned that the lab was entertaining proposals from manufacturers of high-speed, computerized urinalysis machines. Since Peggy had little expertise in urinalysis, she asked Janice to review the proposals and to report back to her after the following week's staff meeting.

A week later, Peggy called her first full meeting of the hematology lab staff. She was introduced by one of the hospital administrators, and the meeting went well. Just as Peggy was about to close, Janice Bowie raised her hand and said, "Peggy, on this urinalysis machine issue, do you think we should get the Megatronic, which has high-speed albumin-scan, or the Synergistic, which has one of the lowest blood-sugar error ratios and has time-saving record-keeping features as well?"

Peggy knew nothing about albumin scans or blood-sugar error ratios. She did know about being put on the spot, however, and she could feel her face flush as she struggled for an answer. She also could feel the eyes of her staff, and sense their curiosity about the "time-saving" (and maybe job-eliminating) aspects of the Synergistic machine. She had to say something to get off the hook. "Well, Janice, as I told you last week, we are nowhere near a decision on these two machines, and you and I need to have a detailed discussion about the relative merits of the machinery before we make a recommendation to the administration. We'll get to it first thing this afternoon, *as we had planned*." Janice looked unsatisfied, but let the subject drop.

What Peggy wanted to do after the meeting was to flay Janice Bowie alive. Instead, she talked to Frank O'Leary, the administrator who had introduced her at the meeting.

"Peggy," Frank responded, "she thinks that she should have gotten your job. She is likely to take every opportunity to show you up to the workers and to your superiors. If you keep her in a position of day-to-day operational responsibility, she'll undermine you . . . and if she can't do that, she may start doing things that undermine the lab."

Peggy considered Frank's analysis of the situation, thought it was an overly competitive viewpoint, and decided to try to accommodate Janice Bowie. After four weeks of hearing Janice's thinly veiled sarcasm ("Oh! You mean you don't *know* about the frimframmis controls?" and "We didn't do it this way when Mrs. Downey ran the show"), Peggy had had enough. Despite Janice's strenuous objections—she even complained to the hospital administrators, whom Peggy had wisely forewarned—she limited Janice's responsibility to training new staff and to training existing staff in new procedures.

With Janice Bowie out of day-to-day management, and mostly out of potshot range, Peggy finally got down to the business of running the hematology lab.

Peggy got off to a rocky start because she did what many new managers do. She failed to consider how her promotion affected the willingness of certain people to work for her. Janice Bowie had reason to expect the promotion and felt doubly cheated when Peggy got the job.

From Janice's perspective, Peggy was "a new kid on the block who doesn't know spit about half our procedures, and kisses the administrators' rear ends besides. Why," Janice asked herself more than once, "should I work for this bitch?"

Managing people is a complicated business that mixes *task management*, *position management*, and *personality management*. When you manage tasks, you direct the actual work that people are doing. When you manage positions, you analyze and, if necessary, modify the way people report to each other as superiors and subordinates. When you manage personalities, you consider the work people do and the positions they hold in terms of their behavior and skills.

Finding the best task-position-personality fit for each employee will be one of your continuing and most crucial jobs. Crucial, because if Steve hates Edie and they need to do something together in order to complete a task, it might never get done—or if it gets done, it might get done wrong. For Janice, doing the assistant's job that she performed ably under Mrs. Downey became an insult to her when Peggy was the boss. So, although in some areas you can know everything about your job—the production processes, the budget, the personnel system, and so on—people management is an area in which that can never happen. New people come, old people go, relationships between people change, tasks change, even personalities change over the years. And each change means a new people-management situation.

Why You Must Evaluate Your Personnel

Your subordinates will have definite feelings about you even before they've met you, and even more feelings if you've been promoted within the company. If you doubt this, just think about how *you* felt when your own boss moved on and you suddenly reported to someone else.

Ignoring the feelings of your new subordinates, or telling yourself that everything will work out just fine once they get to know you for the conscientious, fair-minded person you are, borders on lunacy. If you're unlucky enough to be replacing some beloved supervisor who successfully fought for everybody's raises and brought in homemade doughnuts every Friday, you need to be aware of this as much as you need to know production quotas. Otherwise you might find production dipping and animosity dripping in the wake of your public (or even private) comment that the previous boss's reports (or records or management style) left something to be desired. Your job is to pay proper homage to the saintly boss, even if she was an idiot about some things.

If, on the other hand, you're taking Simon Legree's place, you should know that, too. You are likely inheriting a bunch of workers who, having been beaten into submission for years, are afraid to tell you that the roof is going to cave in (even if they and you are under it). Your job is to reassure them that they can give advice without getting slapped, a task that becomes somewhat easier because you can blame your first dozen mistakes on mean old Simon Legree's system.

Figuring out how the behavior of the previous boss affects the way your employees see you is only one part of the job of handling your subordinates—the part that concerns how they view your position and their relationship to it. In addition, "handling your subordinates" means figuring out how to respond to their *task* and *personality* needs as well.

Just as you will do well to consider your predecessor's style, you must also consider your subordinates' task aptitudes. Is Smith good at detail work? Is Jones a whiz at leading flustered loan applicants through the application process? If you can, distribute the tasks to best utilize your people's different talents.

Then consider personalities. Is Harold shy and withdrawn, but bright? Give him a job that can be done in a quiet corner, and don't give him jobs where he has to boss other people around. Is Cynthia aggressive and dedicated to finishing any task placed before her? Count on her for important tasks (though first be sure of her loyalty to you. That is, does she resent you and your position, or does she appear to be cooperative?) and consider her for supervisory responsibilities.

These are just a few examples to give you an idea of what we mean. People management is a complicated business, and there is little room for the whip-cracking, "There's only one boss around here and I'm it" school of management. With few exceptions (boot camp, the police academy), managers are more successful when they understand that subordinates are individuals who will work hard *and* be more satisfied if you can meet their particular needs and utilize their particular talents.

Your workers are essential but volatile resources. By looking at your staff as "ingredients" to be carefully combined, you'll avoid the wreckage that awaits new managers who are too blind or busy to see that mixing acid with water (à la Hatfield and McCoy) leads to explosions.

We hope this chapter will get you in the habit of looking at your staff the way you'd like to be looked at: as individuals who have competencies and personalities that can be mixed and matched to produce either friction and smoke, or a smoothly running, satisfied, *productive* department.

STEP-UP   SET YOUR GOALS

We repeat: Make your goals specific and definite. Give them deadlines. Get them done. Here is your personnel learning goal:

Within six weeks of my first day on the job, I will:

- Review the personnel file of each of my employees
- Assess task aptitude by asking all employees about their present task(s), and about tasks they have liked and disliked in the past
- Assess supervisory potential by asking all employees about their present position, and about positions they have liked and disliked in the past
- Assess each employee's personality as it relates to my unit's work
- Match my findings about each employee with the tasks they actually do and positions they actually hold

This is all you need to do for now. Later on, you may want to act on your findings (see chapter 7). For now, stick to gathering information that can help you if and when you want to change tasks and positions to give employees more satisfying situations and minimize disruption of the unit by unhappy employees.

Why Not Act Now?

What if you find somebody who's "all wrong" for what he does, and is a threat and/or pain in the neck to you besides? Remember that the person in question may also be the son-in-law of the chairman of the board, or some union shop steward who has filed and won seven consecutive grievances against bosses who tried to move her. Information like this is best gleaned from your own boss when you say, "Gus has been holding up production by arguing with the other quality-control people. I'm thinking of shifting him to solo inspections. Any problems with that?"

Another reason for delaying major personnel actions is that your staff has just gone through a major personnel transition. They've lost their old boss and have to get used to a new one—you. The staff, we can assure you, is nervous. You can paralyze them if it looks like you've put the knife to someone for no reason five minutes after you've arrived. Drastic personnel moves should come when you can show that someone has violated standards you have set and publicized. Task and positional changes should be made after talking with the affected employees and giving reasons for the changes. All of these major actions should wait. For now, your goal is to *collect information*.

And just what information should you gather? The following section provides tools to help you decide how to "Tally Your Resources."

STEP-UP TALLY YOUR RESOURCES

Below are some resources that provide sound information about the people who work for you:

Job descriptions	Salary and promotion
Resumés	histories
Employment applications	Former bosses
Personnel records	Former co-workers
Attendance records	Present co-workers
Performance appraisals	Former subordinates
	Present subordinates

Resumés

If you had to have a resumé to be hired, your subordinates did, too. The resumés are probably somewhere in your department—ask your assistant, your secretary, or your boss. Or introduce yourself to the personnel director and ask for what you need.

As you read through each resumé, see how each person's background matches his current responsibilities. See if he has skills (foreign languages, technical capabilities, leadership training) that he can't use in his current job but that may be useful elsewhere in the company. This information can come in handy whether you want to reward somebody or get rid of somebody—which often amount to the same thing when you are "kicking somebody upstairs."

Be alert for inconsistencies between resumé data and other information that you collect. If, for instance, an employee has a terrific resumé but mediocre evaluations, it's something you'll want to check out. Being familiar with what your people can do—or say they can do—enables you to develop and use them wisely, as well as argue more effectively for them when it's time for raises and promotions (chapter 7).

Job Applications

Usually found in the employee's personnel file, job applications contain career information, and often the employee's reasons for joining the company. (So, frequently, do the letters that accompany resumés.) Job applications may also have the employee's salary history from previous jobs.

Personnel Records File

Personnel records are usually kept in some central location, usually the personnel office. Let the personnel director know that you are new on the job and want to get a better idea of your employees' backgrounds.

It may happen that the personnel director will allow you to see only part of the records, or may ask you to wait a few days in order to review or remove certain information. This is not as unusual as it sounds. Personnel records contain all sorts of information: birth date, anniversary date (the first day on the job), years with the company, union affiliation, grievance history, salary, salary history, health plan subscribed to, insurance carried, marital status, changes in marital status, dependents, promotion history, and so on. Some companies, understandably, will not release all of this information—even to souls as trustworthy as you. Ask for everything you need, and be gracious if you can't get it all.

Performance Appraisals

In most organizations, people are evaluated annually—sometimes more frequently. People are rated on things such as attendance, initiative, amount of work produced, acceptance of supervision, et cetera. In most rating systems, performance is rated superior (or outstanding), satisfactory/good (or acceptable), or unsatisfactory.

Unit managers almost always play a major role in performance evaluations. The unit manager alone may prepare the evaluation, or may fill out the evaluation with his or her boss. What this means is that performance evaluations are either someplace in your office or close by in your boss's office.

What does the performance evaluation tell you? It tells you how your employees have been rated by your predecessor and/or your boss. The performance evaluation does *not* necessarily tell you about how the employee performs his job. It tells you about the *standing* of the employee in question. For example, Chaplin may be one of the less productive workers but has a wit and personality that dazzled the previous boss and your superiors as well. His performance evaluation thus may be outstanding in every respect. Einstein, on the other hand, may produce like a champion but have the personality of a porcupine. Because of his abrasiveness, the people who came before you may have never rated his performance higher than satisfactory, and may have rated it even lower.

Extremely consistent performance appraisals probably convey reliable information. An employee who has been rated "outstanding" for seven straight years by a variety of supervisors is almost certainly outstanding.

However, an employee who has been rated "good" for seven straight years by a variety of supervisors is almost certainly one of your less productive workers. (In many companies, no worker is *ever* rated as "unsatisfactory.")

Salary Histories, Promotion Histories

How quickly have individuals in your new unit been promoted? How frequently have they been given raises, and how large have those raises been? How do the salaries of your subordinates compare with one another? (You should know whether your company grants raises based on a standardized timetable or amount—does *everyone* get a 5 percent raise annually, regardless of performance?)

Frequently these questions are answered by particular reports. Your unit's weekly (biweekly, monthly) payroll report may have annual salaries listed. Salary histories may be available for each person. The personnel department may also have for each of your employees a single listing of all of the positions (titles, jobs) held since the first day with the organization. If salary and promotion reports are not available, the information can generally be pieced together from personnel records and other documentation that you will review.

When you consider each employee's "history," you don't have to memorize the numbers and the years. What you want is some sense of who's moving fast and who's moving slowly, who's paid a lot and who's paid a little.

Why? To gauge your unit's potential for opportunity, threat, and internal dissension. If you have a lot of "fast movers," your new job is ripe with opportunity. Your employees include a bunch of self-starters whose performance makes you and your unit look good. If you have a lot of "bottlenecked" or "blockaded" employees, the situation can be threatening to them (especially if you are seen as having leapfrogged unfairly over them). This is what happened to Peggy in the case that opened this chapter. The passed-over assistant, Janice Bowie, was stuck in place and took out her frustrations on the new boss. Finally, if you have wide disparities in salary between subordinates who have been on the job an equal amount of time and do similar work, the potential for disruption in your unit is great. Few things trigger office strife more rapidly than the feeling of being cheated.

A Warning for Information Collectors

You have a substantial number of available resources to evaluate your personnel. Taken together, these resources will provide a relatively accurate picture of any employee. Taken singly, however, the reports about employees should not be treated as gospel. Otherwise, an embittered ex-boss or ex-employee, or a personnel evaluation from the year Mansfield was getting divorced again, can prejudice you against the employee.

How do you guard against unfairly typing your staff? Wait until most of your information collecting is over before you "peg" your workers. This means cross-checking your written information with other managers and the employees themselves as you enhance your resources.

STEP-UP   ENHANCE YOUR RESOURCES

Now that you've gotten what you can from paper, learn things you can't tell from the files by talking with people.

You'll remember from our discussion of communication in the last chapter that at this stage of the game *asking* and *listening* are more important skills than telling. It's up to you to be as straightforward as possible in letting your people get to know *you* even as you get to know them. The fact that you may have been working there for ten years and already have a good idea of the information you need to get doesn't change this: As a manager, you're an unknown quantity. Despite your being voted Most Congenial at the last company picnic, you're in a new arena now. Asking too many questions, or asking them in a secretive, less than confident manner, only threatens people and makes them defensive. This you can't afford. Let people know you're only after as much information as will help you get to know the personnel situation quickly, and don't press if people act hesitant.

First, be sure to *schedule* appointments with people. If they tell you "just drop by any time Tuesday," tell them when to expect you and for how long. You should call to make the appointments as you are reviewing personnel records, that is, in the first week. The appointments should begin no later than ten business days after you begin reviewing personnel records. Following is a list of people who can enhance your information about the employees who work for you.

· The person who managed the unit before you, if he's still there, and if you're on speaking terms
· Your own superior
· Other managers on your level who have supervised or worked with your employees
· The employees themselves

You are speaking to two sets of people here: colleagues (those who are managers) and subordinates (the people who work for you).

You need to approach colleagues and subordinates differently. Asking "What about Martin's poor performance rating?" will obviously have a different impact on the manager who prepared it than on Martin, who is nervous about you to begin with, and may faint if it looks like you are zeroing in on his shortcomings. In other words, you can be relatively straightforward when asking questions of colleagues. But be very careful not to take an accusatory or offensive tone with subordinates.

The information you get from colleagues is extremely helpful to you as you manage. A series of conversations with your boss, with the former manager of the unit, and with other managers who have supervised your workers can answer these questions:

· Who is a reliable worker? What does the person do that makes him or her so reliable?

· Who has particular task skills? How have those skills been used in the past?

· Who has been loyal or supportive to his unit and to his supervisor?

· How do the various individuals in your unit get along with one another? What personality clashes have occurred in the past?

· Which employees have caused problems for past managers? Were those problems handled successfully or unsuccessfully as far as your colleagues were concerned?

· Which employees present possibly unsolvable problems (because they're the president's second cousin, or their three decades of good service make up for the fact that they've slowed way down now)?

Before you talk to your colleagues, *do your homework.* Your fellow managers, and your superiors in particular, will appreciate some direction from you. Your questions should demonstrate that you have been studying your personnel. You should be *leading* the conversation with statements such as

· "According to the evaluations, Russell looks like the best (technician, salesman, phenomenology teacher) I have."

· "Reichman filed a grievance when you were manager. Anything I should know about that?"

· "Kissinger is really moving along in the company, but his evaluations aren't as good as those for people moving more slowly. Is there something going on that I don't know about?"

If you have read enough to question your colleagues in this way, you've accomplished several things: You've outlined what you want to know (in addition to what you've already read) about each employee, and directed the conversation to those matters; you've demonstrated that you have been active in your first weeks on the job; you didn't give your colleagues (especially bosses) the impression that you were just on a shoot-the-breeze fishing expedition.

Depending on numerous and often unpredictable things like your source's personality, the amount of time he has available to talk, and his past experience with the person in question, you should get plenty of facts, interesting stories, and insight into how to deal successfully with the people who now work for you. In fact, you may have trouble getting people to *stop* talking, so be sure you have your questions prepared. (And be sure to have mentioned an ending time for the meeting. Consider in advance what circumstances will allow you to leave gracefully—e.g., another scheduled meeting, lunch, closing time, a production problem in your unit that needs hourly monitoring. You may need to mention these in order to escape endless war stories.)

Talking to Subordinates

Talking with subordinates in order to flesh out your reading is an altogether different thing from talking with your colleagues about your employees' performance. Some hints:

Act as if you have little information. Your employees will be more willing to help you if it sounds as if you are feeling your way and have few preconceived notions about them. (It's worth noting here that you are not only not lying when you do this, but are behaving in a particularly effective way. True, there's a lot you already know; just as true, there's a lot you *don't* know. Stressing the second truth improves your relations with employees and increases their willingness to give information. Stressing the first truth to your colleagues helps you relate to them better and increases your information.) *Never be afraid to stress facts that help you and suppress facts that hinder you.*

Emphasize to your employees that you have no plans to change things (it's true—you don't).

Emphasize, if possible, the common ground you share with employees: "When I was a staff nurse (administrative assistant, claims clerk, etc.), keeping up with the paperwork used to drive me nuts. I see a lot of paper in this place and was wondering if the paper load makes you crazy around here, too."

When you enhance your personnel information by talking to your employees, your goal should be to get a general idea of him or her. You want to get a sense of Sally's attitude toward her task, her satisfaction with her position, and her relationship with her peers. Some employees may give you much more than this (such as recommendations for task changes or personnel changes, and exactly what unnatural acts the previous boss should engage in with what animal). If this happens, listen without comment. Your behavior should not be seen as requiring such detailed information, nor should you offer your opinion about it. Remain pleasantly straightforward and noncommittal, and thank the employee for his ideas.

Since you are not digging for specific facts from your employees (you have facts from the records and can get more from your colleagues), your questions should be *open-ended*—designed to elicit whatever information the employee wants to give. For example:

TASK-RELATED QUESTIONS
· In general, how do you like your job?
· What is there about the job you do that makes other people doing it unhappy? (Don't ask, "Is there anything about this job you don't like?" It's just too easy for your employee to shrug and say "no" when he doesn't really mean no.)
· How could the job be improved to avoid these difficulties?

POSITION-RELATED QUESTIONS
· How did Mr. Dithers (the last boss) handle delegating the work among the staff?
· How did the staff respond to Mr. Dithers's style?
· What kind of management style do you think the staff responds to best?

PERSONALITY-RELATED QUESTIONS
· The last place I worked, we had a couple of personality conflicts among the staff that had to be delicately managed. Has anything like that happened around here?
· Could you give me a general idea of how the last manager handled the personality clash between Martin and Lewis during the ACSU project?

People are often more willing to talk when they are asked about someone else's feelings rather than about their own. The unsurprising thing is that what Sam says others feel is often exactly what Sam himself feels. You can assume that what an employee identifies as employee gripes (or satisfactions) are at least in part shared by the employee speaking.

What All Those Answers Mean

As you listen to what your people say, you'll formulate some idea of how seriously each employee takes her job and career with the company. You'll also get a feel for each employee's loyalty to the department (and perhaps to the old boss). Finally, from both your meetings and what your employees report, you should get a sense of the personalities of the people who work with you and how they interact with one another.

Listen to tone as well as to words. Consider the feelings behind the content. Is there enthusiasm? Initiative? Do you hear thoughtfulness, or do the answers sound like some party line that hasn't been reevaluated in years (for example, "Management always gets what it wants around here by ripping off the workers")? Does the employee have a false sense of importance? Are there icy statements about how everyone was crushed when your predecessor left for a better position? Or endless complaints (veiled or otherwise) about the job, the people, the salary? Listen also for clues that indicate potential control problems such as the mention of friends or connections in high places in the company. Potential control problems are also indicated by "I put in my time and do my job, period" responses.

In order to manage people effectively, you *must* pay attention to things said between the lines and behind the lines. And the time to start is now, in this initial personnel assessment process.

The main point in getting the answers to these questions is to evaluate who can help you reach your larger overall goal: to make the department more productive than it was under the last manager. Therefore, you must know early on: who the informal leaders of your work unit are, what the competencies of your subordinates are, what problems the workers see as stemming from poor management, and the personality conflicts and compatibilities of your work group.

By answering these questions you get a head start on planning the changes you'll make. Keeping hostile employees apart (or friendly ones together), finding (and bringing out) hidden talents, and neutralizing potential rebels benefits you, the organization, and your employees.

Grains of Salt: How to Be a Healthy Skeptic

A word of caution now about human nature, specifically your own. It's easy to make a snap judgment when one or two people you trust (or want to impress) tell you that "Haynes is a steady worker; everybody seems to like him." In a very human effort to fit in with your new peers, you nod, agree (even if you've never met Haynes) that he is indeed the salt of the earth, put Haynes on your mental shelf with the label "OK guy," and forget him. Where's the harm in this? Not very apparent at first glance, but more insidious when the subordinate's reputation isn't so innocuous. To agree, disagree, or show any strong reaction (especially with a subordinate) can sabotage your information search.

No matter how alarming or juicy a story may be, we repeat: Listen with a poker face. Noncommittal calmness gets you a reputation for unflappability and the retention of maximum discretion to act. Saying "That's terrible!" when an employee's transgressions are revealed almost requires that you take some action. Saying "That's interesting" gives you more room to act or not act.

And take these verbal reports with a grain of salt. No one (even *you*) is completely objective. You will no doubt talk with somebody who paints a rosy picture of weeds, or a weedy picture of roses. This is why you're talking with lots of people. When something is seen more than one way, you may want to trust the majority opinion or, even better, an observer whom you have found to be trustworthy.

Above all, trust your own instincts from meeting and working with your employees. Personnel-folder facts and ex-manager opinions are always subject to your own experience with the employee in question. And that employee works for you now, not for the "old" boss. Relate to your people on your own terms. You may be good enough to confound all of the naysayers, as was Al Davis, the general manager of the 1983 Super Bowl Champion Oakland Raiders football team. He habitually hires players other teams have written off as behavior problems, and just as habitually gets them to produce. If you can get your own "Wild Bunch" to produce more, you're way ahead of the game.

STEP-UP PLAN YOUR ACTION

You have three things to do:

· Gather written information
· Gather verbal information
· Assess the written and verbal information about each employee in order to make tentative plans about the employee's tasks, the employee's working partners, and your supervisory attitude toward the employee

Gathering Written Material

You need these documents:

- Resumés
- Personnel files
- Payroll records
- Performance evaluations

Tell your boss you want to familiarize yourself with your employees' background. Ask where personnel files are kept, and for permission to look through them. If your boss says the files are kept in the personnel office, ask her to call the personnel director and tell him she has approved your request to review your staff's personnel files. (If you must call him yourself, ask what procedures you must follow in order to see personnel files, payroll information, promotion histories, and other such information. These procedures might require a written request and might even require you to go back to your boss for a memo of approval. If this happens, *don't let the aggravation stop you.* You don't have time to waste carping about frustration or making a bad impression on personnel. Your time is better spent getting the memo and thus the files.)

In many organizations, personnel files are not to leave the office. Be prepared to review the files at the worksite, perhaps even in the personnel office. If you have access to the personnel files whenever you want (instead of only at the personnel office and only during business hours), do your file-getting, reading, thinking, and/or copying after work if possible. Going over personnel files during business hours only increases the possibility that your staff will think your reading is a prelude to a purge.

Gathering Oral Histories

Organize your schedule for information gathering, listing the people you want to talk to, and scheduling a time and meeting place. For colleagues and superiors, their office is preferable; for subordinates, your office.

Your list should include all individuals who report directly to you and all individuals who work under you (if practicable), plus your boss, the last three managers who held your position (if accessible), and those who manage similar units (they may have supervised some of your employees; if not, they can still give you general advice). Fill in meeting dates, times, and places as you read resumés and personnel folders.

Check with your boss before you communicate with the people who previously held your position; he may know something you don't know. If you schedule meetings with subordinates of your subordinates, mention your plans to your immediate subordinates first. Tell them the truth—that you just want to get a feel for the employees in the unit. If you sense intensely negative vibrations (your subordinates suddenly become tense, look irritated or worried, start asking a lot of questions, or get evasive), don't push. Quietly drop the meetings for now; you can get this information later.

Assessing the Information

Information must be *patterned* to be useful. What do we mean by patterned? Consider this information:

Height: 5'6" Eyesight: 20/30L, 20/20R
Head size: 7 Hip size: 36"
Waist size: 26" Blood pressure: 120/80
Foot size: 9 Pulse rate: 72
Chest size: 36"

What does this information tell you? A lot—and nothing. That it's a lot is obvious. It will be just as obvious that you are confronting *a lot* of information about your employees. Your personnel information will tell you little that is useful unless you know what you are looking for. For example, if you need information about body shape, the statistics above can be patterned to provide that information: 36-26-36. Similarly, if you specify in advance what information is of interest to you, you can intelligently pattern personnel information as you collect it.

Are you interested in distinguishing up-and-coming employees from stuck-in-place employees? One way to pattern that information is to graph the frequency and amount of their salary increases and promotions (Chart 3A).

Chart 3A helps you identify who has moved quickly and who has moved slowly compared with the average rate of progress. You needn't get this information down to the last dollar, of course. A rough idea is sufficient—which is why you can use promotion histories as well as salary increases.

What you're trying to discover is this: Who's a good bet, and who's a poor bet, for new and challenging tasks. Getty looks good because his salary has increased rapidly over a short time—although you see a leveling off that may be due to his reaching some salary ceiling, or some recent problems which your discussion will probably uncover. Getty's co-worker Rockafel, on the other hand, has received small but steady salary in-

CHART 3A   Salary Increase/Promotion History

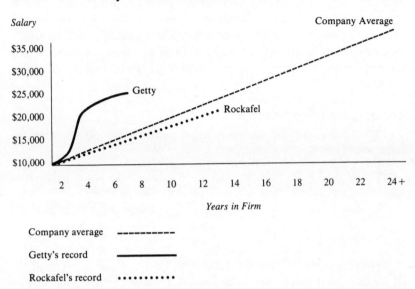

creases. He's not setting the world on fire and, indeed, has progressed more slowly than the average employee. This does not mean that he won't do good work. You may, however, want to give him low-pressure assignments.

Remember also that file information can support only tentative conclusions. You must see for yourself by meeting with and working with the person. You might, to be on the safe side, *begin* with low-key assignments for Rockafel, but upgrade his assignments after reviewing his actual performance.

Assessing Job/Positional Histories

Each of your employees will have a positional history, and most have been subject to a variety of supervisory styles in their careers. Many employees will have had experience as both supervisor (even if it was only of a student intern) and persons being supervised. The attitudes they express about their various positions affect how you will manage your unit.

Chart 3B helps you organize information and categorize experiences regarding the employee's positional history, his experience with supervision (from both ends), and his attitude toward supervising and being supervised.

CHART 3B   Supervision History

EMPLOYEE/PRESENT POSITION	PAST POSITIONS	ATTITUDE TOWARD POSITION/AUTHORITY
R. Jones, Director of records	Probationary clerk Supervisory clerk Administrative asst.	"Boss was an ass." "Liked that job." "Wanted my own shop."
D. Smith, Senior sec.	Probationary clerk Secretary	"I did my job." "I sat down more."
F. Harris, Supervisory clerk	Probationary clerk	

Complete the chart by listing your employees and their present titles; put their past titles in the second column. When you meet with them, ask leading questions in order to get some feedback on their feelings about *previous* jobs. (They're more likely to be honest about what's past. Most people will tell you their present job is okay, whether it is or not.)

Your goal is to find out *how your employees deal with authority.* In Chart 3B, Jones indicates that she prefers that authority stay out of her way so that she can do her job. Smith doesn't indicate any strong feelings one way or the other about authority. You have yet to meet with Harris.

You now have very useful information to help you determine which supervisory style to use with the different individuals. Jones is apparently capable; she has climbed steadily and with good evaluations. Jones also chafes at close supervision. Unless there are problems in Jones's unit that you must attend to closely, Jones is best left to run her own shop. Close supervision will only lead to friction that will impede her performance (and yours).

Smith is another story. His comments have more to do with finding a comfortable corner than with his attitudes toward supervision, although you might try to draw Smith out with some open-ended questions about previous supervisors. Smith's work may be stiflingly boring or he may be content to do the minimum. In either case, Smith's situation demands closer attention than Jones's.

At this point, you may be thinking that doing a dozen charts like this is the last thing you have time for. Wrong—they're the first thing you should make time for, because they'll prove very useful very soon. And you should augment them by carefully monitoring your own experiences with your staff. If the laid-back Smith suddenly becomes a tiger, it's time to reevaluate *your* behavior, no matter what Smith's past history and initial conference indicated you should do.

Assessing Task Aptitude

In your records review, you can draw from resumés and/or personnel folders a sketch of the tasks that each of your employees has performed in the past. The process is the same as with your assessment of positional attitudes. Based on your file reviews, list the tasks each employee can do. When you meet with the employee, draw out his opinion and expertise on those tasks (Chart 3C).

CHART 3C   Task Attitude

EMPLOYEE/PRESENT TASK	PAST TASKS	EMPLOYEE ATTITUDE
B. Lopez	Filed documents	"Too limited."
Manages record room	Directed filing	"Learned a lot."
	Correspondence	"Too isolated."
R. Shapiro	Filed documents	"An orderly job."
Assists manager	Typist	"Overloaded."

These answers indicate that supervisory attitudes and task attitudes can overlap. However, they also show that information about how employees view past tasks can help the new manager. Shapiro in this case is your new secretary. He indicates that he likes order and becomes ineffective when he feels overloaded with work. How can you use this information? It tells you something about how secretarial support can be most effectively utilized. One option might be to consider transferring Shapiro, who is not very comfortable with overloads, if you expect him to have to deal with them frequently. Another option is to feed Shapiro work a little at a time, rather than letting it pile up on your desk for several days and then throwing a daunting heap of it in his in-box.

Again, the solution is not as important as the fact that *information* from records, discussions, and experience underlies the problem-solving process. So use the charts—or your own version of them—to get a reading on your staff. In the process you will get to know them better and in the future you will use them better.

Combining the Information You've Gathered

You have now collected several types of information:

Each employee's educational background and career path (from resumés and job applications)

Each employee's promotion and/or salary track record (from personnel files, resumés, and job applications)

Each employee's attitude toward supervision (from talks with your
boss, other managers, and the employee)

Each employee's attitude toward his/her current task(s) (from talks
with your boss, other managers, and the employee)

With this information, you can build a checklist that will give you a
thumbnail description of your employees (Chart 3D)

CHART 3D The Employee Checklist

Employee	QUALIFICATIONS			TRACK RECORD		TASK ATTITUDE			SUPERVISION ATTITUDE		
	Hi	*Good*	*OK*	*Fast*	*Slow*	*Pos*	*Neu*	*Neg*	*Pos*	*Neu*	*Neg*
_____	☐	☐	☐	☐	☐	☐	☐	☐	☐	☐	☐
_____	☐	☐	☐	☐	☐	☐	☐	☐	☐	☐	☐
_____	☐	☐	☐	☐	☐	☐	☐	☐	☐	☐	☐
_____	☐	☐	☐	☐	☐	☐	☐	☐	☐	☐	☐
_____	☐	☐	☐	☐	☐	☐	☐	☐	☐	☐	☐

This chart is not gospel, nor does it dictate that you act. The chart is
rough, preliminary, incomplete. The full measure of its accuracy depends
on *your own* experience with each employee. The chart does, however,
organize, condense, and compare the employee information you gather.
With any luck you will have several months to see for yourself how each
of your employees performs before you have to make personnel shifts. If
the roof falls in and you have to make major adjustments tomorrow,
however, this chart is better than nothing.

STEP-UP USE AND ABUSE YOUR PLAN

Remember what you learned last time: don't overplan and force yourself to gather so many details that you set yourself up for failure or badly
missed deadlines.

When to Stop Collecting Information

Depending on how many subordinates you have and what types of workers they are, you may be in the pleasant position of being able to cut short your search interviews. You've done enough if:

- Certain key documents such as performance evaluations point to outstanding (or dreadful) performance over the years
- All the information you are getting points consistently in one direction
- Some of the information you need is simply not available
- The previous supervisor fired many people, and most of your staff hasn't been around long enough to have much history
- The employee is invulnerable (you've learned she's the boss's daughter-in-law)

Biases, Stereotypes, and Prejudice

Besides chasing after information that isn't worth getting, you must be careful of something else: *your own bias*. All of us have stereotypes. They can involve ethnic groups (drunken Irish, hot-headed Italians), or they can typecast particular kinds of workers (clerks are unimaginative, civil servants are lazy).

These stereotypes can color what you see when you review records and speak with your employees. So take care. If you feel yourself prejudging a file or if you hear yourself saying "I've seen his type before" as an employee walks into your office for the first time, be extra scrupulous when you assess the person after the records have been reviewed and the interviews are complete. Not only will you use your personnel better, you may avoid legal action.

Another thing that can warp you judgment is the *halo effect*: having once decided somebody is a good guy or a bad guy, people generally perceive only those kinds of behavior that support their existing opinion. Besides being an excellent way to undermine your subordinate's morale and efficiency, you also create problems for yourself by being inflexible ("Don't confuse me with the facts.") Some people are so impressive on one or two measures that it's easy to assume they do *everything* else well. Sadly, this is rarely so. You'll be a sorry manager if you make a supervisor out of your office's most attractive personality before you've fully evaluated his or her other job skills and talents.

STEP-UP PLAN AND PLAN AGAIN

As you go through this learning process, chances are you'll find yourself wanting to ask three more questions for every answer you get. And certainly there will be times when you *need* to ask more. For instance, your unit may have the "Dr. Jekyll" (whom you have found to be pleasant, hardworking, cooperative) subordinate who has a "Mr. Hyde" (mediocre, complacent, careless, troublesome) rating on paper and/or according to the people you've talked to. This could be a case where an individual has had personal issues with her previous supervisor that kept her from producing quality work. An effective new manager (you) will trust your instincts and do what you can to develop Dr. Jekyll, who, while she may be dissatisfied, probably isn't terminally disgruntled—otherwise she wouldn't have bothered to be so nice to you.

When the time comes to talk with Dr. Jekyll, ask the questions listed above and listen for clues that she indeed had disagreements with the previous boss. If that seems to be the case, try a statement like "I get the impression that you and So-and-So didn't always see eye to eye on how the department should be run." This is usually enough of an opening for even the most reticent subordinate to allow that there were differences, and for many subordinates to tell you exactly how their previous supervisor made them miserable. Again, don't agree or disagree with what you hear; just listen and make sure you understand. Then let your subordinate know that your own managerial style will probably be different, and ask a few more questions about the changes *she* would like to see made in the department.

Make no promises, but take notes. Then make it a point to use some of the suggestions (even if it means more work for the employee) as soon as possible. If you think the suggestions are useless or worse, consider a new, slightly challenging task or project for that subordinate. Either way, your subordinates will get the message that you respect their input, need their cooperation, and trust their competency. Obviously these changes don't happen overnight, but it's well worth trying to resurrect people who otherwise would be just so much deadwood to contend with.

Of course, the converse of the above story may also obtain: Dr. Jekyll really *is* Mr. Hyde, as was the case with Janice at the beginning of this chapter. You'll have to keep your eyes open for this: Few subordinates will openly defy you or sabotage the department in any obvious way. Getting someone fired is never a pleasant experience, and right now you have more important things to do. So, if you can, plan to relocate the rebellious employee away from you, where she can't do your profit margin too much harm.

This doesn't mean banishing her to the mail room, however. You'll be dealing with her in some capacity no matter what, so—even if it galls you—give careful thought to where you can find a new spot for her where *she* will be reasonably content. Obviously, this isn't always possible. But it's worth the effort, and the principle applies to separating battling subordinates, grouping compatible subordinates who work well together, and working to match departmental tasks with your people's skills and dispositions.

Let's move now from subordinates to another very fascinating group: your superiors.

Your Superiors

FRED WALCHINSKY hit the ground running. Hired as director of programs for a large social service agency, Fred was a whirlwind. Within two weeks he knew all there was to know about the agency's various programs. Within a month he could tell you the names and positions of all two hundred employees. Fred got all this done because he "had no time for crap," which was what Fred called the almost endless round of testimonial dinners, lunches, after-work get-togethers, and bull sessions that had become a tradition around the agency.

Fred went to none of these. He worked. Fred even worked through the Friday-afternoon cocktail hour in the executive director's office while his peers—the personnel director, the public relations director, and the agency counsel—attended the happy hours, the three-hour lunches, and the other social affairs as well. "No wonder these guys get so little done," muttered Fred for the hundredth time. "They party all the time. If I didn't push them, they'd get *nothing* accomplished."

Six months later Fred had an impressive track record. The poor program structure left by the previous program director had been streamlined. His newly initiated programs were under way. Fred's subordinates were learning to adapt to his high-intensity style and unflagging concentration. Fred was happy and he knew the executive director must be happy too—operations were improving, productivity was up, things were getting *done*.

Which is why you could have knocked Fred over with a feather when the executive director called him in and said, "Fred, I've asked the board of directors that your contract not be renewed for the next year—and they've agreed."

Fred was astonished, then angry, then demanding.

"But why? I got this place running again!"

"Fred, you don't fit in with the organization."

"What the hell do you mean I don't fit?"

"Look, Jack over at personnel and Harry in public relations and

Harriet in legal have all had run-ins with you." (This was the first time Fred knew that what he had considered mere glitches had been reported to the executive director.)

"But I needed to get things done. We may have had disagreements, but we got by them."

"But," said the executive director, "you had another disagreement every week, and we don't need that kind of dissension around here. It wasn't here before you came and I'll be damned if I'll let it continue."

"Did you ever think that maybe they were exaggerating my behavior because they were jealous of how successful I've been?"

"All I know is that before you came, we were one big happy family. Now I have weekly combat reports and a program director who's never around—except to engage in battle."

The discussion continued, but the decision remained the same. Fred would have to go at the end of the year.

Fred's mistake was basic. He failed to figure out his boss.

Yes, Fred did listen to unmistakable orders. (That's why he straightened out program activities.) But Fred failed to interpret the more subtle—*but in the end more important*—messages that his boss was sending. Every Friday that the executive director invited him over for a drink and Fred refused with "No, I've got to write the Flimflam memo" was a nail in Fred's coffin. Not accepting was a deadly mistake because the executive director pegged Fred as unsociable. Not accepting gave Fred's peers a chance to take unchallenged shots at him each week. Not making time for a drink was ultimately disastrous because Fred missed an early opportunity to find out what the executive director really valued—good fellowship among the staff—and what the executive director really hated—people who failed to observe social amenities.

Make no mistake about it. The fault here is with Fred, not with his boss. Bosses come with infinite types of attitudes and expectations, and it is *not* their job to accommodate subordinates. It *is* the subordinate's job to fit in with the boss. Who, after all, gets to fire whom?

All of which means that one of your main jobs in these first weeks is to get to know your boss.

Figuring Out Your Boss

For all the hassle and trouble your subordinates may create for you, you still control them. Your boss, on the other hand, controls you—and is in turn controlled by *his* bosses. Just as your subordinates can't succeed unless they know what you want, you *must* figure out your boss if you want to do well as a manager.

And what do bosses want? Some want increased production, some value informal/social cooperation (as did Fred's executive director), some want yes-men and -women, some want a mix of the three. You need to know what *your* boss wants.

One bossly want, however, requires no study on your part. *All* superiors value loyalty from below. Every boss alive wants and needs to know that you support him and are sensitive to his idiosyncrasies. He needs to feel that you consult and advise him primarily, and that your contacts with other managers at or above his level are few and benign. Indeed, your superior may even bar communications between members of his department and other company officials.

You'll sabotage yourself in short order if you don't take the time to decode your boss's signals and learn to play the game his way. Your boss has enough problems trying to figure out *his* boss; he doesn't need any more from you. The simple fact is that troublesome subordinates (both yours and his) can be moved or let go; troublesome bosses can't.

Some Concrete Advantages to Analyzing Your Boss

· *You'll save enormous amounts of time.* The more you know about your boss, the less time and motion you waste in pleasing him. The time saved can range from a few minutes (when you know that your boss will accept a verbal report instead of a written report) to a few months (when you know enough to avoid doing what drives your boss nuts—rehabilitating yourself in your boss's eyes can take a very long time).

· *You'll learn more—faster.* For better or worse, your boss probably knows more about your new job than anyone else. At the moment, you need her more than she needs you (an inequality that, if you follow the suggestions in this book, will soon fade).

· *You'll acquire a valuable skill.* Learning to work with and for your boss is a skill you can use forever (or at least until you become the chief executive officer).

· *You'll be paying your dues in the managers' club.* Upper management is waiting to see how you fit in with their exclusive group, and this is your chance to become known early as a valuable team player.

· *You'll be healthier.* Figuring out your boss and how to please her is actually healthy for you. You spend nearly half your waking hours working for her; if your relationship is full of friction and confusion, the resulting stress necessarily affects your entire life.

· *You'll go further faster.* At least in the first several months on the job, you need your boss's goodwill. If you're written off early, your most recent promotion may be the last one you enjoy in this company.

STEP-UP SET YOUR GOALS

You've already had structured talks with your boss about production (chapter 2) and personnel (chapter 3), so you've already formed some opinion of him as you've gathered facts. Keep your impressions in mind (but not carved in stone) as you focus on your next goals:

At the end of seven weeks, I will know:

· The pressures in the workplace that affect my boss's expectations of subordinates
· How often my boss needs to meet with me in order to do *his job* as he sees it
· What reporting formats (verbal, written, a combination) my boss prefers for particular situations
· What tone (formal, informal) of conversation puts my boss most at ease
· Something I should always do (because my boss loves it)
· Something I should never do (because my boss hates it)

Let's take a closer look at these learning goals.

The Pressures Affecting Your Boss

Your boss doesn't operate in a vacuum. He is subject to pressures from his superiors (who may have cut his budget), from his fellow managers (who may have complained that he was not doing work they needed), and from the union (which may have complained that he was having the workers do managerial work). If you make an effort to understand the system in which your boss and your unit (and you) operate, the demands he places on you may be easier to take. If you don't try to understand things, you may see your boss as an uncaring slave-driver— which your boss will sense, causing things to go downhill fast.

A caution here: Don't be lulled into a false sense of security because, for example, you work in a friendly social service agency of only seven people. Your boss may be the top executive in the place, but he has a board of directors to please and a community to serve; without their support, you're both out of a job. Even small private concerns have to take the economy, not to mention customers' whims, into consideration.

You may not have to worry directly about the "no-noise" clause in the lease if you're managing a stereo store, but the owner does (or should). And you *do* need to know what's on his mind so you can be ready to help him deal with it.

How Often Your Boss Needs to Meet with You

Some bosses need to meet with their subordinates daily. If you don't report in for a day or two, this kind of boss can have all sorts of hallucinations, most of them visions of you screwing up. By the time you show up, you will be greeted as if you just firebombed his car. Other bosses want to see you when you have accomplished something. They don't want your daily progress reports, or your presentation of problems without solutions, or even your studied opinion of who's going to win the World Series this year. If you see this kind of boss too frequently, he will cringe not only at your approach but at promoting you or increasing your responsibility.

Getting the right reporting schedule for your boss is crucial to keeping him or her happy as well as to using *your* time as efficiently as possible.

The Reporting Format Your Boss Prefers

Speaking of time, perhaps no piece of knowledge will save you more: Know what kind of communication your boss responds to. One of the authors used to write ten-page memos to his boss proposing this or proposing that. Some were accepted, most were not. Another manager working for the same boss had every written proposal approved. The difference? The boss liked to discuss ideas more than he liked to read. If the discussion led to what the boss thought was a good proposal, the memo was just a formality—the proposal had already been okayed without a word going on paper.

How do you find out what your superior prefers? Ask her. If you don't, she may wonder why you're wasting your time on flowery memos when a two-minute conversation would have taken care of things. Conversely, you'll avoid "Why is this guy running off at the mouth when I can't possibly deal with this unless I see it in black and white?"

The Tone of Conversation Your Boss Prefers

Some bosses keep things loose: everyone on a first-name basis, no expletives deleted, howling laughter occasionally allowed. Other bosses want to be addressed by title, even if it's Mister (and especially if it's Commissioner, Senator, Professor, or Doctor). They won't tolerate your outburst of street slang in the office or conference room. And the stigma of "not knowing how to act" is quickly acquired and hard to shake.

So start conservatively—it's easier to loosen up than to tighten up. Pay attention to what tone makes your boss most comfortable, and whether it differs from situation to situation. Nearly all bosses prefer respectful tones from subordinates in public (even the ones who will let you bellow like a moose in private).

Something You Should Always Do Is . . .

Do flowers always make her smile? Does a (sincere) compliment a day keep his blues away? Of course. And most people know the one or two things that are easy to do, yet work wonders in maintaining their personal or romantic relationships. Bosses are no different in this regard from lovers or spouses. They, too, look for simple things in order to make sure everything's okay. It may be promptness, the correct use of titles in letters and memos you write, or your winning smile with every client who walks through the door. Whatever it is, seeing or hearing it makes them happy and secure about your daily performance. If that little touch is absent, they're likely to think "What's wrong with Damopoulos anyway?"

Don't stay in the dark. Don't refuse to provide what your boss wants, even if it has nothing to do with business per se. Successful managers know it's still part of the job.

Something You Should Never Do Is . . .

Think for a moment. Is there anything that so offends you or ticks you off that whoever does it gets written off forever in your book? No? Hmm . . .

How about a person who brings his own condiments to spice up the meal you've just slaved over? Or the horror who tells you in front of five other people that your messy personal problems are all because you left that sweet Henrietta (or Henry) three years ago? You may be a saint, but the rest of us—bosses included—are not. Idiosyncrasies can become stigmas that spell your doom in the organization. Find out what your boss considers utterly unacceptable—and then don't ever do it.

Boss Psychology: Learning about Your Superior's Personality

The psychology of personality is a fascinating subject, and numerous tests have been devised to describe, categorize, and predict what makes people tick. Psychologist David McClelland has developed a theory of personality types that has been widely applied in organizational development. Simply stated, McClelland realized people are motivated primarily (though not totally—everyone has a mix) by one of three basic needs:

· The need for *affiliation/socialization*: interacting with people, getting to know them, working with them to achieve a common goal, relaxing together. In workplace terms, the need for everybody to get along.
· The need for *creativity/achievement*: doing work (or pursuing a hobby) that is meaningful, developing skills or talents, inventing new things (be they toasters or symphonies), improving old ones. In workplace terms, the need to have things done right and done well.
· The need for *power/control*: influencing the world and people around you, arranging things or events the way you want them, directing others for the good of the group or for your own purposes. In short, the need to have things done your own way.

For example, Fred Walchinsky's boss obviously was less concerned about monitoring or rewarding Fred's sterling achievements than he was about seeing that Fred paid attention to the informal (yet very important) social network within the agency. The classic hard-driving impossible-perfectionist boss is, interestingly enough, more often achievement-oriented than control-oriented. In her drive for perfection she works her staff and herself to the bone. The truly control-oriented boss is most often found (and most often succeeds) at higher levels of management. The control-oriented boss may not want perfection but he wants things done *his way*—at least in crucial aspects of the job or in particular ways he expects you to deal with him.

You are likely to have a boss whose personality leans toward a control orientation. (The job calls for it; most people who aspire to bosshood have controlling personalities to begin with.) But don't make assumptions. Observe your boss in the first weeks. Does she pointedly note your absence from an attendance award presentation or a lunch that the rest of your group had together? If so, here is a person who values your touching base socially. Does she go over your work umpteen times, until you're aggravated ("It's only a memo about telephone logs, not an engraved invitation to the White House!") and she's exhausted? A perfectionist-achiever, of course. Do your simple, logical, time-saving ideas get nixed because she likes her own ideas better? A controlling boss can get her people to outdo themselves, or can (unfortunately) quash creativity in the bud.

Boss Psychology: A Questionnaire

None of these approaches is "good" or "bad" in and of themselves (though sometimes it feels that way because we each have one style we're most comfortable with). And although you may be uncomfortable initially with your boss's style, you can learn to adapt. We assure you you'll be *more* uncomfortable in the long run if you ignore her style or think she should adapt to yours.

The Boss Psychology Questionnaire below is simple to complete. For each question, check the phrase that best describes your boss. When you have answered all fifteen questions in a section, go back and add up the checked numbers for

Questions 1–5 (Socializing score)
Questions 6–10 (Controlling score)
Questions 11–15 (Achieving score)

The Boss Psychology Questionnaire

PART I—AFFILIATION/SOCIALIZING INDEX

A. Shooting the breeze with his bosses, his associates, and with subordinates like me takes up about ____% of my boss's time:
   1. 0%
   2. 5–10%
   3. 10–20%
   4. 25–35%
   5. 35% or more
B. When I stay late, my conversations with the boss are:
   1. Strictly business
   2. Mostly business
   3. 50–50 business and social
   4. Mostly social and/or office talk
   5. Strictly chit-chat and gossip
C. As far as I can tell, when my boss is invited to social events such as retirement dinners and award ceremonies, he attends:
   1. None
   2. One out of five events
   3. About half the time
   4. Most events
   5. Every event

D. My boss's relations with his colleagues and superiors can best be described as:
   1. Antagonistic
   2. Careful
   3. Businesslike
   4. Pleasant
   5. Quite friendly
E. The stories or anecdotes that I've heard most often about my boss have to do with:
   1. Disciplining of subordinates
   2. Run-ins with his bosses
   3. Disputes with other unit managers
   4. Devotion to family life
   5. Behavior at parties and get-togethers

Social Needs Index: _____ (25 = highly social; 5 = Greta Garbo)

PART II—CONTROL/POWER INDEX

A. My boss describes events with phrases like "people taking over," "units grabbing turf," and people being "out of line":
   1. Never
   2. Once or twice
   3. Once a week
   4. Twice a week
   5. Almost every day
B. The story or stories that I've heard most about my boss usually describe:
   1. Behavior at parties
   2. Devotion to family
   3. Disputes with other unit managers
   4. Run-ins with his bosses
   5. Disciplining of subordinates
C. When I became manager, my boss *most* stressed:
   1. That the job was mine—sink or swim
   2. That he would be available
   3. That we must meet regularly
   4. The need for written reports to him
   5. The need to clear all matters with him
D. My boss has called me to his office and then made me wait outside:
   1. Never

2. Once or twice
3. Once a week
4. Twice a week
5. Almost every day

E. When my boss calls me, drops by, or has me come to his office, I get the feeling that he wants to know I'm around as much as he wants to know what I'm doing.
   1. Not true
   2. Rarely true
   3. Sometimes true
   4. True half the time
   5. Almost always true

Control Needs Index: _____ (25 = very controlling; 5 = Elmer Fudd)

PART III—ACHIEVEMENT NEEDS INDEX

A. The stories that I've heard most about my boss concentrate on:
   1. Devotion to family life
   2. Disputes with other managers
   3. Disciplining of subordinates
   4. Attentiveness to detail
   5. Workaholism and driving the staff to perfection

B. When I have made mistakes my boss generally:
   1. Casually pointed out the error
   2. Pointed out the error with some concern
   3. Impatiently showed me the correct way
   4. Corrected it himself as I sat there
   5. Took the work away saying "I'll do it from now on"

C. My boss works:
   1. Regular hours and matters move quickly off his desk
   2. Regular hours and matters bottleneck a day or two on his desk
   3. Some overtime but matters move quickly
   4. Some overtime and matters get bottlenecked a day or two
   5. Very long hours and things get stuck on his desk for weeks

D. After getting to know my boss over the past few weeks, I'd say:
   1. She's best at managing people
   2. She's best at getting things done herself
   3. The above skills are balanced
   4. She's best at avoiding errors
   5. What she'd be best at wouldn't involve other people

E. The staff (including me) who work directly with my boss end the day:
   1. Feeling like we've accomplished a lot
   2. Feeling like we've accomplished at least some things
   3. Feeling like we've only provided grist for the boss's mill
   4. Feeling that our work will be torn to shreds
   5. Hoping the boss will die so we can actually learn and things can move

Achievement Needs Index: _____ (25 = Simon Legree; 5 = Laid-back)

We're not saying the numbers above prove conclusively that your boss is a psychotic dictator or a neurotic perfectionist, because they don't. What they do is serve as a rough map of her personality that will help you plan actions to please rather than alienate her.

While you're figuring out what type your boss is, be sure to analyze yourself as well. If you have high affiliation needs (enjoy working in groups, like to spend time with office colleagues after hours, do well interacting with clients, etc.), and your boss is concerned mainly with achievement, you may feel ignored or put off when she doesn't respond to your style . . . and *she* may feel your desire for daily contact with her is just a waste of time. This is why it's crucial for you to psych out the boss's main needs *and respond to them.* If your own style conflicts, don't despair; you can meet your affiliation needs on your own time or with your colleagues and subordinates.

STEP-UP TALLY YOUR RESOURCES

Similar to your investigations about subordinate personnel information, your tally of boss-resources includes both written documents and individuals. Unlke the two previous resource tallies, however, this one will require your constant comparison of incoming information with your day-to-day experiences. The bigger the boss, the more numerous his enemies, and often the greater the admiration from present and former associates. In short, much of your information may be conflicting and distorted. Don't act on anything (with the exception of a "Never do this" warning) right away, and check what you hear against what you see your boss do.

Written Resources: The Organization/Hierarchy Chart

Get the organization chart (the formal one, or the one you create yourself by asking a secretary or fellow manager for help). Locate your own unit on the chart (pencil in your name). Your boss's position is above your unit; add his name immediately above yours. Find the position or unit immediately above your boss's name. Fill in the name of the person who runs that unit: your boss's boss. If she has an assistant whom you know or who is considered to be on your level (e.g., has the same title, or goes to the same meetings you go to), note her name. Find the positions or units on the same horizontal line as your boss's position. Fill in the names of the unit heads (your boss's peers) and those on your level.

Reviewing the organization chart tells you who your boss reports to and interacts with. If you know some of these people, call them up and chat. Mention that you've just started working with Associate Director Big (your boss). Even without your asking directly (which is usually not a good idea with people *on* your boss's level), your contact may tell you a few things about your boss that will help you.

Your lists of "assistants to" serve much the same purpose. Getting to know them makes sense—if they're on your level of responsibility, you'll have considerable contact with them. In addition, they may have revealing stories about your boss.

Written Resources: Outdated Organization Charts

Dig around and see if you can find some old organization charts. They may show your boss as a supervisor in other units, or as a staffer in personnel, finance, or administrative services (perhaps even in a position more powerful than the one he now holds). Research like this helps you figure out where your boss is coming from, which is half the battle in figuring out what your boss is likely to want now.

Written Resources: Judging Your Boss's Resumé

The background information on your employees exists for the bosses in the company too. Look for a resumé or job application from his first position; file memos, reports, or performance evaluations describe his activities since he was hired. These may, of course, be difficult to get hold of.

People Resources: Your Boss Him/Herself

If you cannot get written documentation on your boss, you can ask her directly for this information when an opportunity (an informal getting-to-know-you session or a social gathering) presents itself.

· How long have you been with the company?

· What did you do before you came here? (or, What department were
you in before you came to the Astronomy Lab here?)
· Where did you go to school/get your training?

These are legitimate questions, even if you already know some of the
answers. Don't, however, sound too anxious, demanding, or persistent.
Above all, be ready to stop after the *first* question if your boss gives you a
look like the one your mom gave when you first asked about sex.

On the less personal side, listen closely for any mention your boss (or
anyone) makes of her recent achievements. If she happened to develop the
division's record-keeping system, think twice before suggesting changes.
And if you find the system useful, by all means let her know.

As you gather information by interacting with your superior on any
subject, take careful note of any unusual reactions, positive or negative.
Listen for indirect criticisms. Watch his body language. A grimace is a
criticism whether or not it is followed up by a critical bossly comment
(indeed, a grimace should be followed up by *your* comment: "I'm interested to know if you have any problem with that"). Knowing your boss
disapproves is useless unless you know what to do to change that.

Finally, keep your eyes open. Your boss will be younger, older, or
about the same age as his peers. If he's younger, he is moving fast on the
basis of performance or sponsorship. If he has been a top performer,
chances are he's a demanding boss. The style of the youngish boss may be
less clear if he has a sponsor (like his uncle, the vice president for
finance). In any event, gather this kind of information by looking and
(discreetly) listening.

STEP-UP ENHANCE YOUR RESOURCES

People Resources: Your Co-workers

How do you utilize your co-workers to paint an accurate picture of
your boss's personality? As before, by using what you already know
about your boss to frame leading questions, and by asking those questions
in a conducive environment (not in the office, not during work hours),
such as lunch out.

Let's begin with your peers. If you didn't know them at first, you
became at least somewhat familiar with them while learning about production and subordinates. Your peers will be an even more valuable
resource to you now that you want *subjective* historical information. If
you've been with the organization for years, you may not need an exten-

sive schedule of meetings; you may already know more than you care to about who's going for whose jugular in the boardroom. However, a couple of lunches with other managers on your level can give you more, and more accurate, information while at the same time making you an accepted member of the peer group you've just joined.

Depending on your existing relationship with your new peers (old pals, or strictly business), you have a choice: Tell them exactly what you're interested in finding out, or simply invite them to lunch so you can "learn more about how your unit works with mine in the organization." We can't repeat too often that diving in headfirst and asking "So what's the story with old Witherspoon?" isn't the smartest way to learn anything (and may be an excellent way to sabotage your new career). You *are* having lunch to learn more about your peer's unit, and you'll be smart to ask a few intelligent questions and listen carefully to the answers. Only then is it wise to bring the subject around to your supervisor or manager.

Be sensitive to your colleagues. If a peer seems in any way uncomfortable discussing your boss, let him or her know the reasons you're asking questions: that you want to know the best way to please your boss and avoid confusion or conflict, and that any opinions expressed will go no further. If you get more resistance, back off and talk about less touchy subjects.

Be objective about yourself and your colleagues. If your luncheon companion had a run-in with your boss last year, watch for exaggerations and distortions of your boss's character. If, on the other hand, you've already become a bit turned off to your boss, make doubly sure you act like a fact-finder rather than a prosecutor when you ask questions.

Beware, naturally, of peers who look over their shoulders, wink conspiratorially, and begin with "Well, I shouldn't be telling you this, but . . ." Your aim is *not* to get sucked into taking sides in someone else's juicy gossip or ongoing battles. If you can't get your companion to shut up, remain poker-faced and take what you hear with a grain (or fistful) of salt. Should someone rip your boss apart, remember a cardinal rule: Never, but never, volunteer negative information about your boss. You're new enough to say "I'm just getting to know him," even if you do know something juicy, and your lunch companion is prodding "Aw, c'mon, you gotta know—I'll keep it under my hat." Harmful information can fly through the organization in hours. If it gets back to your boss with *your* name attached, we needn't tell you where you stand.

People Resources: How Your Boss Interacts with Co-workers
Don't be so wrapped up in your work that you miss the important

interactions your boss has with her own peers and superiors. These bear directly on whom you can speak to without jeopardizing your standing with your boss. Evidence abounds for the alert new manager, even one without a formal education in office politics.

Pay attention to how your boss talks about her boss and her colleagues. At company gatherings (picnics, meetings, award dinners), notice who your boss hangs out with. Watch especially for individuals she should talk with but studiously avoids (like *her* boss). When you are in the office, note whose calls she returns immediately, whose calls she puts off, and whose calls she utters a curse about before picking up the phone.

Suppose you get an inkling that your boss dislikes someone (i.e., she calls Riley in purchasing "an ignorant, lying son of a bitch"). Before you call Riley about anything—ever—clear it with your boss first. And be polite but guarded in what you say to him (even if you think he's a terrific guy). Don't worry about being overly careful of the Rileys in your firm. Sooner or later your boss will tell you that you don't need to come to her every time you have to talk to him. If she doesn't tell you that, however, score one for you. The boss wants no one but herself to deal with Riley (for reasons obscure, irrational, or perfectly sensible), and you have demonstrated your sensitivity to her needs.

Your Biggest Resource: You

In no task are you so alone as in the task of sizing up your boss. He or his assistant can help you figure out production or personnel. The comptroller can help you figure out a budget. But no one can provide anything more than background information for the job of figuring out how *you* should relate to your boss.

This is doubtless your most important work relationship. If it sours, so may your career with the firm. If some kindly voice of experience tells you outright how to handle your boss, don't accept the advice blindly; he or she is not you. You are unique and so is your relationship with your boss. Even if his nickname is Godzilla, you might just have the personality and operating style to turn him into Bambi.

STEP-UP PLAN YOUR ACTION

As you plan, remember your double goal: to build a store of information about your boss, and to learn how to interact most effectively with him and his peers. First, get the documents you need.

· Find out where organization charts are kept and get a current chart and several old ones. (Start with the secretary and keep tracking until you have them, or are told that they can't be had by you. If the latter, draw your own.)

- Ask the secretary if the boss's resumé is on file. If she asks why you want it, tell her you are looking for a better resumé format.
- Ask the secretary or the people in the personnel office for access to the unit personnel files. (You can do this as part of chapter 3's personnel assessment—just make sure you see your boss's file, too.)
- Tell the secretary (or your boss) that you would like to review the history of any recent changes in procedures, operations, or unit organization. While learning this (itself useful), note the role played by your boss.

As you pursue and review documents, note the people who can help you understand your boss. In your everyday discussion with co-workers, ask as a matter of course about your predecessors and about whoever used to work with your boss. From this process you should be able to develop a list of several knowledgeable people who have, or recently had, your rank; have had some experience dealing with your boss; have spent at least a year with the organization; seem willing to talk with you about work matters.

Make your list on the form that follows. As soon as you have, call the people involved and arrange a lunch so that you can "Pick your brains for information that will help me get up to speed," or words to that effect. (Remember also that you are making the invitation and benefiting from the information, which means *you* buy lunch.)

Name: Willard Cathay
Position and department: Supervisor—Purchasing
Relationship to my boss: Had my job last
Telephone: X5026
Lunch scheduled: Date 3/12/85 Time 1:00 P.M. Place Domingo's
Questions or topics to cover:
1. What pleases my boss?
2. What displeases my boss?
3. How did you handle him?

Name: Angelo Rasputi
Position and department: Assistant to the comptroller
Relationship to my boss: Assists my boss's boss
Telephone: X8796

Lunch scheduled: Date 4/1/85 Time 1:00 P.M. Place Chun Lee
Questions or topics to cover:
1. How does my boss stand in the company?
2. Any rivalries between my boss and others?
3.

NOW YOU FILL ONE OUT:

Name:
Position and department:
Relationship to my boss:
Telephone:
Lunch scheduled: Date _____ Time _____ Place _____
Questions or topics to cover:
1.
2.
3.

Naturally, be sure to confirm your engagement. If your colleague can't make it, reschedule then and there.

Obviously these lunches will not be your only source of information. Exploit all sources: coffee-break gossip, hallway encounters, washroom tidbits, and water-cooler stories. All can provide you with useful bits of information whether or not you're directly involved in them. While the information from these sources can be unreliable, you lose nothing by retaining the information without repeating it. Remain alert for other, more reliable data that confirms or disproves what you overheard.

Planning What to Ask Your Colleagues

As the luncheon date approaches, flesh out your questions. Write down all the questions listed below and other appropriate ones as well. (Don't bring the paper with you; just be thoroughly familiar with it. If you forget to ask something, you can always find out later.)

After pleasantries and small talk have been made, a few icebreaking questions are in order. They should be easy for your companion to answer; the idea is to encourage her to start talking. Here are a few samples (to which you may add your own, of course):

• "It's my understanding that our departments work together in terms of _____ to produce _____. Can you tell me a little more about how your (budget, schedule, etc.) affects my (schedule, staff, etc.)?" (This should be a question to which you already know the answer, especially if you're not on familiar terms with your colleague—because you also want a chance to relax. That won't happen if your guest gets to say "You mean you didn't know about the Gefleason project?" You could also end up with a dissertation on the Gefleason project instead of on your boss.)

· "What do you wish you had known when you began your job, that you know now?" (This gives your companion lots of room to talk. Her relationship with her supervisor is a very likely subject—which gives you an opening to talk about what you want to know.)

Plan your time at these luncheons. Pleasantries, small talk, and preliminary business questions have a way of taking longer than expected. If you are still making nonbusiness small talk after ten minutes, move on to the questions above. If you are still talking general business twenty-five minutes into the lunch, go on to the questions about your boss. It's going to be a waste of your time and money if you don't get to ask the questions you came to ask: about your boss's work relationships, his history, and his habits.

A few more hints: One way to get your informant to talk about your boss is to have her talk about *her* boss first.

· What did her boss do before he was her boss?
· Did her boss ever work with your boss?
· How did they get along? How do they get along now?
· What did Mr. Big (your boss) do before he was (manager, supervisor, whatever his current position) of the mousetrap department?

Then focus on your own boss's background and work relationships. Try to pick up on:

· How he operates with equals in the company
· People your boss doesn't get along with
· Hints about how your boss gets along with his bosses
· Your boss's recent achievements

as you ask the following questions:

· Did Mr. Bigger (your boss's boss) work in this company, or did he come in from outside?
· How about Mr. Biggest (the boss's boss's boss)?
· How do Bigger and Biggest generally get along with people?
· How does Big (your boss) get along with Bigger and Biggest?

Your lunchmate may know plenty about this, or very little. Even a little is useful to know, particularly if a time comes when you cannot get along with your boss. By asking about the top honchos (a favorite luncheon topic) first, you get the other person up to top talking speed for the really important direct questions about your boss.

· Mr. Big is really interesting to work for. Is it true he was responsible for the timeclock system here?
· Have you ever worked for Big, or know anybody who did? How did it work out?
· Anything I should know about Big that will help me get along with him better?

Your aim is to discover (or formulate) strategies that will work most effectively with Mr. Big. As you talk, emphasize that you want information so you can do your job more effectively; you would rather learn from other people's successes and errors than go blindly on your own. You may still encounter reluctance, but few colleagues will think you out of line for asking questions for these reasons.

If your lunch companion is talkative, you might want to add a few leading questions (couched in what's-the-best-for-the-company terms, of course) to check out your own inferences: "I've gotten the impression that Statler is on less than friendly terms with Hilton, and I'm a little concerned about how that affects convention planning here in my department. Has that ever been an issue in your area?" (We suggest using words like *issue*, *case*, or *concern* rather than *problem*. For many people, the word *problem* is such a red flag, they fail to hear anything else you're saying.) In any case, listen closely to the nonverbal clues—facial expression, coughs, gestures, tone of voice, and so forth—that accompany the answer. Your colleague may not be comfortable telling you the whole truth and nothing but—but you can usually pick up his honest opinion if what he says doesn't match the way he says it.

Also be alert for flashing red lights. You may encounter an informant who in no uncertain terms says "Lie low. Ask no questions. Do your job but don't get too closely identified with your boss Big." This person may be an excitable paranoid, or he may know far more than he's telling. Heed such advice, at least for a while. If guns aren't blazing and your boss (or your informant's boss) isn't fired in a month or two, forget the advice.

A word of caution: Never ask someone to betray a confidence or badmouth anyone. Always couch a potentially touchy question as a statement, in a neutral, unthreatening fashion: "It often seems as if Mrs.

Hatfield is annoyed with Mr. McCoy, but then I haven't seen them together that often. I'm wondering if there are feelings there that I should be
aware of." This approach gives your source more room to sidestep than a
question like "Hatfield is ready to fire McCoy, isn't she? I know you've
been working with her on the Bluegrass project lately, so tell me, what's
really going on there?" You don't say things like this to helpful people,
particularly if you ever want them to be helpful again.

When lunch is over, thank your colleague for his time and input—
even if it turned out to be useless and boring. Remember, you're estab-
lishing working relationships with your peers (for better or worse) even as
you get boss-related information. And insist on picking up the tab for the
lunch, whether it was at the Four Seasons or the company cafeteria.

Planning Strategies to Evaluate Your Boss

You might say that the best place to figure out your boss is from
behind a one-way mirror: You want to get as much information as you can
about him without showing all your cards right away. This is why ancient
history and routine business are safe discussion topics, and why his
touchy issues and personal preferences are best *observed* in the normal
course of work. In planning how to evaluate your boss, you will not so
much use lists of questions as work out *strategies* for getting close to and
understanding him or her.

Bosses are often hard to approach in the heat of the day. Telephones
are ringing. Committees are meeting. Things are going wrong. Therefore, when you do spend time interacting with him directly, the better way
is to spend time with him before or after work: when only you and your
boss are there.

Some bosses are morning *and* evening people: They come early and
stay late. If this is the case, you have the luxury of choosing when you
will put in your extra time during these first several months. If you have a
boss who arrives at 7:00 A.M. every day but goes home promptly at 5:00,
you have little choice but to get up early if you want to spend quiet time
with him. As a rule of thumb, come in at least fifteen minutes early and
stay fifteen minutes late in your first two weeks on the job (if you do
everything we suggested in the last two chapters, staying only an extra
half-hour will seem like a luxury). From the beginning, note closely your
boss's daily schedule; at the end of two weeks, rearrange your own schedule accordingly. You'll want to be at work regularly during at least some
of the boss's "extra hours." Use the following chart:

WEEK 1	Monday	Tuesday	Wednesday	Thursday	Friday
My boss's hours:	___	___	___	___	___
My schedule:	___	___	___	___	___
Best times to be in ofc. with boss alone	___	___	___	___	___
WEEK 2	Monday	Tuesday	Wednesday	Thursday	Friday
My boss's hours:	___	___	___	___	___
My schedule:	___	___	___	___	___
Best times to be in ofc. with boss alone:	___	___	___	___	___

Get used to these hours, and get the people at home used to them. They're probably longer hours than you worked before your promotion, but consider the extra time an investment in learning—sort of an evening graduate class in management. The investment will pay off in a smoother working relationship with your boss and an understanding of office politics that will help you avoid fatal pitfalls.

Talking with your boss is easier when only the two of you are around. It's not necessary to bring up issues that need his decision; you can simply discuss daily matters. In fact, if your boss has a strong affiliation style, he may simply stop in and chat. To the alert manager, even throwaway conversations are revealing. "Those guys in purchasing drive me crazy sometimes," says your boss. "I've just been working on their invoices . . . I know they're bookkeepers, but you'd think they never heard of a dictionary. Here, look how they spelled 'optical'!" You nod in commiseration. It's nice that your boss is talking to you, and even nicer that you now know how important it is to proofread carefully and to keep a dictionary handy. Even if you merely hear him say this to his secretary, you've still learned what's important to him.

For that matter, all kinds of indirect communication provide clues. Unless you're in a coma or on a different floor than your boss is (if you are, be *doubly* sure to spend regular time with him both alone and in the company of others), you cannot help but learn from his interaction with others. Note how he answers the phone when calls come in that are not screened by a secretary. Is he very formal, or loose and casual? Whatever his style, take your cue: This is how he likes phones to be answered (clients to be handled, superiors to be treated). If your natural style is seriously at odds with his, check out his preferences before deciding to be different. "I got used to being very informal with my contacts in the field, both in person and on the phone, Mr. Big. But I expect you'd like me to be a little more formal now that I'm regional manager." You don't have to like it if he says yes; you do have to change your habits, at least when he's within earshot.

His telephone manner, his immediate verbal responses to memos, his manner of speaking to you: They all signal your boss's expectations of you. Obviously, so does direct feedback specifically about your work. How does he give praise? Criticism? Orders? Who gets praise and encouragement, and who's on thin ice? It's difficult to see ourselves as others see us, but take a hard look at yourself: If you do some of the things that your boss finds annoying in others, don't just shrug and think, "Well, I'm a brusque sort of guy, and I can't change my personality. He'll just have to get used to me." You don't have to change your personality, only your behavior—and only with one very important person.

But perhaps you and your boss get along during these tête-à-têtes and even grow to like each other. You might become her confidant; perhaps she even asks you for advice. The best response is to listen closely and answer, "I'm still new and not really sure. But let me run some ideas past you, and you tell me how you think they'd work." Merely listening will win her favor, and offering some intelligent thoughts on the subject will let her know you're awake. But the last thing you need is to send her over a cliff with some bad advice confidently spoken.

Of course, the possibility exists that you'll stay late every night and get barely a nod from the boss. This in itself is a clue—the boss is not a big socializer. But your time is not wasted, because the boss is probably an achiever or a controller. She may not appreciate your sacrifice, but she would definitely think less of you if you *weren't* working overtime.

STEP-UP   USE AND ABUSE YOUR PLAN

As you learn about your boss, you should be ready to cut short your education. It is quite possible that after a week or two, a lunch or two, and an evening or two, you will have accumulated much consistent information about your boss. Your informants agree, she's a stickler for detail who keeps her nose clean in the organization; you see as you work with her that she is a stickler for detail who maintains stable relationships with other executives, and she tells you that she is a stickler who doesn't rock the boat. Do you really need to schedule two more costly lunches with her former administrative assistants? Save your money and get on to the next chapter.

Now the other side of the coin: Your lunches have been discombobulating because nearly everyone you've spoken with has led you to believe that your boss is a humorless, narrow-minded perfectionist. Yet in your brief association with her, she has consistently been pleasant to you, has seemed pleased with your work, and has never hovered over you while you do it. Who's right? We hope you are; and we suggest you ask more questions anyway. Some possibilities of what's really going on:

· She's being pleasant only *because you're new*. You probably would have gathered from your people resources that "She's always nice to new managers, then wham! she lowers the boom," but maybe your peers haven't seen her operate with many new supervisors. One way to check it out on your own is to say, as you turn in yet another high-quality report, "I'm sure you'll expect better work after I've gotten more experience doing these for a while." If she doesn't look surprised but nods or says yes, she may be just waiting to jump on you after a few weeks. Take heed. *Now* is the time to ask her again for specific feedback about what she wants and doesn't want.

· She's treating you well because she *actually likes your work*. Perhaps it's your information that's incorrect. If she answered "As a matter of fact, your reports are perfectly acceptable" or something similar, reevaluate your information sources. Have they had run-ins with your boss in the past? Was their information based on hearsay? Are office politics or the grapevine distorting their evaluations?

There's an interesting line (interesting because so few can identify it) between how Mr. Dithers acts in general—which is quite predictable— and how Mr. Dithers interacts with specific individuals. He may indeed be a detail nut as far as your peers are concerned; that's because they all happen to be creative types to whom details are just so much annoyance. If you, on the other hand, are naturally careful with details, Mr. Dithers is going to see you as one of his own and respond in kind. Don't let erroneous self-fulfilling prophecies damage your relationship before it begins. As always, if there is conflict between your experience and others' testimony, trust yourself first.

STEP-UP PLAN AND PLAN AGAIN

Boss-subordinate relationships are everchanging, often supercharged with emotion, and always crucial to your managerial success. (This is as true of your subordinates' relationship with you as it is of your relationship with your own boss.)

The difference between being the boss and being the subordinate is that subordinates need to respond quickly and often apologetically to difficulties with the relationship. Bosses, for the most part, need neither rush nor grovel. In your role as subordinate to your boss, you may encounter difficulties right away, or down the road.

The most common early difficulty is you and your boss having radically different operating styles and personalities. This gap should be obvious by the time you've completed the steps in this chapter; in extreme cases, it's apparent after a week. If you sense that you and your boss are seriously incompatible, scout around for an equivalent vacant position. Develop a reason for transferring that has nothing to do with your boss ("It's closer to my home and I've always wanted to work in the Lower Manhattan region"). But don't even apply for the transfer unless you have a plausible reason for doing so. And consider carefully what life will be like with this boss if you *don't* get the other position.

Transfers are not always possible, particularly for new managers who are expected to prove their mettle and may have been assigned to Drill Sergeant Attila for exactly that reason. So be ready to live with your manager for at least a year, even if you see the relationship as fire and ice.

If you're stuck, you're stuck—but that doesn't mean you have to be miserable. Very few bosses are truly unbearable tyrants, and you can learn something even from those you have little respect for. Drill Sergeant Attila, director of marketing—quick-tempered, competent, a stickler for detail, hard to please, grudgingly respected in the company, and a cool killer when it comes to getting his way. The hang-glider campaign (which you're working on) is his baby. How do you figure out the best way to work with him?

Start by considering the pluses. Attila knows the business, and knows how to get what he wants: better workers, larger budgets, getting the right people to listen to him blowing his own horn. He may run you ragged, but you'll emerge like an Ivy League graduate—groomed for bigger and better things.

Next, consider what you can do to accommodate yourself to his style. Even if he drives you crazy with his meaningless nitpicking and power games, don't look for ways to avoid him. Instead, force yourself to maintain an open working relationship with him by regularly initiating contact about issues requiring his input *and* discussing less charged topics where you can show off what you've done well. You'll have more of a sense of control (and suffer less stress) if you're not constantly dreading his knock. Attila, in turn, will feel reassured you're not trying to do anything behind his back.

Granted, it can become almost paralyzing to work for someone who gives you little encouragement and less autonomy, *if* you haven't convinced yourself of the wisdom of playing by the boss's rules. Reduce your stress and increase your chances for success by remembering that you work for the company, not the man, and resolve that your boss's way may not be your way, but it's currently the only way.

You have now completed the first section of this book. If you began it as you started your new management job, congratulations: You should have weathered the first two months in good order. You know your product, you know your people, and you know your boss. Once you fully understand these absolutely fundamental elements of your job, you can start building with them: building better products, better employees, a mutually beneficial relationship with your boss, and a solid base for your career.

No one can legitimately claim the title of manager without knowing how to plan, motivate, and get resources. Without these skills, you are a pretender in charge of a drifting, undisciplined, leaderless work group.

The next four chapters, "Stepping Out," concentrate on the practical skills that make an effective manager.

Part Two

Stepping Out:

The Second Three Months

Planning

BARBARA CAVALIERI bit her pencil and reflected that it might as well be a bullet. Only four months into her job as director of employee training for a large bank, she had just been given the news that her department would be the first to feel the budget crunch.

"Don't blame me, blame the new Federal Reserve deregulation policies," was her boss Botts's grim comment when he broke the bad news. Cavalieri's plans to consolidate teller and sales training, and concentrate her efforts on management development, flew out the window and lay in a heap on the grimy January snow.

An hour later she had managed to buck herself up. "I got through the energy crisis by knowing how to economize, and I can get this department through this crunch the same way," she thought. Her staff liked Barbara and cooperated with her; though she was losing one trainer and some support staff, a little streamlining could go a long way and maybe even give the secretaries a chance to show their creative stuff. Barbara vowed not to let it get her down, and the next morning, rather than complain about a fait accompli, she confidently assured Mr. Botts that even in the face of a 15 percent budget cut, she would "find a way to carry on."

During the next six months, Cavalieri worked overtime. She rethought her unit's long-range plans, she reorganized priorities, she redistributed work and consolidated duties wherever she could. She kept her eyes open for special deals from suppliers and asked her friend John in production and copying to let her know about surplus supplies and paper she could use.

Her monthly reports confirmed what she had been shooting for: Cavalieri had managed somehow to provide training for just as many tellers, salespeople, supervisors, and managers as the former director had. Furthermore, she had documented how she managed it on a significantly smaller budget, and hadn't complained or made excuses about shrinking resources. "They're sure to reward my department the minute money loosens up!'' she thought. Barbara's mood was as sunny as the summer day on which she submitted the biannual report to Botts.

And she was utterly shocked and bewildered to find that Botts wasn't joking when he sat her down the next day and unsmilingly said to her, "The figures don't look good, Barbara. What happened?"

What happened was that Barbara Cavalieri, for all her efforts, had failed to produce *more* than the last director. Of course Botts was disappointed; all he knew was that she was "going to carry on," and to him that translated as "I'll do better than last year." With no proof that she couldn't—no written requests saying that she needed more people or materials—all he could do was question her competence and planning skills. Unreasonable? No. Management expects you to produce more than your predecessor.

Some Concrete Reasons Why You Must Produce More Than the Last Manager

· The first reason is obvious: you'll make yourself look good. Your boss, her boss, the head of the company, and certainly you yourself will be pleased. Nothing, after all, succeeds like success.

· *Your* success depends on the *company's* success. A triumph for you is not only a personal victory; it means a healthier bottom line for the organization.

· Organizations don't just encourage growth; they demand it. Maintaining the status quo, no matter how acceptable it is today, is not enough. Like Cavalieri, you're expected to be bigger, better, or both each year. This means you need to produce:

—More of the same (increased quantity): more square yards of carpeting, more cars assembled, more operations performed, more apartments cleaned, than last year
—The same quantity, only better (increased quality): more cost-effective, fewer errors, less waste, fewer customer complaints
—New ideas (for new or improved products or services)
—New markets (new places to sell the same, or improved, products or services)

Other benefits of producing more than your predecessor include the built-in opportunity to manage by objectives (MBO)—that is, to define your unit's goals and to design everyone's tasks to help you reach them. Managers who don't plan end up managing by crisis or catch-as-catch-can.

A goal of 10 percent more output than the last manager's provides you with an "automatic MBO": When your objective is to be 10 percent better or do 10 percent more, it's easier to define specific subgoals. Also, your employees' subgoals (and the tasks necessary to achieve them) are relatively easily broken down from your major objective(s).

STEP-UP   SET YOUR GOALS

Planning is exerting control over the future. As you are no doubt already aware, if you don't control the future, it will control you. You're already more familiar with how to plan than you may think; the **STEP-UP** program itself is a planning method that you've been using for four chapters now, and you can apply it to ongoing and short-term work goals.

Your Planning Goals

By the end of the first six months on my new job, I will have improved the output of my department by 5 to 10 percent through:

· Increasing production
· Producing a new product or service
· Reducing errors or complaints
· Creating a more efficient procedure
· Eliminating wasted time and/or resources

Cavalieri's goals should have included *some* new type of training seminar, as well as written plans to increase the number and classification of trainees. By simply duplicating what her predecessor accomplished, she looked as if she lacked imagination, ambition, and corporate know-how.

It's crucial to keep in mind our discussion in chapter 2: Goals must be *measurable* in order to be any good to you. Five to ten percent over what the last manager produced is a good rule of thumb. You'll need to translate this into hours per piece, dollars per unit, accounts serviced per day, et cetera, depending on your own job and what your boss thinks is important. It's also worthwhile to remember that people understand and respond to *quantity* more than *quality*. If you must choose between them while you're defining your goals, go for more rather than better. Cavalieri would have looked smarter had she provided training for even 6 percent more salesmen rather than having the statistics to prove that the salesmen who received her training had upped their sales by 6 percent (that credit can go, rightly or wrongly, not to training but to the sales department).

STEP-UP TALLY YOUR RESOURCES

Take inventory of what's available to get the work done: personnel, materials and supplies, equipment. Where do they all come from? In-house, or outside? Your own department, or somewhere on the ninety-ninth floor? Find out.

Do you have the same amount available to you as your predecessor did? In chapters 2 and 3, you learned how to become familiar with everything and everyone you need to produce your unit's service or product. Use those same skills to check on resources. (If you need to walk around with a special notebook for a day or two and take more notes, by all means do so.) If by some miracle you have more resources than your predecessor, (1) thank the powers that be, literally and figuratively; (2) make good use of the extra people/money/time by having some solid (i.e., measurable) improvement to show for it. Otherwise, you can kiss that windfall good-bye next time the budget comes around. (See chapter 8 for a detailed discussion of making the budget work for you.)

Often you'll be dealing with fewer resources rather than more, however, so resist the temptation to promise your boss what you're not certain you can deliver. It's natural to want to tell your new boss what she'd like to hear, but be realistic: It's *always* better to be conservative about what you can produce and be able to surprise her—pleasantly—later. If you promise the moon and deliver it, no one will be impressed; you simply did what you said you'd do. Whereas if you document why you can only promise Podunk, and then deliver Cleveland, you'll look like a genius. You're happy, your boss is thrilled, and upper management will be delighted.

If, after tallying your resources, you find you have fewer people, typewriters, and widget makers than your predecessor, *ask* for more, right away, in writing. This should be your top priority. If you get what you ask for, fine; if you don't, you'll be covered when you announce why you can't produce as much. Just make sure you can do a little better than your forecast.

Forecasting: Polish Up That Crystal Ball

Up to now we've been talking about concrete, countable resources. Remember here that your resources include the *demand* for your products or services. This can be measured, but is rather harder to pin down than other resources. Is demand up? Down? Steady? How do you know? You needn't become an instant expert on predicting the market, but take advantage of the expertise of those around you (boss, peers, even subordinates) before drawing up your six-month plan. Don't let them assume you know all about your particular field's supply and demand (even if you think you do).

Following are some external influences that, if ignored, can cripple your company's plans. You may not have to confront them directly at the first-line or middle-manager level, but it pays to be aware of them:

1. *The government:* direct regulations governing advertising, personnel practices, hiring, promotions, equal rights, labor regulations; pricing; packaging, labeling, shipping; employee and product safety; accounting, reporting, taxes; customer relations.

2. *Indirect government influences:* purchasing, employment, and procurement practices; employment subsidies and policies; interest rates; import-export controls; agriculture subsidies, certain anti-inflation programs.

3. *The economy:* capital spending, unemployment rates, new business growth; consumer demand and spending patterns; inflation and credit availability; nonfinancial resources such as labor and material supply and shortages; interest rates and investment patterns.

4. *Social influences:* population size, growth, and demographics; market factors, including fashions and trends, spending patterns based on leisure activities, consumer attitudes; pressures from consumer and environmental groups; the entry of women, youth, minorities, and/or the handicapped into the work force.

5. *Technological developments:* new products, processes, material and energy sources; needs and demands of customer, industry, and government.

For example, if you manage a small branch bank in a "changing" (i.e., deteriorating) neighborhood that services mostly older people who live on fixed incomes, you'll have little success if your plans include "Increase revenue by getting at least ten new accounts per month." You can, however, aim to be the branch with the fewest errors, cleanest building, lowest absenteeism, fewest customer complaints, and so forth. A branch of the same bank in a gentrifying neighborhood, of course, presents different opportunities. Again, your plans depend on who your customers are and what they want and need most. (A college neighborhood needs check-cashing services and twenty-four-hour money machines more than it needs brokerage services. Similarly, a nonprofit health center in the same area will get a better return on reproductive services than on geriatric programs.)

STEP-UP   ENHANCE YOUR RESOURCES

Making Alliances, Making Allowances: Your Support Staff

Developing friends in high places is essential to business success, and will be discussed in chapter 10.

Here, however, we emphasize that it is just as essential to make friends in not-so-high places: the mail room, the copy department, the maintenance department. No unit, even a one-man operation, exists in isolation. You need your clerical people as much as you need your professional staff and customers. It's astonishing how often managers simply assume that support staff are just so many robots, doing consistent, quality work for anyone who requests (or demands) it. Isn't that what they're being paid for?

Don't fall into this trap. Support staff, from the experienced private executive secretaries to the high school dropout who was hired yesterday, will often reward your respect and appreciation of them by giving you speedy service and cutting red tape. Everybody needs it yesterday, and pretty soon so will you; if Housekeeping doesn't even recognize you, why should they run when you call? And what happens if they recognize you and don't like what they see goes without saying. Your plans can be worthless without their cooperation.

How do you show your appreciation? How do you build a good relationship with these crucial people who don't work directly for you? Some suggestions:

· Go in person to the units that help you produce your output. (Be sure it's not their busiest time of day, of course.) Introduce yourself and explain who you are, what you do, and what you understand this support unit does for your operation.
· Call your outside suppliers and do the same.
· In each case, ask the appropriate people what *you* can do (not "*if* you can do anything") to better help them and their department to help your department. Write down the suggestions you hear in that notebook you carry around.
· Ask what difficulties this person or department used to have with your predecessor. Listen carefully, apologize if necessary on behalf of your unit, and ask what you can do to correct the problems in the future.
· Acknowledge the support staff's job pressures and pay attention to individual idiosyncrasies—or, to put it more simply, be nice to people. "Marie, I know how busy you are on Mondays, and (that's '*and*,'

not 'but') I need this report for Mr. Big's stockholders' meeting by five. Will you be able to squeeze me in?'' always works better than a curt "Have this done by five" as you toss another folder on Marie's desk.

· Get in the habit of learning and using your support staff's names, and remembering them and their work during the holidays with wine, a basket of cheese and fruit, or whatever is the custom in your firm. (There *is* no custom in your firm? Start one.)

Charting Your Course: Consider the Alternatives

Let's suppose now that your tally shows just enough people and other resources to see you through a respectable next quarter, but virtually none to implement the changes and improvements you'd like to make. All is not lost. You can probably change how you *use* your resources to increase your time- and cost-effectiveness. Flowcharts and work redistributions are valuable tools to help you get the most out of what you have. Elvira, for example, reduced processing time almost 25 percent by using a chart to streamline the license bureau.

Soon after Elvira took over as manager of the Auto License Bureau, she realized, "There's something wrong with this picture." Once they found the proper initial or renewal window, applicants waited in endless lines for form 12345A only to be told to go to another floor and wait in more endless lines for form 12345B. If they didn't have a check or money order to pay the fee, they had to leave, get one, and wait in line all over again. The written part of the licensing test was given three flights up, and the results often took an hour to be delivered to the proper clerk downstairs. Applicants then walked a thousand feet away to another department to get their pictures taken for the license, and walked back just to have the picture laminated and the license validated. The few signs that told applicants where they were, or where to go next, had long since faded into illegibility. Although the clerks managed to be relatively courteous, they wasted many minutes answering frustrated applicants' questions. In short, the bureau plodded along as it had for years—with the usual complaints and hardly at maximum efficiency. Elvira knew that trying to change an entrenched behemoth would be difficult, so she planned carefully.

Elvira's first step was revolutionary in its simplicity: She had a trusted colleague from another office go through the entire license-renewal process. The colleague timed each step and noted the route taken. She asked "obvious" questions of every clerk she dealt with to see if the answers were clear and consistent. She sympathized just enough to hear comments like "I don't know why they can't just phone down the test results to us as soon as they have them—it doesn't help security any to have them delivered, it just holds us up." She paid attention to what applicants were complaining about as they waited and waited and waited.

When her colleague had finished, Elvira was able to make out the chart below.

CHART 5A: The Old License Procedure

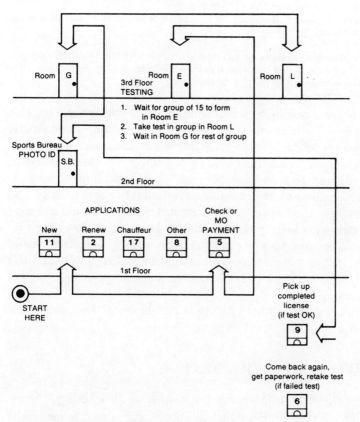

Enter building. Find way to license bureau. (Very small sign in large building directory on wall.)

1. Figure out which of four windows to go to for correct application form (for new, renewed, chauffeur's, or special license). If you were in the wrong line, you must wait again in the correct one. Clerk should explain that you'll need a check or money order to pay for the fee at window 5.

2. Fill out application, get in line again at window 5, pay fee (check or MO only), and get application stamped. If you didn't bring check or money order, leave and get them, wait at window 5 again. Clerk should explain that the next step is to go to the testing area on the third floor.
3. Take application to testing area, take a number, and wait to be called for the license test, which is taken in groups of fifteen.
4. Wait in separate room at other end of floor until all fifteen in the group are finished. Clerk should tell applicants to go to the Sports Licenses Bureau (south end of second floor) to have photo ID taken.
5. Get photo taken at sports licenses. Clerk should tell applicants to take photo to window 12 on first floor.
6. Wait in line at window 12 to have photo affixed to blank license and validated; proceed to window 9, where completed license may be picked up.
7. Wait further at window 9, if necessary, for test results to be sent from third floor before getting completed license.

If you failed the test, you must come back no sooner than one week later, locate your application at window 6, get a special form, and wait on the third floor to be called for the test again. Clerk should explain as necessary, and point out the nearest exit.

Elvira's *goal* was to decrease complaints by 20 percent and increase productivity by streamlining the application procedure. Theoretically, less time spent per application should increase revenue, but since licenses were renewed every four years, Elvira's "consumer population" remained fairly consistent. To accomplish her goal, Elvira planned to cut the average processing time by 25 percent: from two hours to ninety minutes. The applicants would be 25 percent less frustrated; the clerks would no longer have to deal with angry people wanting to know where they were supposed to go next and what on earth was taking so long; complaints should decrease. If the new procedure worked as planned, Elvira would be able to transfer one clerk out of her bureau (and off her payroll) to another department.

Elvira accomplished her goal. How did she do it? She planned her action, of course.

STEP-UP   PLAN YOUR ACTION

It's Lonely at the Top: Mapping Out Your Plan for Change

If your flowchart, like Elvira's, indicates that some changes could make your unit more efficient, start experimenting. You have a lot to keep in mind:

Your company's, boss's, and personal goals (which may not be entirely compatible)

Number and skills of your employees
Equipment, supplies, and space available
Friends in support units
Friends upstairs (i.e., other upper management)
Layout of the physical plant or office
Other relevant factors: _____

However, you can rearrange anything you want on paper (or on your computer, for that matter; see chapter 9, "Better Management Through Computers") and project the results and consequences before you involve anyone else.

Unless a deadline is pressing, give yourself time to plan alone first, allowing yourself free rein to experiment. Then let your alternative plans sit, and look at them with a fresh eye a day or two later.

Now ask yourself on paper:

1. *Personnel:* Who *should* be doing what? That is, what changes in the flow appear to be cost-, time-, or personnel-effective?
2. *Sequencing:* Who should give what to whom, when, and why? Do you have jam-ups and blind alleys where you can build a smooth road? Are efforts being duplicated that could be consolidated?
3. *Physical planning:* Where is each task most efficiently performed? Can people, supplies, equipment be moved, rearranged, divided more conveniently?
4. *Timeliness:* Which start-up times, and deadlines should be extended? That is, what's always late? Why? How can you change it? If you can't, can other parts of the system be changed? Similarly, which production schedules and deadlines could be shortened? Often the answers to the questions in items 1–3 above will suggest ideas.
5. *Deadlines:* When will the plans first be put into action? By what date should all the plans be producing the projected results? If the date is missed, what will the consequences be? (These answers are *crucial*. Without deadlines, your plans will languish, flounder, and expire.)

Elvira asked herself all these questions. When she had answered them, the result was the reorganization plan for the license procedure.

CHART 5B: License Bureau Reorganization Plan

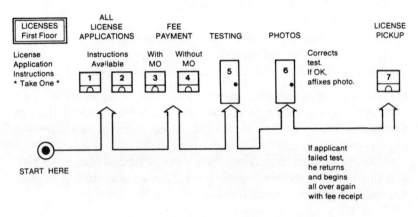

Elvira decided that six months would be sufficient for her plans to be put in place and running smoothly. Her changes included bringing testing and photos to the first floor; displaying large signs directing applicants to the proper areas and windows; making a step-by-step "How to Get Your License" sheet available to applicants, explaining the procedure and requirements (money order, properly filled-out forms); redistributing the work (only two windows would now give out applications, and every application could be obtained at both windows; this freed up another window for fee payments); allowing applicants to take the written test whenever they were ready rather than in a group; having the tests corrected as they were completed, with the results immediately passed along to the validation area. Those who failed the test were told immediately. Rather than saving their paperwork, which was often lost and caused frequent delays and frustration, failed applicants would now be instructed to keep their fee-payment receipt and go through the entire process from the beginning when they reapplied. Elvira also held an hour-long session for her entire staff to explain these changes and their rationale once her plans had been approved by her own supervisor.

Convincing Your Boss and Peers to Support Your Plan

By charting her changes and demonstrating how improved efficiency could mean a 25 percent decrease in processing time (and therefore 25 percent fewer complaints, and perhaps more revenue), Elvira was able to obtain her boss's support for her proposed changes. (Since licenses had to be renewed every four years, Elvira's "product" was in no danger of saturating the market.)

Equally important, Elvira had spoken to Stengel, the head of the Sports Licenses Bureau, and gotten his cooperation as well. The two bureaus shared the photo machine, but sports, being a much smaller office, agreed to make do with a smaller (brand-new) model of their own—to be partially paid for over twenty-four months with a percentage of the money saved by the license bureau's new procedures. The large photo machine could now be moved downstairs to the license bureau. Elvira also exchanged office storage space with another bureau so that testing could be moved to the first floor.

Getting Your Troops On Board: Including Your Staff in Your Plan

Once you have thought out the second (not final) draft of your plan, it's time to discuss it with your staff. Ignoring this time-consuming but crucial step can be fatal. Why? It's been proven time and again that when subordinates have some say in the planning process, they also have a much greater investment in *carrying out* those plans. Don't sabotage your success by struggling through the hard work yourself, and then expecting your staff automatically to be as excited and motivated as you are.

Speak to your people individually and informally, on their own turf if that's quiet enough. Begin by telling them that you'd like their input on some ideas. Tell them that you're enthusiastic about making some carefully planned changes and that you want their ideas before you make anything final. Be sure to explain: your departmental goals and the rationale behind them; the probable tasks and benefits for this employee that your plans will involve; and that you expect everyone's best efforts to produce 5 to 10 percent more this quarter (or whatever your specific goals are). Their cooperation and success will mean rewards that you'll actively seek out for them. (Be realistic about this, or it will have the ring of bribery to it. See chapter 7, "Employee Development, Advocacy, and Discipline.")

Next, ask open-ended questions about what each subordinate thinks of the plan:

· "What serious obstacles do you see that I may not be aware of?"
· "What suggestions do you have for improving the plan?"

Then, *listen*, without immediate comment, to the answers you hear. Jot them down. Whether they strike you at first as brilliant or worthless, thank your employee for his or her ideas, and *think* about them. Your staff is often a gold mine of untapped expertise.

Finally, indicate that you will be sending out formal memos outlining your final changes after you've gotten input from the entire staff. (If the size of your staff makes personal interviews with everyone impossible, at least send a preliminary memo outlining your plan. Ask for written responses to your questions about the plan.) Whether or not you use any of your people's suggestions or ideas (chances are you will), you've improved morale and paid your staff the great compliment of making them feel they're part of a team. The likelihood of your plans and changes being implemented and supported by your people is much improved.

Creating a plan for a one-time (limited, temporary) project involves slightly different concerns than for an ongoing (indefinite or permanent) production schedule. Some of the differences between the two have to do with time: A one-time project succeeds or fails once, while ongoing production must succeed consistently over time. Project management is finite, with an overall deadline; production management is open-ended. Elvira's project, for example, involves production management.

Project Management
The tasks or events to be completed are new; quality and quantity standards are high.

Goal: To create a new product or service (or part thereof)

Example: To design packaging for a new product

Involves: Completing specific tasks with a deadline and subdeadlines, usually only once

Quality control: Measures accuracy, completeness, and timeliness

Deadline (sometimes even more important than results): Fixed

Schedule of tasks (see complete "New Package Design" chart, p. 98)

WEEK

1 Determine costs of materials, etc.

2 Meet with management

3 Discuss and develop management goals with entire staff

4 Refine goals with art/design staff

   Et cetera

Production Management
The tasks to be completed remain consistent; quality or quantity standards change.

Goal: To measurably improve, continue, or institute an ongoing process

Example: Processing auto licenses

Involves: Doing a continuing series of the same events well and consistently

Quality control: Measures and monitors change per day, week, etc.
Example: Current production: 500 accurate, complete licenses per week.
How many more? Goal: +125 licenses processed per week
Current complaints/errors: 20 per week
How many less? Goal: −20% complaints per week
Deadline (usually less important than results): Flexible
26 weeks to achieve goals completely
3 weeks to implement changes
Schedule for changes:

WEEK	LICENSES PROCESSED	COMPLAINTS MADE
1	+10	+5%
2	+10	+3%
3	+15	+1%
4	+15	−1%
5	+20	−4%
6	+25	−6%
. . .	. . .	. . .
26	+125	−20%

Note that Elvira, realist that she is, has planned for more, not fewer, complaints at first. Although part of her plan is to *reduce* complaints by 20 percent, her changes will discombobulate her staff enough to make things worse, not better, for a few weeks. Errors should start to decline after a month, as Elvira plans.

Planning for both one-time projects and ongoing production is similar in these ways:

· *You must set specific, measurable goals:* Realistically ambitious, they should be clearly written, just as your own **STEP-UP** goals have been, and distributed to everyone involved.
· *You must check out whether your goals are compatible* with other units' goals. Departmental goals are too often self-defeatingly incompatible; some managers adopt "sensible" objectives like "Expand organization by 18 percent," while others resolve to "Pay back 75 percent of outstanding debt"—both within the next fiscal year. No company can do this, and much effort is wasted working at cross-purposes. If your unit's goals turn out to be incompatible, what can you change? Consider making tradeoffs with other managers, or setting different (alternative) goals that do not conflict. In every case, discuss with your boss the firm's overall objectives or five-year plan and keep them in mind as you replan.

- *You must create alternative plans* for achieving the goals. Elvira's final plan was not the *only* workable one she developed. If Stengel in sports licenses hadn't cooperated about the photo machine, she would have used an alternate plan. She talked with more than one other bureau director before she found some who were willing to exchange space with her.
- *You must evaluate the alternatives* in terms of time versus money, people versus equipment, speed versus quality, and so on. Which gets you where you want to go in the fastest, least expensive way? (You're right—this is not always immediately apparent.)
- *You must choose the best* (or least intolerable) *plan*, and put it into action after figuring out the personnel you'll need to carry out the plan, the resources it will take to implement the plan, the timing and sequencing (priorities), and building in checkpoints (discussed more fully in "Use and Abuse Your Plan").

Project Management: Carrying Out One-Time Plans

Project management involves tools and techniques you use to plan, organize, staff, direct, and control the activities that are necessary to meet a single set of objectives.

Let's trace a specific goal from the overall long-term objectives of a cosmetics company down to you as manager of the design department, where it becomes one three-month project you're in charge of. Note how the goals that affect you here (marked by ≫) progress from very vague to very detailed.

Overall Company Objectives of a Cosmetics Manufacturer

    1. Create customer satisfaction
≫ 2. Make profits 6 percent of sales
    3. Grow in size

Supporting Objectives

≫ 1. Improve product quality by using higher quality, more expensive ingredients, materials and packaging.
    2. Increase market share to 15 percent.

Specific Goals for Next Twelve Months

    1. Improve manufacturing productivity by 10 percent
    2. Reduce wasted material in production by 35 percent
≫ 3. Develop new line of sun-care products

>>> 4. Advertise higher quality of products
(Note that all these objectives work together and are compatible: that is, the goals are not in conflict with one another.)

Specific Objective

>>> Develop a new after-sun moisturizer and have it displayed for sale on counters of 8,000 drug and variety stores in the Southwest within 12 months.

Departmental Plans to Reach This Objective

1. Budget money to develop, produce, advertise, and distribute this new sun-care product. (Finance Dept.)
2. At 3 months: Have product developed (Research and Development Dept.)
3. At 5 months: Complete field tests for new moisturizer in four consumer test markets (Market Research Dept.)
4. At 6 months: Secure necessary Food and Drug Administration approvals (Legal Dept.)
5. At 6 months: Review progress, take necessary corrective steps (General Manager)
>>> 6. At 6 months: Have new package design approved (Art/Design Dept.)
7. At 7 months: All new production and packaging materials purchased (Purchasing Dept.)
8. At 8 months: Production of moisturizer under way (Production Dept.)
9. At 9 months: Advertising and promotion campaign completed (Advertising Dept.)
10. At 10 months: Sales force has initial distributors' orders secured (Sales Dept.)
11. At 11 months: Have 35,000 cases of new product shipped to distributors' warehouses (Shipping Dept.)
12. At 11 months: Print advertising begins (Advertising Dept.)
13. At 12 months: Television advertising begins (Advertising Dept.)
14. At 12 months: Check to see that new moisturizer is on shelves of 8,000 drug and variety stores in the Southwest (Market Research Dept.). Any problems will be corrected by the General Manager.
15. Develop plans for next 12 months for new objective and specific plans to increase distribution of this new product, and add other products to the sun-care line. (All departments mentioned, including quality control.)

Adapted from Ronald A. Burke and Lester R. Bittel, *Introduction to Management Practice*, New York, McGraw-Hill, 1981. Reproduced with permission.

YOUR UNIT'S PLAN   As manager of the design department, one of your unit's plans must be based on step 6, "At 6 months: Have new package design approved." Control of this subproject is now in your hands. As project manager, you're responsible for:

· Developing the schedule, preparing the budget, and building in appropriate checkpoints (that is, the "Plan Your Action" step in **STEP-UP**)
· Acting as the focal point for all project tasks, i.e., coordinating activities and preventing things from "falling through the cracks."
· Evaluating progress, preparing written status reports, and taking cor-

rective action when necessary (the "Use and Abuse Your Plan" and "Plan and Plan Again" steps).

As you brainstorm about it on paper, you realize the package design project involves numerous concerns:

- The actual calendar date on which the project is due, and the "real" date (which may actually be several weeks later) that upper management really expects it. You probably have some idea of the time leeway allowed in your firm; if you don't, listen between the lines to the grapevine, or ask your boss directly. There are very few good excuses for being late.
- When to begin work on this project, based on how much time it will take your unit to produce an acceptable design. (A solid estimate, made with the help of your experienced staff, is essential. Whatever the time line, *allow 20 percent more time for error, delays, and miscalculations.* This is known as obeying Murphy's Law, i.e., "If anything can go wrong, it will.")
- Which managers need to approve the design, and who has power to veto it. (Make it a point to find out and meet their standards and preferences.)
- How many alternate design choices you must produce.
- Whether you must produce a new container as well as box design. If so, should the container be hard plastic? A squeeze bottle? Does the product formula require light-resistant packaging? The cost of each may affect your design.
- How much money is available to finance your role in meeting the overall objective to "improve product quality and sales by using more expensive ingredients/packaging and more advertising" (that is, the product budget you must meet).
- Photos, drawings, design elements that need to be produced.
- Sample of bottle must be made by company's usual plastics supplier.
- If time is short, can you hire temporary help or new staffperson? Or can your existing staff handle the work adequately?
- Deciding who should do the work: Your best artist, someone new who needs the experience, the least busy person, et cetera (discussed in detail in chapter 6, "Leading and Delegating").
- Meshing the work with your other ongoing projects and production.
- Evaluation (by you) of initial ideas, designs.
- Scheduling first, second, and additional drafts of packaging to be shown to your boss and upper management (how many levels?).

- Probable time needed to incorporate recommended changes of appearance and cost of packaging, et cetera.
- Advertising copy must relate to package copy and design.
- Initial brainstorming sessions with creative staff.

You've looked at cost, performance, and time lines; now put your ideas in orderly sequence by answering the following questions:

- Which task must be done first?
- Which tasks can be done concurrently?
- Which facts must you get from other participating departments to prevent wasted time and effort?
- Which tasks depend on certain people or equipment being free? Will these plans conflict with seasonal overloads or other busy times in your unit? What about predictable outside influences? (See the list in "Tally Your Resources.")

Having considered these questions, you're ready to prepare a chart (known as a Gantt chart, after its inventor) to keep track of who needs to be doing what, when. A bar chart indicates how long a project phase will take, whether other phases can be done concurrently, and milestones or deadlines for various tasks.

Note that not all the above items appear on the chart; you must see to budget considerations and delegating the work before you schedule activities.

According to your projections, it will take a total of seventeen weeks for the project to be completed. Now add 20 percent to your estimate (about three and a half weeks); you can now tell your supervisor that you need to begin work five months before the due date of the package design.

Everyone involved with completing tasks for this project (everyone you supervise, that is) should have a copy of this chart. This includes the appropriate people from advertising (the copywriters and their supervisor) and your suppliers. In addition, memo the project's boss, with copies to Mr. Big and Ms. Bigger, a week before their review dates come up. This reminds them that you're depending on them to have their comments back to you by a certain date and that your department is working hard and on schedule.

Note that you can—indeed you have to—break down some of these steps further into subtasks and sub-subtasks. The staff to whom you've delegated certain work might want or need subdeadlines, or you may direct them to set their own.

CHART 5C   New Package Design

WEEK NUMBER

ACTIVITY MILESTONE	1	2	3	4	5	6	7	8	9	10	11	12	13	14	15	16	17	18
1. Get projected production costs from suppliers, etc.	1–2																	
2. Meet with selected upper mgmt. to discuss initial ideas, costs		2–3																
3. Initial staff meeting: explain project, delegate tasks			3															
4. Meet with art/design staff				4														
5. Meet with advertising dept., copywriters, and design staff				4														
6. Design development package				4–6														
7. Review design development work					5–7													
8. Arrange container production (sizes, materials, deadline)					5–6													
9. Meet to review production							7											
9A. Sample container and package completed								8										
10. First review (your boss, Mr. Big) of package, container									9–10									
11. Redesign according to Mr. Big's suggestions										10–11								
12. Arrange another sample container (if necessary)										10–11								
13. Second review (Ms. Bigger)											11–12							
14. Redesign according to Ms. Bigger's changes												12–13						
15. Final review by CEO													13–14					
16. Redesign according to CEO's suggestions														14–15				
17. Finished art, copy, sample containers submitted for final approval																16		
18. Deliver packaging and container design to suppliers and production dept.																	17	

In short: The whole idea behind charting and planning is to *save you trouble*—by getting a realistic idea of *what* needs to be done and *how long* it will take to do it. Obviously, when a tight deadline is part of the assignment, planning is even more important: By "controlling the future," you avoid the stress of wasted time, effort, and supplies.

STEP-ⓊP   ⓊSE AND ABUSE YOUR PLAN

Does It Work? And Does It Help? Controlling Plan, People, and Production

At first glance you may think the two questions above are redundant. They're not. A plan can work as smoothly as a canoe gliding down a stream, and one wrong turn can leave you miles from where you really wanted to go. And a poor plan can look at first like it's getting terrific results ("Hey, it's really helping!") only to hit serious obstacles farther down the line from unforeseen problems involving other production units, federal regulations, or opposition from individual superiors. In fact, the monkey wrenches that may land in your works are virtually countless. This is why **STEP-UP** has contingency planning steps built into it: abusing (modifying) your plan while still using it, or junking what doesn't work and getting a new plan in place without losing time and money.

How will you know if your current plan is working? By using the milestones on your Gantt chart and measuring the standards you built into your goals after the plan has been put into operation (this may take as little as a few days, or extend over months).

Elvira, for example, might exert control by keeping track of weekly or monthly statistics: how many more licenses are now being processed accurately and completely? She may note how much, if any, new revenue is coming in compared to the costs of making the changes. She may keep track of how many complaints are being made and whether they reflect problems with time or other concerns. She should also ask the clerks what problems the new layout is presenting to them. If their concerns are real, they'll show up consistently in the appropriate production statistics.

Such concerns may, however, be due solely to changeover confusion; remember, Elvira *planned* for more complaints at first. Initial difficulties require Elvira's support and leadership skills rather than a reworking of her new standards or policies. She may go through the licensing procedure again herself (or send a colleague) in seven or eight months (once all her changes are in place) to see how much time is saved. And she can spot-check applicants to see whether the new signs and directions are helpful, and how long the process now takes them.

We remind you again: trying to keep track of every single step in any new plan or procedure is self-defeating, exhausting, and will leave you suffocating in paper. Choose beforehand the 20 to 25 percent of the people and procedures that produce the most, or most important, results: results on which other activities depend. Focus on them.

When your changes have taken hold and the system is running fairly smoothly, you can see to the rest of the details (which more than likely will have taken care of themselves).

STEP-UP PLAN AND PLAN AGAIN

Though we sincerely hope your plans work as well as our example does, life is often more complex. You may find that indeed your milestones are not being met, your staff seems confused or disgruntled, and problems no one could have predicted are botching the works. Some typical reasons why Murphy's Law was passed and affects us all:

· *Seasonal changes:* If you work in a department store or tuna cannery, these are obvious; if not, learn from your boss or peers the signals that predict slowdowns or hectic periods.

· *Bottlenecks in your system:* There are all kinds of possibilities here:

—You created a change, and everyone *(everyone)* needs time to adjust to even the smallest or most positive of changes. Therefore, your staff's output is (temporarily) down. Offer support and praise whenever something is done right, insist that things continue to be done the new way, and keep your cool. They'll get through it.

—Equipment or supply shortfall: See if you can trace it, untangle it, or go around it to get what you need. Call in whatever favors may be owed you, reschedule where possible, and memo your boss about what you've done.

· *Unexpected absences:* illness, vacation, the weather, an urgent project for which your people have been appropriated by a higher power. Can you have your people work overtime? Hire temporary help? Borrow from another manager?

· *Employee conflicts:* Productivity can nosedive, especially in a small office, when people aren't getting along (and there doesn't have to be a rational reason why they're not). Separate the battling parties, if possible. If not, call them in together, and without mentioning their conflict directly, explain that personal stress must not be allowed to affect the quality and timeliness of the work. This is usually enough to give people the idea that their differences should be settled outside the office.

· *Overoptimism:* Maybe you forgot Murphy's Law and your plan hinged on every piece of equipment running perfectly. *Always* add 20 percent to your best estimated time, especially when telling your boss how long it will take. In the meantime, can you hire temporary people or equipment?

· *Inadequate fact-checking:* influences and facts you were honestly unaware of, as well as those you should have checked out. Next time you'll know.

· *Poor communication:* Did you get feedback from all your people that they understood what they were to be doing? Those in your unit and appropriate outsiders need to have adequate, factual, written information about your plans (a Gantt chart) as well as a clear idea of what results they should be producing.

Be prepared to do all you can to solve these problems as soon as you identify them. Investigate quickly, thoroughly, and impartially. Meet with the people involved, and be sure all of them know they're there to define the problem and solve it with your help. You may offer only unbiased support while your staff irons out the details, or they may require your concrete advice and direction. Certain employees may need training or reeducation in a certain aspect of their job; see that they get it, quickly, if you can't provide it yourself.

When Your Work Is Progressing but the Project Itself Is Stalled

Your unit plans are rolling right along, but your boss is telling you that work on the new sun-care product (and your design for packaging it) has been postponed—again. The project you were hoping would single you out as an up-and-coming, promotable manager may never see the light of top management's day. What do you do? What *can* you do?

First, make sure there's a real project slowdown and the delay is more serious than overwork on some vice president's part. Warning signals: your boss is evasive or snappish when you ask why things have slowed down, or is heartily reassuring but vague when you ask when the project will get in gear again.

Listen to what your reliable peers have to say, without asking direct questions. If things look bleak, don't play ostrich. Instead, find out why the project is stalled: Is it because of an apathetic boss, or one who has a personal gripe against this project? Have personnel changes left everyone confused about who's in charge of what? Have new marketing information or pending regulatory changes put everything on hold?

If necessary, give yourself a chance to be angry and regroup—but not on company time. (See chapter 11 for some stress-management techniques.) Determine the exact status of the project by asking your boss directly, or, if this isn't feasible, using his secretary as a go-between. Perhaps you know someone on your boss's level who can call him because she's "wondering what's happening with the new sun-care project."

Depending on what you hear and the other work your staff is doing, you may put this project on the back burner, perhaps indefinitely, or be ready to revive it on an hour's notice. Either way, cut your losses where you can, and direct your own and your staff's efforts elsewhere.

Next time, plan a safety net: Be enthusiastic when you're given a new assignment, *and* make sure you're also working on some important project that will definitely be carried through. There will always be some projects that never get off the ground. No need to spin your wheels in frustration; rather, write up what you did accomplish, and CYA.

CYA (Cover Your reAr end)

If the problem or obstacle is out of your control, memo your supervisor immediately. Tell her what's going on, how it's affecting your unit's output, and what you've done (or tried to do) about it. Most likely you've already asked your boss for help or guidance, so to some extent she's aware of conditions; if not, the memo is doubly important. If the situation deteriorates further, you can show that you were aware of problems, took steps to solve them, and advised the proper superiors.

A word of warning, however: If a superior would like to see you go (for any reason), or if your unit is in a weak or vulnerable position, written records proving you're "right" may not be enough to settle the problem.

When Things Just Don't Work Out

Making judgments and decisions is difficult at best, and more so when you've invested yourself in your plan. Force yourself to read the writing on the wall: If you can't salvage anything worthwhile and your plan dies, take responsibility for it. This means letting your employees know what happened and why it happened, without specifying blame of any kind. Thank them for their efforts. Then go right on to explain how production will change and what will be expected of your staff in terms of new plans and projects.

This hurts, especially if it's the first time for you. Don't yell at yourself or allow your staff to think you've lost confidence in them or in your own ability. *Everyone* makes mistakes, screws up, and gambles wrong from time to time. The real mistake is to waste hours or days being angry, finding someone to blame, or trying to justify your actions to yourself (you may be wise to justify them to your boss, of course) when you could be planning again, using what you learned.

Run Your Plan; Don't Let It Run You

Whatever you do, however you plan, remember this: A plan is just a managing tool. Don't let your plan assume, like Frankenstein's monster, a life of its own. Don't let it hide or submerge the goals and objectives it's meant to help you reach. If it isn't doing its job, or if circumstances make it obsolete, junk it—now—and plan again. The more you plan, the more you'll learn to build flexibility into your plans; the more flexible your plans, the more time, money, and effort you'll save yourself and your staff.

Leading and Delegating

MALMQUIST knew how to get grants for the college. Malmquist wrote proposals; foundations wrote checks. And the special projects office of the college grew and grew. When the special projects office needed a new manager, Malmquist was chosen thanks to his almost single-handed funding of all the office's various activities.

Malmquist hadn't chosen to be a crackerjack writer for nothing. He liked working by himself because he hated confrontations. As manager, he seized onto a cliché he had once heard and made it his motto: "Delegation," he would say, "is the better part of management." So he let his subordinates run the shop while he pursued more grants. He checked on people infrequently and corrected them even less.

After eight months of nonmanagement, Malmquist suddenly found that his subordinates had but the slightest idea he was the manager; Malmquist's assistant, Machiavelli, had been running the department for all practical purposes. Everyone in the special projects office assumed that Machiavelli, not Malmquist, was the boss.

Machiavelli thought so, too. In eight months of unfettered activity, Machiavelli had made himself the only channel through which the staff could communicate upward. He was beginning to make power moves against other organizational units and had illegally mingled funds from one grant with funds from another grant.

Machiavelli was caught—not by Malmquist, unfortunately, but by a sharp-eyed auditor. Malmquist was fired along with Machiavelli, and left with the college president's words ringing in his ears: "Your job was to *lead* them, not abdicate your power to whoever felt like using it! You gave up your leadership, but the responsibility is still yours. *You* let the unit be led astray, and *you*, damn it, are going to pay for it!"

Mildred Harrison, who had gone to school with the unfortunate Malmquist, was anything but shy and retiring. As the director of community relations for a social services agency, no detail escaped her overview, and no worker changed a comma without her okay. Nothing got by Harrison, but plenty of work waited forever before getting *to* her. Half-completed reports sat around for weeks because Harrison had only so much time in a day to go over things with her fine-tooth comb.

The work coming out of Harrison's office was letter-perfect, but the perfection was all Harrison's. Her employees got so used to her changing things, no matter how hard they tried to do a perfect job, that they stopped trying. Harrison found herself doing more and more work, with more and more of it under crisis conditions as she pulled from her in-basket half-completed reports that were due yesterday.

A year of this made Mildred Harrison very tired. Finally, under doctor's orders, she took three weeks' vacation to Europe. Without Harrison, the work of the community relations office ground to a halt. When Harrison's boss, Chambers, came by during her absence, she found a bunch of people trying to look busy while they did nothing. When Chambers asked questions, she was struck by how little the employees knew and by their utter lack of energy and initiative.

When Harrison returned, agency director Chambers was waiting. "You," said Chambers, "are not immortal. And your people have about as much ability to carry on after you as my pet cocker spaniel. Now you give them work and let them do it, mistakes and all. If you don't delegate to them and develop them, you're slowly going to kill yourself—and I'm not going to keep you here while you do it."

Mildred Harrison decided to change her ways.

In the end, Harrison fared better than Malmquist. It's easier to ease up on a well-controlled staff than to rein in a runaway staff. Harrison gave more authority and work to her people, stayed out of their hair while they did it, and conducted reviews of finished products with suggestions for the next time. Endless drafts became a thing of the past, along with the listlessness and ignorance of her staff.

Some Concrete Reasons Why You Must Delegate Work

The moral of these stories is simple. You cannot delegate effectively unless you demonstrate leadership—that is, present yourself as being in command, plan direction and assignments for others, and stand by to help and to review end products. By the same token, you cannot lead well without delegating work to your subordinates. By failing to delegate, you lead only yourself, and armies of one go nowhere.

Some further reasons:

· Most of the business of management, in case this is not already abundantly clear, *is* delegation. You've moved from taking orders to giving them, from doing to directing. (You're still ultimately responsible for the results.) Your staff relies on you to coordinate the work of the unit so there are no gaps, no duplications of effort, and consistent quality.

· You now are responsible for training people to do their jobs well. One way to do this (besides formal training) is to let employees take on and complete tasks.

· You are not physically capable of doing all the work yourself. (This doesn't stop some managers from becoming overextended, ineffectual workaholics, but we suggest it should stop *you*.)

· You may not have the expertise to do all of your subordinates' jobs. And even if you do, reread the preceding sentence.

· Your job is to see that people's skills are used, and mesh well, to produce your output and meet your departmental and organizational goals. It may be hard to give up the title of "Best Damn Widget Maker This Company Has Ever Seen," but if you don't, you might as well go back to making them.

· You'll save time. And you'll need all the time you can get, especially while you're learning the job and refining your delegation techniques.

Some Concrete Reasons Why You Must Lead

Delegating work is not the same as leading your staff, and both are essential to your long-term success. As a leader, you must give direction and orders with authority, set examples of quality and timeliness, act as peacemaker in the work group, and protect your work unit. Your staff looks to you for help in emergencies, making major decisions, settling squabbles among themselves, and even for behavior and dress guidelines. As much as people complain about how the boss runs things (you did, didn't you?), one of the luxuries of being a subordinate is letting someone else make the decisions. And now that someone is you.

You may be thinking "All that leading is a little much for me . . . Anyway, some of those old-timers know the job better than I do at this stage of the game." Even so, if you want to be an effective manager, you cannot long evade a leadership role.

Why? If *you* don't lead (consciously, deliberately, carefully) no one will follow you. They will, however, follow *someone*, and that someone may not necessarily be going where you want him to. In fact, like Machiavelli in the story above, he may be aiming to roll right over your laid-back body on *his* way to the top. Furthermore, leading your people means you'll get better cooperation and better work from them. When a boss is respected (not necessarily liked, but respected), people are interested in her approval and will work to get it. And, moving now from the practical to the political, remember that your success or failure depends on your *own* boss's perception of how well you lead your subordinates. Don't undermine your own authority by having to call in your boss to settle your staff's infighting, or complain more than once that your people don't listen to you.

Leadership is hard to fake; even if your styles differ, your boss will look at the omnipresent bottom line as the real test of effective leadership.

STEP-UP SET YOUR GOALS

Leadership Goals

From month three to month six (and beyond, if applicable), I will:

- Establish a schedule for meeting with my immediate staff
- Develop a plan for contacting all my employees at least twice a month
- Develop and adopt the style of leadership (ways of conveying information, directing work, and responding to the staff) that best fits my personality
- Demonstrate a leadership style that will encourage my employees to be productive and content

Clearly these last two goals may conflict. You may be a quiet soul who has been made manager of a unit that needs a drill sergeant. You may be a stern and forceful type in charge of a unit that goes to pieces when yelled at or pressured. Someone has to change—will it be your staff, or you? Figure it out: You are one person. Your staff is four, fourteen, or forty. Who can adjust more quickly? And minimize the sheer quantity of change? That's right: You. And what's more, the work habits that grate against your "principles" may be the habits that work best in the office that you now manage. Striking a compromise between your style and your staff's needs means adjustment on your part as well as on your subordinates'. Fortunately, it also means less tension for your workers and a better chance for you to watch, evaluate, and plan. You can always take off the kid gloves later, or, if you've become manager of a sweatshop, ease up on the dictatorship.

Delegation Goals

By the end of my fourth month on the job, I will:

- Assess my employees' aptitudes and skills for various tasks and jobs
- List the jobs I now do that can completely or partially be delegated to my staff
- Delegate at least two of my jobs to two staff members who have the skills and aptitude to learn and carry them out
- Assign, explain, and monitor the delegated work without creating resentment or bottlenecks

STEP-UP TALLY YOUR RESOURCES

But What If I'm Just Not a Natural Leader?

If you've never led anything before, not even a Cub Scout pack, you have plenty of company. You also have this book, which is about to tell you how to figure out your own leadership style: how to capitalize on your strengths and develop the skills you may be lacking.

Remember that your most important leadership resource is *you*: your personality, how you deal with people, and your motivation to get the job done well. Other resources include: your past managers whose leadership you admired or envied: What is it about them you can emulate? Your past supervisors whose leadership made you want to scream and tear your (their?) hair out: What horrible habits of theirs must you studiously avoid? Current co-workers at all levels: When you see them trying to lead, what works? What doesn't? And how do they respond to their own boss's attempts to lead?

All these resources can give you useful advice about how to practice good leadership. However, *you* must apply the information to your own personality and style, and you are the one who must, ultimately, lead your staff. You are your own best resource.

As a manager *learning* to lead, you may of course have crutches. Your boss may be such a holy terror (or such a saintly presence) that your leadership is an extension of hers. But what do you do when she retires, drops dead, or otherwise departs? Suddenly all leadership depends on you.

You may have a staff that does everything for you, and willingly—at first. But what happens when you have to fire someone, or a budget cut hits, or an emergency occurs that your staff simply can't handle? Suddenly, it all depends on you.

Don't kid yourself that every successful manager you've known is a natural leader; the good ones were simply smart enough to study and practice some perfectly learnable skills. To find out which skills you need to develop, complete the Leadership Self-Assessment below.

Leadership Self-Assessment

Rate yourself against each of the following descriptions, on a scale from 1 (This is not very much like me at all) to 10 (This is exactly like me).

1. I provide phone numbers when I leave the office so I can be reached almost any time if my people really need me. (Availability)   Rating ____

2. I like some people on my staff more than others, but am not extreme in my feelings and show little favoritism. (Fairness)   Rating ____

3. I rarely advertise my unit's work as "mine," but instead stress to the outside world that my staff did the work. (Credit sharing)   Rating ____

4. When something goes wrong in my unit, I see a problem that I need to work on (and may have caused) rather than labeling it a screwup by an employee. (Problem solving)   Rating ____

5. I have little difficulty admitting to others in the workplace that something is my fault. (Acceptance of responsibility)   Rating ____

6. I pay attention to how I dress and how I talk, because it affects the workers' image of me and of themselves. (Image-consciousness)   Rating ____

7. I have patience when people tell me about their "new ideas" that I thought of two years ago, or when people at meetings consume time debating what to me are trivial issues. (Tact/Patience)   Rating ____

8. My first reaction—and it is a strong one—is to defend my staff if anyone criticizes them. (Protectiveness)   Rating ____

9. I would rather decide, be wrong, and scramble to fix things than put off a decision until I think my action plan has a 100% chance of success. (Decisiveness)   Rating ____

10. I realize that certain of my employees might feel cheated by their co-workers' (and superiors') salaries,   Rating ____

office space, or promotions. (Equitability)

Total Rating (add items 1–10) _____

If you scored more than 90, go straight to the Management Hall of Fame; you have excellent leadership qualities. If you scored above 70, keep up the good work. If you scored 60 or lower (and even if you scored higher), look again at the items where you gave yourself less than a five. What can you do for your staff that will demonstrate the qualities indicated in parentheses?

Availability, decisiveness, tact, credit sharing, and the rest are essential characteristics of good leaders. Poor leaders (including nonleaders) don't have them, as will become clear when you think of your own bosses who were never around, played favorites, couldn't decide anything, or blamed you for everything. Is this the way *you* want to look to your staff?

Your Delegation Resources

Like leadership, effective delegation depends on your personality as much as it depends on your communication skills.

To be a good delegator you must be willing to give up some of your favorite work (which suggests—heaven forbid—that you are dispensable). To be a good delegator you must be a patient teacher (which means accepting occasional mistakes and helping your staff learn from them). You must be willing to give your staff the authority to complete the assignment along with the accountability for doing it. Finally, you must advertise the accomplishments of your subordinates, which means saying "I couldn't have completed that report (or project, or reorganization) without their efforts."

Most of us have an understandably hard time considering ourselves dispensable, or a manager of mistakes, or only as good as our subordinates. Yet this is exactly what managers are, and an effective delegator accepts these facts and works with them. The questionnaire below is designed to show you how ready, willing, and able you are to delegate work to your staff.

If you make similar remarks, even to yourself, check the box.

Delegation Self-Assessment

1. ☐ If you want something done right, you have to do it yourself.
2. ☐ By the time I finish teaching them how to do it, I could have done it and two other things myself.

3. ☐ Most of the things that I do couldn't be done by my staff.
4. ☐ You have to be on top of them every minute if you want them to finish the job.
5. ☐ If they were as committed and enthusiastic as I am, I wouldn't have to recheck all their work.
6. ☐ When my boss gives me a job, I do it myself so that she has nothing to complain about.
7. ☐ Between union rules and position descriptions, giving anybody new responsibilities isn't worth it.
8. ☐ We can't afford to have errors around here, so a person who masters a job should stick to it.
9. ☐ I really don't mind going over all the delegated work, and redoing it (without telling my subordinates) if necessary.
10. ☐ I consistently work longer hours than I should.

If you checked even half of these ten statements, we suggest seriously reconsidering and adjusting your attitude. Yes, delegating often feels like more trouble than it's worth, *at first*. But any successful manager (who at one time doubtless held at least some of the beliefs above) can guarantee you that in the long run, the payoff is worth it.

STEP-UP ENHANCE YOUR RESOURCES

To repeat: You are *the* resource when it comes to leading and delegating. Your effectiveness in these areas, however, depends equally on your knowledge and on the approach you use with your subordinates.

Your subordinates are the field in which you exercise your leadership. If they are rebellious and you lead feebly, your leadership may amount to nothing. Similarly, you'll undermine your leadership (and your output) if you overmanage bright and industrious subordinates.

Effective delegation hinges on your ability to figure out which of your employees can already do what type of task, which employees are ready and willing to do other tasks, and how best to approach your employees with major delegations.

Overload timid, inexperienced Tina with too large or too complicated a task, and you've created a frustrated, demoralized, ineffective employee. Give menial, boring jobs to bright, ambitious von Braun and you've created a frustrated, demoralized, ineffective, resentful employee.

Leadership: Assessing Your Staff as a Group

You lead workers as a *group*. You delegate to individuals, but as a leader, it's your standing with the group that counts. Your staff is extremely sensitive to the way you fit into their group, and they (and your boss) can easily withdraw their cooperation and support if the fit isn't comfortable.

Part of your job as manager is to give your workers the kind of leadership they *need*, which may not always be the same as what they want. Some work groups (usually after extended periods of poor management) reach such a level of rebellion and low productivity that the manager must be a dictator (preferably benign). Most managers, however, can adopt more moderate and cooperative styles for leading their work groups.

Work groups can be characterized in several ways: A *mature* group has worked together for some time. Its members have sharp job skills and a secure association with the company. A *cohesive* group's members stick up for each other, work well together, and frequently carry on their association after work. A *highly stressed* work group often exists where time clocks are punched, when worker production is closely checked, or when a crisis every minute is the rule. Examples include assembly lines, advertising, certain hospital jobs, and highly technological jobs.

Different levels of work-group maturity, cohesion, and stress call for different leadership styles. Complete the questionnaire below to diagnose your own work group.

Leadership: Assessing Your Work Group

Circle the letter on the right that corresponds to the answer you have chosen to the following questions about your work group.

1. The average age of my staff is
   (a) 20–25 (b) 25–30 (c) 30–35 (d) 35–40
   (e) 40+   A B C D E
2. My subordinates average ＿＿ years with the
   firm.
   (a) less than 1 (b) 1–2 (c) 2–5 (d) 5–10 (e) 10+   A B C D E
3. The average employee has been in this unit for
   (a) less than 6 months (b) 6–12 mos. (c) 1–2 yrs.
   (d) 2–5 yrs. (e) 5+   A B C D E

4. Years of job-related education (average for all
   employees)
   (a) 0 (b) less than 1 (c) 1–2 (d) 2–3 (e) 3+　　　A B C D E
5. My company is ___% unionized.
   (a) 0% (b) 20% (c) 50% (d) 75% (e) 100%　　　A B C D E
6. My employees work together on projects ___%
   of the time.
   (a) 0% (b) 25% (c) 50% (d)75% (e) nearly 100%　A B C D E
7. My subordinates see one another socially ___
   (a) never (b) once each month (c) twice a month
   (d) weekly (e) twice a week or more　　　A B C D E
8. The average job in my unit takes ___ minutes.
   (a) less than 5 (b) 5–60 (c) 60–120 (d) 2–7 hours
   (e) 7+ hours　　　A B C D E
9. ___% of the work in my unit is done under tight
   deadlines or other crises.
   (a) 100% (b) 75% (c) 50% (d) 25% (e) almost 0%　A B C D E
10. ___% of my employees' work is subject to
    quotas and quality checks.
    (a) 100% (b)75% (c) 50% (d) 25% (e) almost 0%　A B C D E

Now draw a line down the page connecting all of your answers. If your line is mainly on the right (*D*s and *E*s), your work group is experienced, cohesive, and relaxed. They'll probably do their best with low-key leadership from you.

If your line is mainly on the left (*A*s and *B*s), your work group is relatively inexperienced, not very cohesive, and is laboring under stressful working conditions. In this case, you'll need to exercise more forceful leadership. In the "Plan Your Action" section below, we'll discuss specific leadership *behavior* in more detail.

Delegation: Measuring Individual Potential

You assessed your staff as a whole in order to figure out the leadership style they would best respond to. You assess individual members of your staff in order to figure out what work to delegate to which worker.

By now you should have a good idea of not only *what* your employees do but *how* they go about doing it. Does Hernandez work slowly or quickly? Does Lafayette produce the most when you keep your distance? Does Gruber's output take a nosedive when you put a daunting pile of work on his desk? Is Ellis good with detail work, while Washington will get any job done even if the edges are a little rough?

In order to delegate each job to the most appropriate person, keep in mind what each of your workers can do and prefers doing. Look back at the charts you completed in chapter 3, "Your Subordinates," to refresh your memory about your workers' skills, ambitions, and attitudes. Then complete the assessment below to round out your knowledge of your people. Capitalize on your people's natural strengths and aptitudes, especially at first.

Delegation: Assessing Individual Subordinates' Work Styles

Pin down each subordinate's work style before you delegate. Complete the following questionnaire by blacking out the terms that do *not* apply to him or her.

EMPLOYEE'S NAME _____ DATE _____

1. Works (quickly) (slowly).
2. Needs (little) (much) direction.
3. (Does) (does not) seek out new assignments.
4. Makes (few) (many) mistakes.
5. (Does) (does not) handle large new assignments well.
6. Writes (well) (poorly).
7. Gives (clear, strong) (unclear, faltering) verbal reports.
8. (Likes) (dislikes) getting things perfect.
9. Is (organized) (disorganized).
10. (Likes) (dislikes) general office chores.
11. Enjoys working (alone) (with others).
12. Prefers (structured, predictable assignments) (opportunity for creativity).

Note: this list is most definitely *not* something to use to make decisions about raises, promotions, and transfers. It's only to help you decide what kind of project to delegate to a particular subordinate. Unless you supervise an assembly line, your department probably has a sufficient variety of tasks to occupy almost any individual. Some jobs require speed (the paste-up of the new Sunday section that has to be on Kane's desk first thing in the morning); others don't (updating the annual customer Christmas card list). Some jobs require good verbal or presentation skills (handling phone calls, especially from clients, or reading material to summarize verbally for you); others can be performed without a word being spoken (checking and compiling statistics, taking inventory). Some require careful thought and decisions (market analysis, product development, creating and delivering in-house training); some are simple, straightforward, cut-and-dried (preparing monthly reports, sending out yearly questionnaires to all regional divisions).

Even employees who resist new assignments can and should be delegated projects. It's up to you to define jobs that, especially at first, fall within the scope of the person's existing tasks and skills and will *reasonably stretch those skills* so the subordinate learns something. In other words, we come right back to the key delegation resource—your ability to define jobs and creatively match those jobs to members of your staff.

STEP-UP   PLAN YOUR ACTION

Planning Your Leadership Style

If you're a take-charge whiz kid who finds herself managing a mature, cohesive, and relaxed group, you must tone down your gung-ho leadership act before the group decides that it can do without you as their manager. If, on the other hand, you are by nature a laid-back type who now has a frenetic work group beset by crises, you must learn to take charge before your boss decides you don't have the right stuff.

You must lead the way your work group needs to be led, by word and manner, by deed and by dress. Below is an outline of the elements of leadership style for two types of work groups:

· Type 1 (High maturity, high cohesion, and low stress), and
· Type 6 (low maturity, low cohesion, and high stress)

Obviously, most groups are types 2 through 5, according to their maturity, cohesion, and stress levels. The suggestions below are for groups at the two extremes.

Your own group will almost certainly fall between types 1 and 6. If your staff tends toward a type 3, your leadership behavior can be more midrange as well. Take another look at the work group assessment on pages 112–13. The first four questions measure maturity, the next three measure cohesion, and the last three measure workplace stress. The lower the cohesion and maturity levels of the group, the more you must set a high standard of behavior and discipline. The more stressed a group is, the more you need to be an active force giving daily direction and support to the group.

Type 1 Group
HIGHLY MATURE, VERY COHESIVE, LOW (I.E., MANAGEABLE) STRESS

Example: A group of highway engineers, architects in a design firm, nurses in an orthopedic or maternity ward.

Your tone:	Informal, down-to-earth. The group knows what they're doing and enjoys doing it. Consult *with* them, rather than talking down *to* them.
Your style of dress:	Halfway between your boss's and the group's.
Your new ideas:	Consult individually and quietly with group members. Because your idea will be only as good as their reception of it, take time to "sell" the idea based on the group's preferences and your common goals.
Frequency of group meetings:	Once a month, unless the work process itself calls for more.
Meeting style:	*Moderate* the discussion, listen for problems. Keep your proposed work changes open to discussion while stressing that several of the work group have already been consulted.
Disciplinary issues:	Seek "Let this cup pass" solutions such as transfers and "kicks upstairs." If you must directly discipline somebody and the rest of the group finds out about it (see chapter 7), express your discomfort to key group members. To avoid a coalition against you, stress that the disciplined person's behavior exposed the group to penalties from upper management.

In other words, if your group is skilled, experienced, relaxed, and operating smoothly, leave it alone. An excellent way to sabotage your operation is to poke your nose into every corner and insist (or even imply) that your way of doing things is better. Don't let your initial excitement and energy cause you to dive in and "take charge" if your staff are already a cohesive, productive bunch who turn out a good product. Encourage the positive behavior you see, and reassure yourself that a good staff will be receptive to your leadership and specific advice. (Furthermore, you'll learn from them how they got to *be* so productive.) If you must change procedures, inform the group and explain why you need their cooperation. Allow yourself time to sell your changes, rather than forcing them upon the group.

Sylvia had been assigned to manage a dozen teenagers working in a busy fast-food franchise. The pressure had been too much for the previous manager, who had literally stopped managing. As a result, the employees were running the place exactly as they pleased. Breakfast ended whenever they liked, depending on when they got tired of cooking breakfasts and decided to switch to hamburgers. The dress code didn't exist: some wore uniforms, some wore jeans. Most were less than courteous to the customers, who, annoyed with the delay and careless service, often complained.

Sylvia knew exactly what she had to do. Dressed to the nines, she arrived every day at 6:30 (half an hour before the employees were due) and her daily staff meetings began at 7:00 on the dot. Late arrivals were not only docked for clocking in late, but were warned not to disrupt further meetings, which were essentially uniform checks. Those with sloppy or half-complete uniforms were required to straighten up in front of the group; those without were given one chance to go home and try again.

Sylvia gave the orders for the day and kept close tabs on whether they were followed. Those who resisted or fell short were immediately disciplined: warned and sent home on the first offense, and fired (as promised) on the second.

Type 6 Group
VERY INEXPERIENCED, LOW COHESION, HIGH STRESS

Your tone:	Formal, official, authoritative.
Your dress:	Just a notch below your boss's; several notches above your subordinates'.

Your new ideas:	Run them by your bosses first. Stress that the change may cause problems and you would like support. Present them to your group as orders, not suggestions, with detailed directions for completing them.
Frequency of group meetings:	At least once a week.
Meeting style:	Steer discussion away from volatile issues even if you have to be heavyhanded, e.g., "We're not discussing the new sign-in policy here, Cagney. See me afterward if you have any questions." *Announce* work changes. Permit discussion on implementation; accept and praise sensible suggestions and ideas for modifications.
Disciplinary issues:	Stress compliance with rules. Keep careful records. Discipline violators promptly and according to policy (see chapter 7). The rest of the group will find out about the punishments without your having to advertise them.

The type 6 group is, as we said, an extreme case, often a work group that has been without a manager (and without direction, discipline, or company loyalty) for a year. Your management aim and leadership style are to impose fair, consistent discipline and be the sole director of the work.

Planning How to Delegate

Below, you'll be listing and analyzing the jobs you do as a manager. Unless you're dedicated to working yourself to death by exhaustion from job overload, or by boredom from job stagnation (if you don't get fired first), you'll give some of those jobs away.

But "What jobs?" you ask. What jobs indeed. Do you go to meetings that subordinates could attend? Almost certainly. Do you do things (such as answering certain correspondence) that once helped you learn about your unit, but could now be done just as effectively by a subordinate? Of course. Give them away tomorrow!

Are there jobs that others need to learn so that the unit can operate when you're on vacation (or promoted)? The only correct answer is yes. (If you dare to answer no, come back to this question after you have analyzed your job.)

Assessing Your Tasks

The mother lode of delegation is work that comes to the unit through you. One of the worst things you can do is ask your staff to do more (of what they're already doing) without giving them more to do. Too many managers go by the credo "My staff should be able to find enough work to do." This is crazy. Why should the staff "find" work to do? That's your job now: directing, coordinating, assigning work. And why should anybody's subordinates invent jobs (or stretch out the ones they have now) to placate a boss who says things like "I don't want to see anybody sitting around with nothing to do"? Even if your people sometimes pad their work day, there's no reason *you* should choose inefficient, directionless management.

If you're blessed with an army of self-starters, we envy you. In general, however, unless you think of yourself as the main supplier of new work and direction for your staff, few new things will be done. And if you merely encourage everybody to "look busy," old tasks will be done with less efficiency and more dishonesty.

Since your own work forms the main source of responsibilities to be delegated, making a detailed list of the jobs that you do is crucial. And the key word is *detailed*.

Learn to think of your specific jobs in terms of two things: the *results* they're intended to produce, and their constituent *subtasks*.

For example: If you think of yourself as a boss who has to go to a lot of meetings, your fate is sealed—endless and boring meetings forever. If you think of yourself as a boss who goes to the executive committee meeting to discuss policy and new projects, and to the computer coordinating meeting to monitor how your unit will fit into the officewide system, you already have an option. Maybe your data-processing manager, Descartes, could be your representative at the computer meeting. You save time, and Descartes gains valuable experience. You've made her feel necessary while developing her talents—another important managerial task! (More on developing your staff in chapter 7.)

Attending the weekly managerial staff meeting involves representing your department's interests and presenting production reports. Your effort in preparing for the meeting can be halved if you let the writers of the report *give* the report. You're still there to answer questions, but haven't spent three valuable hours studying the information from scratch.

You'll need to give careful thought to what you do before listing the jobs you could delegate. When you make the list, be clear and precise, just as you've been with your goals:

- "Prepare standardized monthly report of mousetrap production statistics" (*not* "write statistical reports")
- "Meet weekly with administrative director to discuss my unit's support service needs. Push for new clerk" (*not* "Meet with officials from other departments")

Then, break down each job you've listed into tasks. For instance:

JOB	TASKS
Monthly report of production statistics	1. Collect reports from my unit heads
RESULT	2. Enter unit statistics on department report form
Get correct, complete production information to persons A–G	3. Calculate total and subtotals
	4. Write summary memo
	5. Recheck statistics against unit reports
	6. Recheck calculations
	7. Proofread memo
	8. Make 10 copies
	9. Distribute copies
	10. File office copy

We cannot overemphasize how important it is for you to analyze your jobs this way. Your jobs and tasks (and new ones your unit acquires) are your primary delegation resources. If you don't exploit them, no one will.

Delegating versus Dumping

Many managers, drunk with newly found delegating power, carry it to self-defeating extremes. They "delegate" everything from implementing entire projects to watering the office plants. But there's a big difference between just *assigning* tasks (often perceived by subordinates as "dumping") and truly *delegating* a project or chunk of work. Compare:

ASSIGNING (OR DUMPING)	DELEGATING
"Sarah, I want you to bake three rhubarb pies, four dozen lemon cookies, two dozen chocolate cupcakes with vanilla icing, and one strawberry mousse. Don't forget to clean up the kitchen and turn off the lights when you're finished. Then call Joe in the mail room and tell him when it's all ready. And get it done by 4:30. Oh, and use the ceramic cookware, not the stainless steel."	"Sarah, the company bake sale is tomorrow. We've been asked to donate the equivalent of four pies, four dozen cookies, and a specialty item. You're the best pastry cook in foods research, and I want you to handle it. Will you have any problem preparing it and sending it over to the auditorium by 4:30 today?"
"Sam, about this memo: make a thousand copies on company letterhead, and send one to every salesperson. Get on it right away."	"Sam, we have a thousand salespeople in the firm and I need to let all of them know about the policy change on this memo as soon as possible. I'd like you to handle it. Would you give it some thought and discuss it with me in half an hour?"

Sam may surprise you by suggesting you include the memo in the avidly read company sales newsletter, which is about to go to press. He may know of a reliable, informal network among the salespeople that will spread the word. Or he may say that the only way to do it is to send out one thousand form letters . . . and isn't it lucky that he's on the best of terms with Christine, who can squeeze in a mass mailing tomorrow morning. Sam may also surprise you by not having the vaguest idea of what to do. Good. You now have the chance to teach Sam two things: that there are several ways to disseminate information to a thousand people, and that you rely on his ideas as well as his help, and will continue to ask for both as you delegate.

Note that assigning work—giving detailed directions about what's to be done and how to do it—offers little if any room for choice, let alone growth, on your subordinate's part. (Often the employee may not even know *why* she's doing certain things, or how those tasks relate to what other departments are doing.) Assigning tasks has its place, of course, and occasions will arise when your staff will have to be trained, or told exactly how to carry out orders. This, however, is not actually *delegation*. True delegation means you've given the subordinate some freedom to make decisions about the task. You've explained the *final result* that's needed and the deadline. After some discussion about potential problems (see outline that follows), you allow your employee to accomplish the task the best way he sees fit.

This is the point at which so many managers get scared and shrink from delegating. "What if it's not done the way I would do it myself? I'm still ultimately responsible for the work; why *shouldn't* I make sure it's done the way I think best?" If you're unsure of the answer to this question, go back to the beginning of this chapter and let Mildred Harrison explain why overcontrol can be as bad as none at all. Then remind yourself that your way isn't the only way; in fact, if you're running an unfamiliar department, it may not even be the best way!

A DELEGATION EXAMPLE   Lou had been assigned major responsibility for a new project by his own boss, so he decided it was time to let his administrative assistant Reed do something more. "What job do I want to give away?" he thought. "Ah! Reed can manage the support staff—it's mostly typing, filing, and routine reports. He's helped me out with that kind of thing already."

Lou sat down with a piece of paper and figured out just what he was currently getting from the support staff. Ida, Lee, and Sid were responsible for typing, copying, distributing, and filing. Lou set priorities for them so the most important work got done first. Lou made sure Ida typed the important letters and reports, and let Lee take her time on less crucial internal memos. He was careful to give Lee other clerical duties, since Ida did so much more typing (they had the same job description, but certainly not the same skill level). Lou checked Lee's work frequently so that he was sure it was done on time with (at least) acceptable quality. Ida required fewer checkpoints. Sid's work was flawless, but he was a bit unreliable about deadlines; he had to work overtime occasionally to get major reports copied and distributed on time.

Lou hadn't realized how much work went into keeping the support staff running smoothly. Just giving a written report to Ida or Lee meant:

1. Figuring out how much work each of them was doing at the moment
2. Deciding how important the report was (acceptable error rate, deadline, et cetera)
3. Telling the typist (if necessary) which paper, typeface, and layout to use
4. Keeping records of when work was due and who was doing it
5. Checking and proofing completed work, making corrections, and evaluating the typist's performance for her annual evaluation
6. Thanking the staff, especially for rush work

After explaining to Reed the reason for their meeting, Lou said that a new project would be taking up much of his time in the future. "I know I can depend on you to learn quickly and do a reliable job with the support people, Reed. You've always been an excellent employee.

"Another reason I'm delegating support functions to you is so that you can take a fresh look at the job. I've established a system of my own, but that doesn't mean there isn't a better way. For example, I've always had Lee and Ida make copies of short letters and memos rather than bother Sid with them, but you may decide it's more efficient if Sid takes care of *all* the copying and distribution.

"So feel free to make whatever changes seem sensible to you. It's gotten so rote for me that I've probably missed making some improvements. In any case, instituting a change or two will let the staff know that you're the one in charge now.

"Whenever you decide to make a change, I'd like you to run it by me first. Not that you have to justify it to me; it'll just give me a chance to tell you if the change might inadvertently bruise any egos.

"Reed, once I listed what the support people do for us, I was surprised at how much was involved in keeping support functions running smoothly. Fortunately, you've already had some experience directing Lee on this when I was at the conference, so there's nothing that will come as a surprise to you. But let me explain some of the finer points about how things need to get done.

"First, our top priority, the most important thing the support staff needs to get out, is the production report: how much we've produced, number of defective units, and number of customer complaints. Getting this on Mr. Rasputin's desk by the second of the month is—repeat—the support staff's *top* priority. After that come the divisional sales reports, quarterly reports, and then special reports, memos, and letters. I'm relying on you to judge what's most important. Obviously, Mr. Honcho's work is number one; but you know the pecking order around here.

"If you need copier repair, call Wolfson's—the number is in the Rolodex, and Ida's a friend of the repairman. I've already told her to give you a hand with machine maintenance.

"I'll be giving you the actual reports and letters that need to be typed, but you may at times have to ask questions of whoever wrote the report. Watch out for Hayes, he's the worst. He'll give you stuff without clear instructions as to format, typeface, how many copies he wants—half the time you won't even know his deadline. So don't let him get away with it, because you'll just waste a lot of time. Pin him down on everything before you give his reports to Ida, and always have Ida do them. He can be a real stickler.

"Now, Reed—what questions do you have? I know this is quite a job, so don't hesitate to ask."

Reed had no questions at this point. Lou then asked Reed to tell him, in his own words, the basic duties he would now be responsible for. Lou was satisfied that Reed understood.

Lou then took Reed over to Ida's desk. "Ida, you know Reed, my assistant. From now on he'll be doing the distribution of the office work for you, Lee, and Sid. I'm still division manager, and since I'm taking over the Clone project next month, I'm delegating support staff management to Reed. I want you to do for him what you've been doing for me . . . which should be easy, since Reed's much more organized than I am."

After similar introductions to Lee and Sid, Lou asked Reed to write memos describing any future procedural changes and give him copies. "This will keep me informed, and give us both a reason to meet briefly to discuss how things are going for you. Of course, you'll keep copies of everything the typists do in our chronological file here in this cabinet."

Although Lou had every confidence Reed could handle the support staff, he didn't expect Reed magically to do a perfect job right away.

Back in his office, Lou said, "Reed, here are the statistics and handwritten text for a special report Gallagher wants in ten days. Some of it requires bar charts and pie charts, and I'm not sure the staff has had to do those before.

"Assign the work as you see fit, and then we'll meet in four days to see the first rough draft of the report. Then let's get together again in two days to see what you and the staff have come up with before giving it back to Gallagher for his approval. He always has a few changes, so that should allow time for you to let me have a look at the final copy the day before it's due." Both Lou and Reed noted the checkpoint dates on their calendars.

Although the first draft looked different than Lou would have ordered it, he managed to refrain from puncturing Reed's confidence with comments on the order of "Here's how I usually format a report like this." Instead, he complimented Reed on his timeliness and readable layout, correcting only minor items that he knew Gallagher would catch.

Lou spent most of the meeting asking Reed how he was getting along with Ida, and whether Hayes had given him any problems. "The work rarely changes very much—it's keeping the people running smoothly that can be difficult. Be sure you let me know if Sid has had to put in much overtime, or if you foresee any glitches coming up. Although I expect you to handle them, I'll be happy to give you some suggestions if necessary."

In the next week, Reed expressed concern only about Lee's attitude. She was angry at having to retype several memos and said, "Lou never made me do these over just because the margins were a little off." Lou listened, and encouraged Reed to be pleasant but firm with Lee. Although privately he thought Reed was being overly picky, he said, "You're deciding procedures now, and it's up to you to make sure the staff carries them out. You have my backing." Because Lou's support of Reed was apparent, Reed's changes were adopted with only minor friction.

Task Delegation Outline

The outline below (which is simpler than it looks) lists every step Lou took in delegating to Reed. You can apply it to whatever task or project you want to give away.

A. Explaining the Task or Job to Yourself
    1. Define the specific *results* you want from the task in terms of our old friends Who, What, Where, When, and Why.
    2. List everything you now do to complete the task: the materials you need, where you get them, how you use them.
    3. List relevant time lines: starting dates, regularly scheduled reporting dates, completion deadlines.
    4. List others involved in the task: those who do subparts of the job, who supply necessary materials, or who use the results.
B. Explaining the Delegation to Your Employee
    1. Allow enough time for the meeting (add 10 percent to be on the

safe side) to discuss the task itself, and to allow the subordinate to give some initial thought to *how* he will go about the task and *when* he can complete it. (Allowing the subordinate to set his own deadline is far preferable to forcing yours upon him, though circumstances may dictate this.)

2. If appropriate, introduce your subordinate to everyone involved in completing the task: superiors, co-workers, support staff. Make it clear that your subordinate now has the authority to do the job, and that you expect him or her to work through any problems that arise.

C. Monitoring the Delegation

1. After the introductions, get feedback from the staff member: Make sure he knows what results are expected, and ask what problems he foresees.

2. Together, schedule the necessary checkpoint meetings. For a simple task, one or two may be sufficient; more complex tasks require regular meetings with specific agendas.

D. Making the Delegation Stick

1. Emphasize your confidence in the employee at every opportunity, even if you have to force yourself. Review work only at scheduled checkpoints, or when the employee comes to you with a problem. Refrain from looking over the employee's shoulder.

2. If your employee decides the delegation is too hard, be ready with a "We all take longer the first time; how can I help you past this obstacle?" speech. Don't show empty confidence, but don't plant more doubts in his mind about his abilities. You'll sabotage the whole process.

3. Compliment the employee *throughout* the task whenever she does something well. Your support often means more than your specific advice; in fact, employees often ask for advice when what they really want is support or a word of encouragement.

STEP-ⓊP   ⓊSE AND ABUSE YOUR PLAN

Steeling Yourself for Mistakes

Remember our friend Harrison from the beginning of the chapter? Harrison fell into the classic new-manager trap: she panicked, decided that her subordinates couldn't do anything right, and took the weight of the department on her own shoulders (all the while muttering, "If you want something done right, do it yourself!")

There's a little of Harrison in all of us. How you feel about delegating and directing others depends in large part on how comfortable you are giving control (no, not giving *up* control) to them. It takes quite a leap of faith to trust people to do something important. It's difficult to focus on your own job until that first checkpoint meeting comes up. When it does, the important question to remember is this: Is the work getting done reasonably well and more or less on schedule? (Don't expect perfection; you're bound to be disappointed.)

If the answer is yes, you've been delegating effectively. Give yourself and your staff a large pat on the back (see "Rewards and Incentives," chapter 7).

Even if the answer is no—even if the delegated work is seriously and consistently below your expectations, resist the urge to jump in and "fix" things for your people. The chaos created by any change is inevitable, and usually settles down if you manage by consulting and giving suggestions.

Controlling Your Expectations

The temptation to yank back the authority you've given Sam to arrange the company convention in Tahiti can overwhelm you at the first hint of problems. Don't do it! You'll sabotage not only the task but the whole delegation process, and damage your relationship with Sam as well.

Too many managers see that a change isn't working out perfectly, hear gripes from their staff, and precipitately snatch back the power they just delegated, in a misguided attempt to put things back "just the way they used to be." This is a mistake, because it makes you look like you didn't carefully consider the changes you made, but just took a shot in the dark; it also teaches your staff that if they complain and/or screw up enough, you'll change your mind and take the work off their hands; and it makes your management style look arbitrary and unpredictable by imposing yet another change on an already unsettled group.

To avoid the temptation to seize control again, estimate in advance the performance time you expect, based on the time it took *you* when you first attempted the job (add 50 percent for your faulty memory). How many mistakes (or drafts) did you make the first time? (Add 50 percent here, too.) Plan ahead for mistakes and foul-ups wherever possible; you'll save your sanity as well as the project.

Although it's not part of delegating per se, this is a great opportunity to be your staff's advocate (more on this in chapter 7). Let your boss know, in the subordinate's presence, that he or she has ably taken on a new job.

Why Change Makes People Crazy, and What to Do About It

Hard as it is for many people to believe, implementing even the most *positive* change means things will get worse before they get better. (Computerizing any department you care to name has become the classic example of this.) Learn early to foresee and accept that things will go to hell for a while, ride the bumps and offer support while people get used to it, and then—and *only* then—evaluate whether you need to make further changes.

At that point, the most important question to ask yourself is: How are your employees responding to your leadership style and task delegation now that they've had time to adjust to it? The answers lie in the following: positive and negative verbal feedback, direct to you or through the grapevine; cooperative behavior versus uncooperative behavior (that is, do your staff initiate work, show good attendance, and produce quality, or are they sloppy, in need of a push, and often absent?); high versus low productivity, as measured by quotas; the undefinable quality of life in your office: Do the people appear and act reasonably content?

Okay, You Goofed: Reversing Leadership Errors

If most of your people are negative or unproductive, then it's time to rethink your own approach to leadership. This is not to say you've done anything wrong; it simply means that what you've done (which may have made perfect sense on paper) hasn't worked in the real world. You probably feel frustrated, perhaps indignant, maybe even furious. Irritating as it is to see your plans go awry, remember that **STEP-UP** provides for just such eventualities.

Begin by looking at your own responsibility in the situation:

· Is my style appropriate for my staff? What have I done that's worked, and what specifically hasn't worked? (Be brutally honest with yourself here. Keep in mind that it's easier for you to change your style than to get ten subordinates to change theirs.)

· How did I misread the group? (Be specific: Was it personalities, work skills, power coalitions, etc.?)

· Are there bigger-than-all-of-us things to contend with—company failing, major union problems, and so on—that could be affecting the group's behavior?

Besides talking to yourself, talk to one or two respected subordinates who enjoy high standing in the work group. If no one in the work group qualifies, ask your boss or one of your peers some variation of the following leading question. "The crew seems a bit off these days. I know I've instituted some new things, like _____ (fill in the blank). I just wonder if any of this has upset the staff for reasons that I might not be aware of." Be ready to hear some direct criticisms. And be equally ready to say sincerely that you will consider changing some of your nettlesome behavior. After all, the changes are not only being criticized, they're *not working*. You'd be crazy not to consider reversing or altering them, even if somebody else did have to tell you what the problem was.

If you've misread the group or are just plain lousy at being a taskmaster, your alternative is simple: Act differently. Behave in ways that are more responsive to the group, and work to stretch the limitations you may have.

Okay, You Goofed II: Reversing Delegation Errors

Recovering from a delegation mistake is much easier than recovering from a leadership mistake. Generally, you must intervene in a misguided delegation when it threatens to damage your unit's reputation. Take action if important deadlines are in danger of being missed, or if the quality of work your subordinate produces will be embarrassing to you and your department.

Intervene first by working more closely with Reed. Set up joint working sessions so that you can train him more intensely while *both* of you are producing an acceptable product. Only *after* a job is complete should you consider whether the delegation should continue. If you've made a mistake (and remember, the responsibility for best using Reed's skills is yours), thank Reed for his efforts and resume doing the job yourself. Explain that "I didn't realize how much of your time this would take up. At this point I need you to continue doing _____ (Reed's original tasks) and we'll talk next month about _____ (other new assignments)."

When you put it this way, Reed won't feel criticized for trying something new and will be more amenable to the next delegated task . . . which, now that you've learned more about him, should be better suited to his talents.

STEP-UP PLAN AND PLAN AGAIN

If things didn't work out the way you thought they would, take heart. Depressing as it may be at the moment, you've still learned some valuable things about your people. Go back to "Plan Your Action," and reappraise which employee should be doing what. You may not have to change everyone and everything; in fact, the fewer changes you make, the better. Just be sure you're satisfied with the *reasons* for the changes you're making.

If it was your delegation or leadership style that caused some of the problems, spend some time considering how you'll approach your staff this time. It's perfectly okay, and refreshingly human, to explain why your last plan didn't work out the way you thought it would, *as long as you have a sensible alternative to offer*.

Your next step is to present these alternative changes in a full staff meeting. Make it clear how long your staff will be expected to stick with the new plan to give it a fair try.

Then meet with each subordinate individually, as before, to debrief the problems and discuss the new tasks at hand. This last step is essential to everyone's understanding, and gives you an extra chance to show that you're flexible and willing to modify some of your behavior and ideas for the good of the department.

Of course, it's likely that your delegations have neither broken every previous production record nor caused your unit to fall flat on its face. Most of the staff have probably adjusted to their newly delegated tasks and are performing them well. But if one or two subordinates are unhappy, an effective manager will do what she can to accommodate them.

First, meet with the employees who are disgruntled or falling behind. This is not for disciplinary purposes (that, if necessary, comes later, in chapter 7). Rather, ask unthreatening, open-ended questions, and *listen* to the answers: "The task I delegated to you was a complicated one. How could we have worked together to make it more successful?" "What would you do differently next time on the same type of task?" "What else got in the way of your completing it by the deadline?"

Making a sincere effort to understand why Reed behaved as he did means being prepared to hear some complaints and comments about your own style. One way to stay objective about this is to memorize any negative things you hear and write them down when Reed leaves. Let the criticisms cool, and think about them before responding.

Ask for, and listen to, Reed's ideas about how to improve his effectiveness. (Here it's all right to take notes in front of him.) If it's a relatively simple matter that you can decide right away, do so. (For example, Ida's expertise and rapport with Lee may be so much better than Reed's that it makes sense for her to explain new procedures to Lee.) Tell Reed what you plan to do, what you will look for from him (in terms of specific, measurable results and deadlines), and follow up with checkpoint dates.

Despite the temptation to be defensive (or aggressive) and justify why you did what you did, consider the possibility that you indeed made an inappropriate delegation: Maybe Reed really *isn't* right for the job, at least not now.

One Last Caution

You rise or stall in an organization because of how well you lead and delegate. You are *stuck* if you let a few bad experiences freeze you into an inappropriate leadership style, or make you cynical and disrespectful of employees, or cause you to take on too much work yourself. Your bosses will see you as an unimaginative, simpleminded, overworked individual with little influence over your staff. Don't cheat yourself out of your next promotion by working too hard at the wrong things.

7

Employee Development, Advocacy, and Discipline

IT HAD BEEN a rough time for Steve, new account executive at a growing advertising agency. Working overtime, he had managed over eight months to keep a step ahead of the work: his staff consistently turned out print and film commercials that both clients and superiors were wild about. Not one to hog the credit, Steve made a point of frequently telling his people how much he appreciated their producing under pressure. "I hated it when my old boss acted as if those storyboards got done by magic," he often thought. "I swear I'll never ignore my staff like that." So Steve was bewildered when his people turned from a grateful flock into a rampaging herd.

"Steve, I don't like to bother you again, but it's about that promotion we discussed. It's been two months since you said you'd talk to Mr. Doyledane, and since then you told me that if it weren't for my copywriting, we would've lost the Intercontinental Megaconglomerate account. I mean, isn't this the perfect time to talk to him? What gives?"

"Steve, you've just got to send me to that presentation skills seminar you mentioned when I started in your group. I'm still a wreck whenever I have to give a presentation to a bunch of clients, and Jack practically had to pick me up off the floor after the last one. I'm afraid I'll just go blank one day."

"Steve, that raise you promised me for taking charge of the Planetwide Platinum account . . . I didn't see it on my check again this week."

"Steve? Listen, I just wanted to thank you for that 'good' rating on my evaluation sheet. I know I've missed a lot of deadlines, but it won't happen again. By the way, I need tomorrow morning off for a dentist appointment."

"Steve, I just read my performance evaluation, and . . . well, I'm shocked. You've been telling me for months what a terrific, creative artist I am—how could you only rate me 'good'? That shoots my merit raise all to hell!"

Steve's response deteriorated as the days dragged on, from "Listen, you're right—I've been swamped, but I'll get to it the minute I can" to "Listen, I'm swamped! I do all I can, and I can't change company policy. Talk to (Mr. Doyledane, the personnel department, your landlord, your analyst) yourself—I just don't have the time!"

Steve's time became even more limited when his hardworking team decided that pitching in and working overtime weren't getting them anywhere: not creatively, not financially, and most certainly not into a corner office. And Steve's blood pressure rose yet higher as he tried to explain to Mr. Doyledane why his formerly fantastic group just wasn't creating the knockout campaigns it used to.

Some Concrete Reasons Why You Must Develop and Discipline Your Staff

Before you became a manager, you probably didn't give much thought (beyond wishful thinking) to moving people up, down, or out. Now you have not only the power but the *responsibility* to do so. To assume you can just let things take their Darwinian course ("The good workers will ask for promotions, the bad will get themselves booted out") is to invite a slowdown, if not disaster. Think for a moment about your own past supervisors. Whom did you do better work for: the one who made it clear he was actively on your side when you deserved a raise or promotion, or the one who, like Steve in the story above, fell back lamely on "company policy" whenever you broached the subject?

Virtually everyone understands why discipline—clarifying goals and standards, pointing out mistakes, imposing penalties, and firing if necessary—is essential in an organization if people are to produce consistently and correctly. Therefore, "Plan Your Action" will focus on *how* to use discipline effectively rather than rehash *why* it's important to set standards and expect your staff to meet them.

Far more important than discipline, however, is *developing* your staff: training them and motivating them to take on more responsibility and, ultimately, promotion. Few brand-new managers have ever had to think in terms of anyone else's career path. But it's the foolish manager who arbitrarily decides "Well, Joe deserves to move up. Maybe I should talk to him—but I have too much else to think about right now."

We're sure you have plenty to think about. We're also sure you're expected to develop your people's skills and talents, through training and delegation, for the good of the company. This necessarily means that soon some of your staff will be prepared for bigger things; you *must* also be ready to help them move up (if such is their goal), or to reward them in other ways. We guarantee their efforts won't continue without recognition from you.

That's what's in it for your subordinates. What will development and advocacy do for you?

· You'll get more and better work from your staff. Active concern for their status and well-being keeps morale high.

· No company, no matter how successful, got that way by maintaining the status quo. Your staff need to expand their skills, functions, and ability to fill in for one another (and for you, in emergencies) to keep your department productive.

· Helping your outstanding employees move into more powerful positions builds you a network of allies in high places.

· You'll avoid rebellion: the passive rebellion of the suppressed (like Steve's group above), and the more active rebellion of the staff who, lacking discipline, soon think they can get away with murder.

· When your own boss is ready to promote you, you will have already trained and groomed a replacement for your own position.

· You'll reduce costly turnover. Though any manager can name one or two exceptions, the fact is that investing time and energy in developing your staff is putting money in AAA triple-tax-free bonds. The employee who's been trained to enhance his skills, who knows you support his advancement, and who respects you because you respect him, isn't likely to leave the firm for a few more dollars in another position.

STEP-UP SET YOUR GOALS

Following are your goals for your fourth, fifth, and sixth months on your new job. By the time you finish this chapter, you'll be able to:

· Assess your subordinates' work against
  —Production standards
  —Performance goals
  —Timeliness
  —The priorities and particular expectations you've set for them
  —The company's priorities and expectations of them
· Write useful (fair, objective, detailed, comprehensive) performance evaluations for each subordinate
· Further your subordinates' advancement (or demotion) by initiating and utilizing meetings with upper management to
  —Document problem subordinates

—Obtain your own boss's support when an employee's performance warrants promotion (raise, title change, more responsibility) or firing
· Motivate your staff through
   —Positive incentives, challenges, and rewards for everyone
   —Fair and appropriate penalties, formal and informal, when necessary
· Utilize employee training
   —As a reward, by learning what training and educational benefits are available and making your employees aware of them
   —As development, through formal training (in-house and outside) and informal training (on the job, by you or by an assigned subordinate)
· Evaluate and hire applicants based on
   —How their job skills and talents will meet your unit's needs
   —How they will "fit in" with your existing staff

STEP-UP TALLY YOUR RESOURCES

Your Best Resource: Positive Reinforcement

Your resources include both positive rewards and incentives as well as disciplinary measures. Furthermore, you have both formal and informal ways of getting your people to produce what you want them to produce. We're very much in favor of positive reinforcement (noticing and rewarding behavior you like, rather than punishing behavior you don't like) as a motivator, simply because it's always more effective and every manager in every organization can find some way to use it. As we mentioned earlier, however, many supervisors are (sadly) conditioned to respond only to infractions and screwups; the habitually tardy employee gets docked or written up, the salesperson not up to quota gets more training seminars and personal attention (albeit not always pleasant) from the boss, while productive workers are lucky to hear "Great job, Bill" maybe once a year.

Many managers agree with positive reinforcement in theory, but complain about built-in restraints on bonuses and other rewards. "Why should I go after raises for my staff? We're locked into (salary scales, endless red tape, civil service ratings, union rulings, etc.) and everybody knows it." We maintain that even in a government job you have the resources to get your staff *some* type of meaningful reward and recognition for work well done—if you'll only use them. Here are some tools.

Resources on Paper: Employee Performance Evaluations

You'll remember using performance evaluations in chapter 3 when you were learning about your subordinates. At the time, you made a note to yourself about whether the evaluation form provided meaningful information, or whether you'd have to change its format to reflect actual employee performance. If your unit has *had* no formal evaluation form or process up to now, you'll learn to create one here in the "Plan Your Action" step.

Let's assume for now that your unit has a procedure to be followed, and you have several years' worth of evaluations in your files. If the information on them is specific, objective, adequately detailed, and actually tells you something about what the employee has accomplished and where she needs to improve, our congratulations to your predecessor. You already have the form and hard documentation you need to back up your advocating promotion (or training, demotion, or firing) for your people. If, however, the evaluations are of the variety where the idea "All persons are created equal" means that virtually everyone is rated "Satisfactory" regardless of performance, you have more work to do. Not only must you learn to write an evaluation that says something, you must find out why such meaningless consistency has become acceptable, perhaps even expected, in your organization. Before you try to convince your boss that a new method will work better, consider and check out the following:

· Did your boss create the existing evaluation system? Don't alienate him by criticizing it (even intelligently) or suggesting sweeping changes, no matter how brilliant. Even if you know for a fact that it was Swanson in personnel who cooked it up, you may not know that Swanson is your boss's favorite poker buddy. Introduce your new ideas carefully.

· Is the existing system the result of a lawsuit or union ruling? Managers saddled with terrible workers have often found less-than-straightforward ways to get rid of those employees—only to discover that a piece of paper saying "He was incompetent and obnoxious, and everybody was glad to see him go" doesn't hold up in court when said employee sues for wrongful termination. As a result, many employee evaluations have, in an effort to be safe and "fair," become watered down to the point of meaninglessness.

The possibilities, then, are three: you already have a good evaluation system; you can improve on what you have; or you're stuck with filling out useless forms every year. In the first two cases, you'll be using formal performance evaluations as major proof in discussions with your boss that certain individuals deserve more money, a bigger cubbyhole, more time off, a title change, specialized training, or a transfer to the Waikiki office. In the latter case, it'll take a little more ingenuity and clout to wangle these "perks" for your people—but you'll have plenty of time to do so, since it won't take long to fill out those useless (but necessary) evaluation forms.

Written Resources: Training and Development Courses

Managers too often think of training, like discipline, only in remedial terms: to teach someone something he doesn't know, or to teach him to do it the right way. Worse, employees get the idea that training is punishment! Since you're already responsible for training your staff to do their jobs, don't make your own task even harder. Let your people know that you regard training courses as a useful way to refresh and improve on existing skills, to keep abreast of new developments in the field, and to learn more with an eye toward future promotion. In other words, you support training because it's essential to their career development.

No matter what you do, where you work, or whom you supervise, some type of training—from informal, on-the-job advice to week-long off-site seminars—is always available to your subordinates. How do you find out exactly what's offered and how to take advantage of it? If you were promoted to manager in a small company, you may already be aware of all the in-house courses and educational benefits available. Don't just assume, however, that you already know all there is to know. If it's not in your desk or bookcase, ask your secretary or office manager where the file of routine training and seminar offerings is kept. It should be full of announcements and brochures sent out by established training organizations and independent consultants, as well as the company's own programs. Spend a *limited* amount of time going through it, pitching outdated or irrelevant offerings and retaining those that apply in any way to your current and future work. (You'll use these in the "Plan Your Action" step below.)

If you work in a large company, an entire unit may be devoted to providing and keeping track of employee education. Such departments are often affiliated with the Personnel office and are called Employee Education, or Human Resources Development (they may also be part of the union). Find out from your boss or peers, call the head of the department and introduce yourself, and make an appointment for a brief interview. Your purpose here is to familiarize yourself with all the training courses available to your staff (and to yourself as well); any courses that are mandatory for promotion or raises; and all the educational benefits (partial or full tuition to college courses in the community, etc.) your staff may be eligible for. Add this information to your own training file.

If you find yourself drowning in details after all this, it will be tempting to issue a blanket memo to your staff saying "The folks over in personnel are very helpful. See them any time you have a question about training." This, unfortunately, will defeat your purpose, which is to let your staff know that their development is *your* concern. In "Plan Your Action," you'll use your employee-history charts from chapter 3 to tailor each subordinate's training to his needs, and use the plan to motivate them.

Material Resources: Rewards, Incentives, and Motivators

Positive reinforcement falls in and out of favor from decade to decade, depending largely on the state of the economy. When money is often plentiful, it's easy to pay a worker more to stay; management knows he can quit and get a job elsewhere with little trouble, so the company makes itself more attractive with fringe benefits, extras, and so on, to keep him. Hard times, of course, tell a different story; monetary bonuses become scarce or nonexistent, and management knows jobs are hard to come by. Fringe benefits dry up, and disgruntled workers become experts at doing only enough to keep their jobs. Thousands of new managers, caught between deserving subordinates on one side and the budget crunch on the other, feel helpless to motivate their valuable workers to produce as much as they used to, let alone more. This is precisely why the canny manager must be imaginative and aggressive in securing rewards for her people that don't necessarily depend on cash.

Fortunately, this is probably easier than you think. Recall our discussion about your boss's style in chapter 4: She's primarily an achiever, a controller, or an affiliator. The same principle applies to your subordinates, and provides an excellent clue to the most effective incentive for each. We'll discuss this at greater length in the "Plan Your Action" section.

For now, list the rewards at your disposal that you can offer your staff:

More space: larger office, bigger desk, more bookcases and file cabinets, etc.

More time: extra days off, longer lunches, permission to come in late or leave early, a flexible schedule of four ten-hour days, etc.

Desirable assignments: more (or less) travel, opportunity to work with preferred co-workers, special projects, training seminars or conferences, etc.

More status: new title, more responsibility, office with windows, company car, companywide recognition awards, etc.

More convenience: better typewriter, new furniture or carpeting, first pick of vacation dates, better parking spot, office in a different area or building, etc.

Miscellaneous goodies, all of which have worked for real-life managers we know: bringing in doughnuts on Fridays, flowers or a bottle of wine on birthdays, occasionally having a catered lunch in the office or taking everyone out when a major project is completed; thoughtful (i.e., nonidentical) holiday gifts; informal World's Best Secretary (Salesperson, Physicist, Patternmaker) awards; "business" (but really vacation) trips, etc. (One caution, however: these informal treats rarely work if your staff has reason to believe you've scrimped on their deserved raises.)

And, when possible, money: raises, bonuses, stock options, bigger expense accounts.

By now you have a good idea of what your people value and what you can do for them. List those things here, even if they seem barely possible right now:

STAFF REWARDS AND INCENTIVES

_____   _____

_____   _____

_____   _____

These are your resources. Even if you're fully satisfied with what you have to work with, learn to enhance them with the people around you.

STEP-UP ENHANCE YOUR RESOURCES

People Resources: Your Boss's Support

Too many new managers think it's not their place to talk about their subordinates to their boss. "That's what I'm being paid to take care of;

why should my boss care who's doing what? Anyway, if I tell him Rizzo is screwing up again, won't it reflect badly on me?'' Not if you present Rizzo's case in the right way. Complaints alone are counterproductive; letting your boss know your disciplinary plans is another matter. If you've made it a point consistently to give your heroes credit where it's due, on a weekly if not daily basis, the bad news (along with your proposed solution to it, of course) becomes much easier for your boss to hear. Furthermore, you're setting the stage for your boss's cooperation when you ask for better money and/or titles for your people, you sound as though you're in complete control of your unit, and you avoid giving the impression that you're taking credit for everything that goes right and for nothing that goes wrong.

So what do you do if one or two subordinates are real performance (or personality) problems? Even if the boss's favorite expression is "Don't bring me problems, bring me solutions," there's still a way you can approach him with bad news. In so doing, you gradually let him know that there *is* a problem (i.e., a potential termination) that may require his backup later.

Most staff problems build up over a period of months; few are full-blown emergencies. Once you've taken some action on the problem and monitored the result, you can tell your boss what you've already done to correct the situation. Should the same problems recur or become worse, you have then covered yourself well enough to ask your boss's advice without appearing to throw the problem into his lap. Present your own proposed action or considered solution first; if your boss knows you've already worked on this, he'll respond more readily when you ask him whether he's ever had to deal with the same situation and ask for his suggestions about what to do next. You may discover that although you supposedly have adequate documentation to fire the person in question, company politics or some technicality makes that impossible.

People Resources: Your Peers' Support

A trusted co-worker on your level can be an invaluable source of information and encouragement. Use the same approach as you did with your boss: Ask your peer if you can have ten or twenty minutes of her time to bounce some ideas around. Explain the problem, what you plan to do about it, and why you think your plan will work. Ask your colleague's opinion of your ideas—don't put her on the spot by asking "What do you think I should do about that maniac Rizzo?''—and you'll probably get much more detailed, sensible suggestions. (If your colleague is hesitant or has other reasons for not discussing this with you, ask her who else has handled this kind of situation.)

While you're at it, you might want to pick a competent co-worker's brain about:

How she handles discipline in general
Which nonmonetary rewards she uses to motivate her staff
Whether she's ever had to write up or fire anyone
How she's helped secure promotions for her people

People Resources: Enhancing Your Own Skills

Although this chapter includes all the basic facts about employee advocacy and discipline, we suggest you think carefully about skills you have—and those you lack—as a manager of people in some very delicate situations. Announcing Mother Teresa's raise is easy; calling Chuck Manson in for the fifth time to announce that his poor performance means his services are no longer required is a responsibility many managers would sooner die than face.

If you suspect that a course in assertiveness training or basic communications would make you a more confident, effective manager, don't hesitate; find one and take it, even if it's on your own time and paid for out of your own pocket. Learning, practicing, and getting feedback from a living, breathing, qualified instructor will be worth it. You won't be able to avoid uncomfortable situations as a manager, and this is one area in which learning on the job is the less-than-ideal route to expertise.

STEP-UP   PLAN YOUR ACTION

Now down to brass tacks: how to write effective performance evaluations, motivate your people, plan for training and development, and plan an advocacy campaign that works. (In "Use and Abuse Your Plan," you'll learn how to document and remove a poor employee through transfer or dismissal; in "Plan and Plan Again," how to hire new employees you can count on.)

Writing Effective Performance Evaluations

Most of us consider ourselves fair-minded, discerning individuals, yet few of us like to sit in judgment on others. Most managers have a very good idea of what each of their subordinates is accomplishing, yet few of them can put their ideas concisely on paper. Every manager would like to see her staff enjoy their work while producing more, yet few think to use the (often dreaded or ignored) performance evaluation as a tool to achieve just that.

But you can. And you can do it with the skills you've already learned in chapters 2 and 3.

PEs: What's in Them for You and Your Staff

Performance evaluations (hereafter known as PEs) are used in virtually every organization of more than fifty people. If your department doesn't as yet have PEs, now is the time to initiate them. If people resist the change, here are some facts that may sell them (and you):

1. *PEs confirm or correct past behavior.* A cook will never improve unless he can taste what he's cooked, and a swimmer can't know what his form looks like without a coach. Your staff may be honestly unaware that their work is below par (or excellent, for that matter) unless you tell them.

2. *PEs provide an opportunity for communication*, and communication is essential to your success. If you manage a large department, you may rarely see some of your staff. For that matter, you may have little time (or inclination, if you're not an affiliator) to talk with the people at the next desk. Recognition for work contributed—superior or barely average—is essential to motivating your staff.

3. *PEs provide a record of your judgment, your communication, and your employees' mutual agreement.* Without documentation, you *may* be able to convince the powers that be that Sally deserves a promotion. Without documentation, you'll never be able to convince them (nor should you) that she should be demoted or fired. Objective information protects all of you.

4. *PEs provide the most common basis for salary increases*, or for nonmonetary rewards where preset salary scales exist.

What Should Be Included in the PE?

Get a blank copy of your firm's PE, or use the following sample.

Employee Performance Evaluation

Employee_____ Department_____

Unit_____ Evaluator_____

ASSESSMENT

PERFORMANCE FACTORS	Outstanding	Very Good	Good	Standard	Poor
Attendance	_____	_____	_____	_____	_____
Timeliness of Work	_____	_____	_____	_____	_____
Following Directions	_____	_____	_____	_____	_____
Co-worker Relationships	_____	_____	_____	_____	_____
Customer Relationships	_____	_____	_____	_____	_____
Quality of Work	_____	_____	_____	_____	_____
Overall Rating	_____	_____	_____	_____	_____

Comments:_____

_____

_____

_____

_____

_____

_____

Supervisor's signature_____

On the sample, you see a list of performance factors and a range of assessment categories. Before diving in and checking off the categories, stop and think: What *are* the best things about the employee in question? Make notes to yourself about his or her strengths and contributions, including things that don't necessarily have to do with performing the job itself (i.e., her reliability, his soothing way with irate clients). Then do the same with areas that need improvement. What do you want the employee to do that he isn't already doing? What is she doing that you want her to stop? Get a true, broad idea of the employee's performance before filling in the blanks (in pencil, of course). The tendency for managers to over-react to an isolated bad incident, or to overrate people because of one or two endearing traits is what makes PEs so often meaningless. Take your time, and give your subordinate your honest consideration before you decide.

Halos and Horns

The halo effect means that once you've decided you like Jake—for whatever reasons, professional or personal, rational or not—even his questionable behavior or below-standard performance somehow doesn't seem so bad. After all, you know Jake's heart/attitude is in the right place; you're sure he's just having a bad day and will do better tomorrow. Just as important, you will prefer to keep the opinion you have of Jake, even in the face of much negative evidence, rather than revise it. Why? Simply because it's easier, and because none of us likes to admit we've been wrong or mistaken. His likeable qualities are perceived as more important and noticeable than his disagreeable characteristics. The horns effect is the other side of the coin. If at some point you decided the quality of Brunhilde's work was marginal and her attitude difficult during those first weeks on the job, you're likely to keep thinking that, even if Brunhilde graduates with flying colors from a Dale Carnegie course and buckles down to produce more and better output.

This is why *objective, consistent standards* are so important for all your staff, and why completing the comments section is essential. You needn't like all your people, but you'll never regret being fair. In the space reserved for comments, you can provide all kinds of positive rein-forcement: show recognition for adequate work, give compliments on better-than-average work, and offer clear goals for improvement to every-one, not just those whose performance is lacking.

When an Employee Is Inadequate

As always, *be specific* (just as you've done for your own goals) when you write evaluation comments. You know exactly what you mean when you say "Joe's too fussy—wastes time," but your subordinate won't, and he may resent your opinion of his meticulousness. Hold your fire if you can't be measurably specific about a shortcoming (i.e., "Elaine's weekly production reports were late eight times during the past six months and lacked statistics from the Timbuktu office").

If you've had chronic problems with an employee, the PE is a place to note them briefly, along with any corrective action you took and the result. If Elaine finally started getting those reports in on time, for heaven's sake say so in no uncertain terms; she needs to know you've noticed and you're pleased. If she didn't, state the facts specifically (i.e., don't write "Elaine still has trouble getting reports in"). The PE must match other documentation you have on employee foul-ups should termination ever be necessary.

Finally, *every* employee does *something* adequately, if not outstandingly. Say so (see below). Few things are more demoralizing (for an employee you would like to keep) than a PE with no redeeming comments.

When an Employee Is Adequate

In your comments remember also to give ample recognition to those satisfactory employees. It's easy to motivate employees who are seeking promotion; they know they have to excel to earn the new title. Not so with certain clerical or assembly-line workers, or any staff who are not interested in moving up. This is why letting them know that you acknowledge and appreciate their work is so important. So ask yourself: What is it they do that keeps the works oiled? "Jim photocopied over 100,000 letters and managerial reports this past year," sounds far more impressive than "As always, Jim has done a good job in the copy room." If your customer service staff has met the standard of thirty-two people a day, translate it into "Carol successfully serviced over (32 people × 250 working days =) 8,000 accounts and opened 350 new ones." Saying "Carol is a reliable worker and her customers seem to like her" is a cop-out. It's nice, but it means next to nothing.

When an Employee Is Outstanding

The same principle applies to outstanding achievers, of course. "Terry initiated and developed a new patient care/medication system that saved four nurse-hours per day and resulted in monthly savings to the unit of over $500" is both a motivator and a strong argument for Terry's merit raise. And it will jog your memory with something solid when Terry's new employer calls you for a reference two years from now. Nor should nonmeasurable contributions to the unit be overlooked. "Ethel's unfailing good humor and diplomacy in chaotic situations made it possible for the rest of the staff to maintain their quotas following the fire and our move to new quarters last summer."

Still uncertain what to say, especially if PEs come around shortly after you begin your new job? There's a simple solution: Just ask your staff. Two or three weeks before PEs are due, ask each of your subordinates for a list of his or her accomplishments during the past year, along with one or two areas they'd like to improve in. Most employees will be surprisingly, refreshingly candid, and you'll learn plenty about how your people regard themselves and their performance. A few more tips:

- Base your evaluation on the job description and goals that your subordinates are familiar with. *A good PE never comes as a surprise!* If you followed the guidelines for planning and delegation in the last chapters, your people should be fully aware of what you expected from them.
- Keep notes now and then on anything memorable, good or bad, your people do. You have too much to think about to trust your memory for a year, or even for six months.
- Don't defeat your own purposes by failing to give immediate, verbal positive reinforcement (that is, compliment your staff on what they're doing well) on an ongoing, informal basis. Only when necessary should you point out—privately, of course—their mistakes or poor performance and make clear how they must improve. This in itself keeps the formal PE from being a surprise.
- Be fair and consistent, using the same objective criteria for all concerned. Since virtually all managers are human, too many of them are victims of the halo effect (and its corollary, the horns effect) when writing evaluations.

The Performance Evaluation Interview

Writing the PE is often not in itself the task managers dread most. It's giving the evaluation to the employee, allowing him or her to read it (often while you sit there feeling nervous, hoping he or she agrees with it with no argument) and discussing it afterward. Although most of your people probably haven't given you a great deal of trouble, several may present a problem, and all deserve to be heard. Hence, a few guidelines about the PE interview.

- Be absolutely sure you allow sufficient, uninterrupted, and private (i.e., in your office) time for the interview. Thirty minutes to an hour should do it, depending on the quality of the PE and the type of job being rated.
- Check with your subordinate to set a time for the interview that won't

interfere with his schedule. Then give him the actual PE to read the day before your appointment (don't give out all the PEs at once; comparisons may work against you). Many employees feel uncomfortable having to respond immediately to an evaluation they may not agree with, and some may overreact but calm down after a day's thought. In either case, interviews work best when your staff has had a chance to think about what you've written.

· If an employee disagrees with some negative point you've made, hear him out; really listen, even if you're convinced you're right. You may have overlooked extenuating circumstances or misjudged certain situations. If you have, be honest and be big about it: Change the evaluation. Your staff will respect you for it far more than if you shake your authority in their faces and insist you're right.

If you have too much negative evidence to warrant changing the evaluation, however, explain this to your subordinate. In no case should you let your emotions color what you say here, no matter how upset or angry your subordinate may become. If you've done enough homework to write a solid evaluation, you have the facts—and the facts will speak for themselves. If emotions become too volatile, however, tell your subordinate to think the facts over for a day or two, and set another interview when he (and perhaps you) have had a chance to cool off.

Performance evaluations are work, but the work really pays off for everyone when they're done well. Your staff will respond to your fairness and recognition, and it's the manager who knows how to motivate her people who gets promoted first.

Motivating Your People: Carrots, Not Sticks

"Why should I have to motivate them? They get paid—they should do the work they're being paid to do."

"You can't motivate people. They're going to do the same as they've always done, and all you can do is hope you inherited a decent staff."

"My subordinates are basically a good team, but you've got to keep on people's backs all the time if you want them to perform."

"If you're just nice to people, they'll cooperate."

If you firmly believe any of the above statements, be warned: You're unlikely to get as much work and cooperation as you can from your staff. These oft-heard sentiments are incomplete at best: There's a grain of truth in all of them, but a little knowledge, in management as elsewhere, is a dangerous thing.

Motivation is one of the most misunderstood, misused, and mismanaged skills in any business. How you treat your people *does* make a difference; understanding and applying some simple facts will make your job enormously easier and more successful.

First, let's see what you think people want from their jobs. Rank the following ten items twice: First, rank them in the order of importance you think your subordinates would rate them; second, in the order that is most important to you personally.

Motivation Self-Assessment

Rate the most important item 1, the second most important 2, and so on, for each column.

	WHAT YOU THINK YOUR SUBORDINATES WANT	WHAT YOU WANT
Interesting work	___	___
Job security	___	___
Full appreciation of work done	___	___
Personal loyalty of supervisor	___	___
High salary or wages	___	___
Tactful discipline	___	___
Feeling of being "in on things"	___	___
Promotion in the company	___	___
Good working conditions	___	___
Help with personal problems	___	___

Did you mark "High wages" and "Promotion" as the most important things your subordinates want from their jobs? If you did, you have plenty of company—the majority of managers tested think so too. The fact is, however, that this belief is based on myth.

Myth: More money (or benefits, or bonuses) is the best—in fact, the only—real motivator.

Fact: Management experts and psychologists have shown that more money is *not* necessarily the ultimate motivator.

We invite you to prove the wisdom of this seemingly heretical statement by recalling the last time you got a raise (which, if you were recently promoted to manager, may have been just last month). How did you feel when you were told that you would now be getting X percent more dollars per year? Probably pretty good. And how long did this good feeling last? Jot your answer here: _____ (If you're like most people who've answered this question for us, you're lucky if it lasted a month. Several managers we know have seriously answered, "About ten minutes.")

Unless you cannot live on your present salary, more money is often a weak motivator. In the classic ten-item study you just completed (the results of which have remained consistent in many management training seminars we've conducted), psychologists found the following:

What Workers Want

	HOW SUBORDINATES RATED THESE ITEMS	HOW MANAGERS *THINK* SUBS. RATED THEM
Full appreciation of work done	1	8
Feeling of being "in on things"	2	10
Help with personal problems	3	9
Job security	4	2
High salary or wages	5	1
Interesting work	6	5
Promotion in the company	7	3
Personal loyalty of supervisor	8	6
Good working conditions	9	4
Tactful discipline	10	7

You'll notice the rather startling fact that the supervisors and managers in the study were dead wrong about the three most important things their staff wanted from work: Subordinates rated "full appreciation," "help with personal problems," and "feeling of being 'in on things' " most important. Their bosses thought they would rate these items *least* important. This is even more surprising (and unfortunate) considering the managers themselves rated "full appreciation" and "feeling of being 'in on things' " as *their* top two motivators. Your staff isn't so different from you in this respect!

Then why has the myth of money-as-ultimate-motivator become so widespread? Often it's because ambitious, productive workers (frequently the power-control individuals discussed below) openly expect and respond best to merit increases at raise time. Salary, for them, becomes a very visible status symbol, as important for the prestige it conveys as for what it buys.

Money, however, is simply not your most effective *day-to-day* motivator. It's been shown again and again that men and women work best when they receive regular attention and recognition for their contributions, and are helped to feel like part of a team. These are two things money simply can't buy.

While we're on the subject, let's shoot a few holes in another favorite motivation fallacy:

Myth: People basically don't like to work, have little ambition, and therefore must be monitored all the time so they actually accomplish the tasks at hand.

Fact: Putting forth mental effort and physical activity in work is as natural as playing or resting. Thousands of people work who are wealthy enough to retire—including those who have independent means, those who have amassed their own fortunes through hard work and risks, and some million-dollar lottery winners.

Surprised? Not if you remember the control-achievement-social needs we talked about in chapter 4. Those needs apply to the lowliest laborer, the wealthiest CEO, and everyone in between. The vast majority of people come to work every day not only to earn enough money to live on, but to satisfy the need for structure and predictability in their lives. Almost all jobs provide structure. But as an effective manager you can motivate your people to give more than their minimum effort by attending to their control-achievement-social (CAS) needs.

How can you identify which subordinate has which need? Here are some basic types of behavior to watch for.

CONTROL/POWER NEEDS
Talks frequently about his/her own accomplishments
Takes fixed positions and doesn't like to listen to others' arguments
Is a natural leader
Spends more time talking or arguing than listening
Volunteers to take over stalled projects
Tends to dislike being told what to do or having too much company-
imposed structure

ACHIEVEMENT/CREATIVITY NEEDS
Does extra work or asks for more responsibility
Uses new or difficult methods to complete assignments
Takes pride in work
Tends to keep a low profile
Asks for feedback and recognition for accomplishments
Finds unusual solutions to problems

SOCIAL/AFFILIATION NEEDS
Talks to you often about work- and non-work-related things
Volunteers for group work
Very agreeable (sometimes overly so)
Prefers to work with others (customers or co-workers) rather than
alone
May take overlong lunches, coffee breaks; socializes with co-workers

Take a moment to note on your subordinate assessment from chapter 3
which style is dominant for each. Remember, everyone has some need for
each thing; we simply have them in differing amounts. If you have people
who seem equally concerned with achievement and control to the exclu-
sion of social needs, just mark them an A–C combination.

Now your task is to figure out how you can meet these needs during
the work day. Look back at the list you created in the "Tally Your Resources" section above. Our list is reproduced below, along with control,
achievement, and social needs each item fulfills.

Rewards and Incentives: Control, Achievement, Social Needs

CONTROL OR POWER REWARDS
Larger office
Bigger desk
More bookcases and file cabinets
More computer time

Extra days off
New title with more status
Office with windows or in better location
Company car
Companywide recognition awards
First pick of vacation dates
Better parking spot
Sole responsibility for a project
Being appointed to take over for a few days in your absence
Raises, bonuses, stock options, bigger expense accounts

ACHIEVEMENT AND CREATIVITY REWARDS
More work space
More bookcases and file cabinets
More computer time or access to computers
More specialized equipment
Special projects
Training seminars or conferences
Revolving duties
More challenging responsibilities
Acceptance of and recognition of new ideas, accomplishments
Raises, bonuses, stock options, bigger expense accounts, etc.

SOCIAL AND AFFILIATION REWARDS
More (or less) travel
Opportunity to work with preferred co-workers (rather than be
    switched from job to job)
Longer lunches
Permission to come in late/leave early
Flexible schedule (four 10-hour days, etc.)
Companywide recognition awards
First pick of vacation dates
Thoughtful gifts on birthdays or whenever extra effort was required
Being taken to lunch
Raises, bonuses, stock options, bigger expense accounts, etc.

A word here on another motivator that is so obvious it may be overlooked: simple justice. If the last boss for whatever reason shortchanged
your staff out of their appropriate rewards, by all means right these
wrongs as soon as you can. This kind of information is best discovered
through the grapevine (although more assertive subordinates may tell you

in no uncertain terms how they or their friends were cheated by your predecessor). Fix it, and your PR will zoom without your having to say a word.

Different Strokes for CAS Folks

Rewards, of course, are not the only motivators. Everything you do and say affects your staff in some way, so tailor your interactions with each one, keeping in mind his or her needs. Here are some guidelines about what to do, what to avoid, and the dangers to watch for with each type of employee:

CONTROL- OR POWER-ORIENTED

- When you delegate, outline the results you want, and allow him authority and leeway in deciding how the task is to be carried out.
- Whenever possible, don't give orders.
- Comment on and reinforce the positive aspects of his natural leadership. Don't ask for reports or check on him unnecessarily.
- He is often best motivated by knowing a promotion or new title awaits if he does his job well.

DANGERS TO WATCH FOR

- He may "forget" to get your approval when it's required, create conflict by acting bossy with his peers, and in some cases create his own coalitions and power bases behind your back.
- If his ambitions don't include getting your job, he can be helpful if he believes you'll help him get ahead. Check him out carefully and avoid power struggles by insisting he keeps to whatever reporting schedule you've set up, and by dealing with infractions promptly and firmly.

ACHIEVEMENT- OR CREATIVITY-ORIENTED

- Whenever possible, avoi. giving her repetitious or routine work; if you must, be sure to give her other assignments (even if you have to create them) that utilize her creativity and problem-solving skills.
- She probably won't mind being switched around to different tasks or projects from time to time, and may even welcome the chance to learn or do something different.
- Her new ideas can be a terrific help if they're not quashed by "But we've always done it this way. . . . Upper management won't like it."
- Reinforce her by recognizing and using her creative endeavors and contributions. As with the control-oriented employee, allow her freedom to design and carry through on projects when possible without dictating exactly how it should be done.

DANGERS TO WATCH FOR
- She may be a fussy prima donna, respected for expertise but disliked by co-workers.
- She may do poorly on routine tasks and/or try to weasel out of them so she can spend more time on projects that pique her interest.
- She may do poorly working with others, customers and co-workers alike.

SOCIAL OR AFFILIATION-ORIENTED
- He likes to spend plenty of time with his co-workers, including you, and may find pretenses to talk with you about almost anything. Give him work that involves dealing with others, and pay close attention to which people he works best with.
- Reinforce his good work by paying him some sincere personal attention once a day—even for five seconds—about something he's done well (but never point out his mistakes in front of others).
- Capitalize on his style by allowing him plenty of customer or client contact; train him for this, if necessary.

DANGERS TO WATCH FOR
- He may spend too much time socializing with others, or distract certain co-workers from their own tasks.
- He may do poorly (or do nothing) on tasks that must be done alone or with people he dislikes.

A final word: You've probably figured out by now which CAS category you fall into, and which motivators work best for you personally. And you no doubt know people among your co-workers, friends, and family whose styles are different from yours. Listen to these people: They're an excellent source of advice about precisely what you can do (and avoid doing) to motivate and reward your staff. The key is flexibility; if you're willing to use different strokes with different folks, as the song goes, the folks will reward *you* with increased output and improved morale.

When Nothing Seems to Work

The few subordinates who don't respond to your honest effort at motivation are either in the wrong job completely (words on this later in "Use and Abuse Your Plan") or gain almost no personal satisfaction from their work. Their needs are met elsewhere. Docking them for unacceptable work and withholding bonuses, etc., can be an effective though negative motivator, and must be used carefully.

It's also worth noting that if such employees are already earning enough money to live on, giving them *more* money won't necessarily make them do a better job.

Training and Developing Your People

If you're fortunate enough to have a training program in-house, or access to various training seminars, take care not to fall into the classic trap of thinking "Oh, boy! Once I send my staff to the ten-day Creative Widget Development seminar, all my production problems will be solved!" The seminar content may be just what they need, but remember: You're also asking them to do the most difficult thing of all—change.

We mentioned change in the last chapter when delegating was discussed. People resist change because it feels different, and anything different rocks the proverbial boat. No matter that the boat is a leaky, grimy tug; if it's *your* boat, you'll hang on to it through hell or high water. So remember this: People resist change *mainly* when it comes too fast; you'll enjoy much better cooperation and success if you plan ahead for effective training.

Get together the information you gathered about training and educational offerings in "Tally Your Resources." Familiarize yourself with what's already available. Then find your production plans for the following year, and decide what new or different training courses your staff will need to meet your new goals. If these aren't offered, find out from the personnel department or from your boss if they can be arranged or initiated. (This job may fall to you, so give it careful thought beforehand.)

The first thing to do, of course, is pin down *who needs what kind of training*: to learn necessary skills they haven't yet mastered; to augment or improve their existing skills for their current job, based on their PE; to learn new skills to achieve upcoming project goals. Chart 7A gives you the means to plan all this.

Your second goal has more to do with staff development per se: determining *who wants what kind of training*, based on their desire to transfer to another department, your desire to increase their responsibility in their current job, their desire to move up in your department or to acquire particular new technical skills.

Once you have completed this chart (again, in pencil), talk to each of your staff who requires training. It's best to go to them this time, during an unpressured time of day. If yours is a small firm or department where everyone needs the same training, you can have a staff meeting and give everyone the same information at once. Explain to the group what the company's goals are, your unit's upcoming projects, and any current

CHART 7A   Unit Goals and Training Needs

1. Your year's goals: _____

_____

2. Skills required to meet those goals: _____

_____

3. Subordinates' training needs:

Name: _____   Training required: _____

Name: _____   Training required: _____

Name: _____   Training required: _____

4. Training available: In-house   On the job   Outside seminars

_____   _____   _____

_____   _____   _____

5. Subordinates' desired or requested training needs:

Name: _____   Training requested: _____

Name: _____   Training requested: _____

Name: _____   Training requested: _____

shortcomings. Then outline what training will be required to meet those goals. (You needn't be specific if certain people require individual training.) Mentioning your own needs and projected training during this discussion isn't a bad idea, especially if you're asking for major changes from your people and want to foster the feeling that "We're all in this together."

Depending on the type of work and the situation, you'll also want to ask your employees privately about their personal goals and needs. (This might also be a part of the PE interview for subordinates who seek promotion.) Providing a course in basic supervision skills for the woman who wants to move up is not only an excellent motivator and reward; it will save you time and effort because you can delegate more tasks to her as you give her the chance to *use* the skills she's learned. Don't automatically assume, however, that everyone wants to be a leader or hankers after a promotion. Identify, develop, and use your people's *natural* inclinations and talents. Give them the opportunity to learn and expand their knowledge and responsibilities, but don't insist that they change if they really don't want to. Their job satisfaction may lie in doing more within the position they now hold.

Even more frustrating than the good worker who prefers to stay with what she's doing is the Neanderthal who responds to none of your efforts to correct, let alone develop, him. How to deal with this type will be discussed below in "Use and Abuse Your Plan." In the meantime, however, keep in mind that the chance to unload such a lemon on another department is often irresistible. ("I'm sure Neander will be happier in Murphy's unit anyway" is the usual rationalization.) Again, resist temptation. Don't fob off your problem worker on another department without explaining the situation to his new manager. You can slip this maneuver by once, but you'll be suspect forever more . . . and inevitably some other disgruntled manager will do the same to you.

Employee Advocacy: Moving Your People Ahead

Now that you've evaluated, motivated, and trained your staff, they're probably knocking your socks off. There's one more step: advocating. To *advocate* means "to support by argument, to recommend publicly." In other words, speaking up for them when they deserve raises, promotions, or other rewards, sticking up for them when their well-being may be threatened, and supporting them in the ways you want to be supported by your own boss.

Although not all your staff will deserve (or desire) a promotion, everyone responds well to merit raises and recognition from above. Because your boss is the one to approve those raises, make her job easier by selling your best workers throughout the year—not just at performance evaluation time when a dozen other managers will be championing their favorites.

How do you choose whom to advocate for promotion? Obviously your PEs provide solid information (especially if you've written them as suggested above). Besides your whiz kids, also consider:

Subordinates who for whatever reason were "victims" under the old regime—if they were cheated out of raises or promotions, right these wrongs first

Those whose PEs document flexibility, above-average output, and ability to meet deadlines

Those motivated enough to ask and campaign for themselves, even if they're not totally outstanding

Those willing to take on new tasks, to do more than their share, and/or who are natural group leaders

Those you want to "kick upstairs" to get them out of your unit and your hair (like Peggy Sanger's nemesis Janice in chapter 3)

A note of caution here: While you're deciding whose flag to carry, decide also who's going to *replace* this paragon. One of the first things your boss will want to know is how the promotion will affect your unit's performance. If you've been training and developing your staff, of course, it should be no problem.

Planning Your Campaign

Effective campaigns of any sort work because they convince the right people at the right time. The right people for you are the individuals and/ or committees who have the authority to award more money, better titles, and formal recognition your staff deserve.

The right time is at least once a week, all year long. It's a mistake to save up all your wonderful tales about Jerry's devotion to detail and constant willingness to work overtime and trot them out in one lump *only* during PE time. To be effective, you must call your boss's attention to Jerry consistently and persistently during the rest of the year.

How to sell Jerry's sterling qualities? As with so much advertising, keeping the product's name before the public is the main thing. You can:

· Leave Jerry's name on a (usually anonymous) report that he did particularly well, and circulate it to your boss(es).

· Write at least four memos, with copies to Jerry and your boss, thanking him for his overtime, pointing out how much money and hassle he saved you, and praising his programming skills to the skies. This is much more effective than one big memo about how Jerry single-handedly saved the project by working overtime three weeks running and devising a new computer program himself.

· Bring Jerry along when you have to talk about work Jerry's involved in to your boss and any other individuals or committees who have the power to okay promotions, raises, and awards.

· Always mention Jerry's name (and Gail's, and Steve's, and Harriet's) to your boss *whenever* some accomplishment warrants it. This not only makes you look good, it prevents long-winded explanations of who these faceless creatures are when you're asking for their raises.

Warning: Even your best employees can be stopped by bureaucratic regulations. Check out early any job prerequisite or company rule that could prevent their raise or promotion. If the job requires more or higher college degrees, or an employee is already at the top of the salary scale, or there's an informal freeze on raises or promotions, or the company is seriously in the red and no money is available, you won't be able to keep the promises you made, even if you made them in the best of faith.

Contingency Planning

If some or all of the above apply, however, you still have options. Ask for a title change for the employee: Paul may need a Ph.D. to become an associate professor, but his M.A. can still get him an assistant deanship (with the same raise). Cheryl may not have enough experience with the company to become a full project director, but her accomplishments qualify her for a research director's post. Gus has done such a terrific job as a service rep in six months that, even without official sanction to give him more money, you can create a "Senior Service Rep" title and talk your boss into budgeting a raise for him. Cite precedents of such rules that have been waived for others. This type of information is best discovered through the grapevine; ask your staff to help you find out.

Few rules in any firm, public or private, are rock solid. Identify who has the authority to bend policy, get your boss's support (once you've convinced her that Jerry is God's gift to the company, of course), and ask for what you want. *Always* ask, even if you're sure of a no, because: It keeps you in practice, and you have nothing to lose; you're more likely to get what you request the next time; it marks you as a concerned leader; and at times you'll be pleasantly surprised with a yes! It's in upper management's interest to hang on to good employees, and they won't know what gems they have unless you tell them.

Accentuate the Positive, Shut Up about (or Relabel) the Negative

There's no need to mention Jerry's drawbacks while you're selling him to Mr. Big. However, be prepared if your boss knows Jerry well enough to be familiar with his shortcomings: occasional tardiness, complaints from co-workers about his "pigheadedness," and the like. You want to be able to argue that Jerry's bad points are minimal—certainly no worse than anyone else's—or even *helpful* in certain ways. ("Jerry's stubborn, it's true, but only when he's right; and he's right more often than anyone else." "I can't deny people's complaints that Joe can be an abrasive SOB; maybe that's why he gets more work out of the construction crew than the other foremen.") If Gail had several correction conferences with you or was written up by the past manager, be ready to explain how she's fixed, or made up for, her mistakes. ("She's a poor teacher, but a great researcher. If you promote her, she'll have fewer classes and more time to work on grants for our department.")

If all else fails, agree that Gail does have her failings, *but they are no worse than Sam's, Gary's, or Helene's* (none of whom work in your own unit, of course). Repeat your positive arguments, then gracefully accept your boss's decision. She may have her own reasons for putting you off, such as timing. Examples:

Is practically everyone in her division due for a raise this month? (Gail's merit raise may have to wait.)

Is the company seriously in the red?

Is your boss having a bad week because of other pressures, and likely to say no to any request?

Timing, of course, can also work for you:

Has it been two full years since Cheryl's last merit raise?

Has Cheryl just accomplished something prominent as well as cost-effective?

Have profits been up recently, and you've just heard that another unit on your level is now getting more money? (Equity is almost impossible to argue against, profits or not.)

Even if you don't manage to get the raises you've been fighting for, don't give up. Continue advocating your people, and let them know you're still actively on their side. There's always next quarter, and persistence wins many a battle.

STEP-UP   USE AND ABUSE YOUR PLAN

There comes that time in every new manager's life when he finds himself with subordinates who, for a variety of reasons, do not perform as they have been directed. Few people enjoy pointing out another's mistakes or, heaven forbid, firing anyone. This is part of your job, however, and in this section you'll learn about:

1. Correcting your subordinates' mistakes and below-standard performance

2. Disciplining them when simply correcting them hasn't changed their behavior

3. Documenting and dismissing them should it become necessary

Correcting Your Staff's Mistakes and Performance: Where, When, and How

Where is easy to answer: in private. There really are no exceptions to this rule (unless you see Naomi about to accidentally run over Harriet with the forklift, of course). For nonfatal errors you needn't call Naomi into your office, but *don't* correct her in the presence of another. The rule "Praise in public, reprimand in private" is one of the few truly eternal verities of management. To break it is to invite embarrassment, resentment, low morale, even vengeance. And who needs that?

When to correct or reprimand your staff is also a relatively easy choice. If Sadie's work is consistently late, or full of errors, or sloppy, or missing any essential ingredients, you need to mention it in a brief, private talk with Sadie as soon as you notice it. The longer you wait to give Sadie feedback—whether it's a compliment or a correction—the less it will mean to her.

A big caution here: People do make honest mistakes and overlook things occasionally. Yes, you should surely mention the error (again, privately) and allow the perpetrator to correct it. But to pounce on the first mistake you see *and treat it as a reason to have a full-blown conference* is to paint yourself as a fussy Simon Legree who doesn't trust his staff's competence or dedication. (Exception: brand-new workers, who rely on you to tell them if they're doing something wrong, so that they learn the correct way right from the start.) Many "problems" just go away, with no action from you. Don't be so zealous that you end up creating unnecessary havoc.

How to correct your staff: a much more complex and delicate task. Some workers take any criticism as an insult or undeserved attack on their entire personality, some as proof that you have it in for them, and most, fortunately, for what it is. When your people perform poorly, especially more than once on the same issue, you must find a way to correct them while motivating them to improve.

You can minimize interpersonal friction and maintain morale by criticizing and correcting the *behavior, not the person*. That means being factual and helpful while you talk to Sadie about those late reports, or about the figures she always seems to "forget" to include. No matter how upset, angry, or frustrated you may be, taking out your feelings on Sadie via shouting or sarcasm is 100 percent guaranteed not to make her a better report-completer. Sure, you can scare or browbeat your people into doing what you want—for a while. But the loss you suffer in good working relationships and resulting productivity is never worth it.

When you think of your own experience being corrected by past supervisors, you'll agree that the good ones provided both factual and helpful criticism. So when you correct Sadie:

· *Be sure she knows what's expected of her.* Go over the relevant task descriptions and standards. Avoid using accusatory words such as "You never remember to get those sales figures from Herb in accounting, and the report is useless without them." Instead, say, "The sales figures from Herb in accounting are essential to this report, and they've been missing several times in the past three months. What problems have you encountered in getting them, and how can I help?" If Sadie really needs your help, she now feels comfortable asking for it. If she's been merely forgetful or too lazy to see Herb, you've still gotten your point across.

· *Explain the nitty-gritty consequences of the mistake.* Do your people know what happens to their work after it leaves their desks? Strange as it may seem to you, Sadie may have only the haziest idea of who sees or uses the reports she's responsible for. (Too many employees have seen some evidence that "Upper management never reads this stuff anyway, so what's the big deal about a few mistakes?") Explain in a calm, factual way how you and other department(s) in the firm rely on the accuracy of her monthly reports to, for example, plan weekly shipments, analyze regional needs, and plan future marketing strategies. Don't give Sadie the impression that you're blaming her for the company's being in the red; rather, let her know that her work is necessary to the team's success and you expect her best efforts.

· *Know exactly what you want her to change, and by when.* As you've done for your own goals, give Sadie something specific and measurable to shoot for. Have the goal in mind before you even call her in ("I want to see fully complete and accurate reports, using the standardized form, starting next week"), and be flexible in case she explains how unavoidable circumstances have prevented her from meeting standards in the past.

Whenever possible, ask Sadie how *she* would solve the problem before you tell her how. Similarly, ask her how long it will take her to correct the problem and meet the agreed-upon standards. (If she says "six months" when you expect six weeks, ask her why she thinks it will take that long. If her reasons aren't solid, reiterate clearly why you insist on improvement by a certain date, and stick to it if you know it has been a reachable goal in the past.)

· *Ask for her feedback and get her agreement to change.* You may be uncomfortable enough in correcting people that you jump at the chance to end the interview the minute Sadie says, "Don't worry, it won't happen again." Grit your teeth if you must, but be sure to have Sadie put in her own words specifically what she has agreed to change. Nothing is more maddening (to both parties) than to have the same problem next month, only to find there was an honest misunderstanding. Write down the standards and time lines, if need be; just be sure you understand each other.

· *Let her know you're serious.* We've already mentioned that yelling at your staff or accusing them (directly or subtly) of deliberately screwing up is counterproductive. Equally ineffective is the manager who is *so* nice, *so* careful not to hurt feelings—and so vague in explaining the problem— that Sadie leaves thinking the correction interview was nothing more than a pleasant chat. We know managers who have actually apologized to a subordinate for having to correct them, and then wondered why that employee felt no impetus to change.

· *Keep a brief written record of the meeting*, which you may later add to Sadie's permanent file if necessary. At the very least, keep a note of the agreed-upon expected changes. Any other information or notes to yourself will remind you, should the problem continue, of what has already been done and said, and can form the basis for formal documentation.

The suggestions above presuppose that Sadie already knows how to do the report, where to get the necessary information for it, and has a desk to sit at while she completes it. When one of your people is performing poorly but seems to have no attitude problems, you owe it to yourself to check further.

Did Sadie get the proper on-the-job training when she started? Does she really know what the job entails? Are there certain skills or knowledge she needs that a seminar could improve? Find out and train her.

The wrong environment may be causing problems: If it's too hot or too cold to work, or if Sadie has faulty equipment that keeps breaking down, it's your responsibility to fix it. Similarly, make sure Sadie *has* the proper equipment and supplies in the first place.

In certain work situations, there's enormous peer pressure to do only average work. It's the rare individual who's willing to make her co-workers look bad, no matter how much she wants to succeed. If this is the case in your unit, think about how to restructure things so that peer pressure is reduced.

Are *you* doing anything that makes it more difficult for your staff to perform well? Inadvertently sabotaging your own people and interests is deceptively easy. For example, suppose your top salesman reports his best month yet (and is hoping for a word of congratulation from you). You say, "Good—then you won't mind taking over Harvey's territory this month.

He's been slipping lately, so I'm sending him to some sales training in the Bahamas." Don't punish your best people by loading more work on them simply because they're competent.

CORRECTING THE QUALITY WORKER   Sadie is the typical worker with performance problems. Jack is the typical worker who performs well consistently, but arrives late, or leaves early, or spends too much time on personal phone calls. It doesn't affect his work quality or your unit's bottom line yet, but he's breaking the rules—and everyone knows it. The same guidelines that apply to Sadie apply to handling Jack, in spite of his heartfelt argument that his behavior isn't damaging the department in any way. This just isn't so; if it's affecting morale, sooner or later it's going to affect productivity.

This type of infraction often lends itself to creative problem solving. Can you let Jack work late whenever he comes in late? Can you let everyone else have flexible schedules should they wish it? Can you let the staff know that Jack will indeed be arriving half an hour later than anyone else, but will be taking over some other late-hour task that no one else wants? Can you assign Jack to an early-morning task in another part of the building so that his tardiness isn't so obvious?

In other words, to suggest that Jack set his alarm clock twenty minutes earlier will inevitably not work—and we would be astonished if Jack hadn't already tried that one himself. Don't set yourself up for frustration by suggesting the obvious; put the responsibility where it belongs, and be willing to consider some not-so-obvious solutions.

If Jack's tardiness persists, however, you must:

Be sure Jack knows what's expected of him: starting time is 8:45, and you expect him at his desk every day at that time.

Explain the nitty-gritty consequences of his failure to abide by that rule: peer resentment, not being there when you need him, and so on.

Know exactly what you want Jack to change, and by when; in this case, effective immediately.

Ask for Jack's feedback and get agreement to change. If there were extraordinary mitigating circumstances, you probably would already know about them. But give him a chance to explain.

Let Jack know you're serious by stating, in an unthreatening way, that your own job descriptions require that you write him up and consider changing his performance evaluation if his tardiness continues . . . and you want very much not to do that.

Keep a brief written record for yourself of the meeting, which you may later add to Jack's permanent file if necessary.

Tardiness and overlong lunch hours are, by the way, one of the banes of managerial existence. You can, if you want to, stand over Sadie all week and make sure she gets that report done correctly and on time; you can't very well knock on Jack's front door every morning and get him up in time for work. (Well, maybe you could. But—in both cases—you'd be a fool to do it.)

Discipline: Fair, Prompt, Dispassionate, and Consistent

To your dismay, the improvement Jack and Sadie showed after your first meeting has deteriorated. You've already spoken with each of them again, repeated the above steps, and said that a second failure to improve would affect their PE and/or yearly raise. You let them know the record of the second meeting was documented and put in their file.

After a brief period of quality reports and punctuality, both of them have slipped a second time. You now need to carry out the disciplinary measures you cautioned them about last time. Theoretically, this should be no problem. You simply tell them that due to thus and such behavior on their part, they will not be getting a raise next month. In practice, however, telling an already strained staff member that she won't be receiving the increase in salary she was expecting—well, it makes strong men want to weep.

If you're nervous because you've never had to discipline anyone on the job, ask a trusted co-worker (boss or peer) who's been in the same situation to listen to what you plan to do. (If there's no one you trust, ask a friend or acquaintance at another company. You need support, not questioning of your abilities.) Do inform your boss before you act, however. Find out whether any union rules or personnel guidelines apply. This is no time to be unsure of what you're doing, and your boss should know who's being disciplined so he can be ready for any appeals.

By now Sadie should certainly know what you want done, so don't spend time elaborating on standards and descriptions. Instead, be brief and direct with her; tell her the reports are still below par, and that the next time a faulty or incomplete report is submitted, company policy requires you to demote or terminate her. Make absolutely clear the *time lines and consequences* Sadie will face if she again fails to improve. Usually one to two weeks is plenty; be realistic, however, if the job is unusual.

Suitable disciplinary measures are usually prescribed by the company; if they're not, keep in mind that good discipline is like a traffic ticket: fair, prompt, dispassionate, and consistent.

Fair: The penalty has been carefully considered according to accepted guidelines; it is not haphazard, arbitrary, or subject to whim.

Prompt: Discipline loses its impact if much time elapses between the infraction and the consequence.

Dispassionate: No matter how angry you (or that traffic cop) may be, browbeating or emotional exhortations have no place in correcting another human being. The discipline is given from adult to adult, and enforced fairly.

Consistent: Everyone who fails the same standard will face the same consequence.

There may be cases where, in your heart of hearts, you have begun to hope your subordinate *will* fail (so you can terminate her), while at the same time you want to be utterly fair. Bide your time—few employees are patient enough to keep their work hovering at "barely acceptable" for very long. As long as you mention and document mistakes and infractions, the law—in letter if not spirit—is on your side, not hers. Be sure to explain clearly, as soon as it's appropriate, that one more infraction will necessarily result in her termination.

Meanwhile, beware of our old friend the "horns effect" and make a conscious effort to treat Jack and Sadie as you always do, neither coldly nor apologetically. Perhaps it's a holdover from being made to sit in the corner in grade school, but some managers *inadvertently* isolate an employee who hasn't been working up to par. Letting a staff person know, even nonverbally, that "You're not part of the team anymore" is a great way to demoralize him.

Whatever discipline you decide on, of course, is worse than useless if you don't follow through on it. To renege on eliminating Jack's raise, or to feel soft and allow Sadie first dibs on choosing vacation time after all, is a mistake. It might make you look like a great guy for an hour, but like a schmuck for years afterward (and not just with Jack and Sadie—the news will travel fast). Don't invite disrespect and more poor-quality work; do what you say you will.

THAT OLD DEVIL INSUBORDINATION   Unfortunately, all the logic and supportiveness you can muster will be useless with the insubordinate employee. For reasons of their own, insubordinates will, with hostility or sarcasm, question your leadership or expertise at a meeting, go over your head, badmouth you to clients or colleagues, or undermine your authority to other subordinates. Often this is done in such a subtle way that you have no solid ground on which to challenge the worker. You need special ways to handle such behavior before it turns into a maddening, energy-sapping cold war. An anecdote will illustrate.

Zachary, not unlike our friend Peggy Sanger who opened chapter 3, found himself pinioned at a staff meeting by a subordinate who brought up a small erroneous point in Zach's report and refused to let it drop. Though Zach thought the subject was closed when he said, "Yes, of course, I meant the Lexwriter 3L software instead of the 3N," Mark continued to dog him with remarks like "That would change a lot of specifications about the work, wouldn't it? Using the 3N? You made a mistake there, right?" Everyone at the meeting could sense the growing tension, and Zach realized he had to let Mark know his behavior was unacceptable. But how? Mark obviously had a grudge against Zach, and simply telling him "Don't do that anymore" would be absurd. Zach had to find a way to demonstrate to Mark, not just tell him, that he did not want to be rudely questioned in public.

What Zach did was to have his secretary call Mark to his office shortly after the meeting was over. He then kept Mark waiting for ten minutes (even though Mark was five minutes late himself). After Mark was finally shown into Zach's office and sat down, Zach said, "Oh, it's two o'clock. I have a phone call to make. You won't mind waiting outside for a few minutes." Mark did mind, but had little choice.

When Zach called him back into his office after ten more minutes, he spoke to Mark only about legitimate, upcoming work topics. At the end of the discussion, Zach calmly continued, "If you have any issues to raise about anything at future meetings, don't hesitate to bring them up—and if I say we'll discuss them later, that's exactly what I mean. Your behavior today was unacceptable. I don't want to take formal action against you, so don't force the issue to a win-lose argument in public."

Predictably, Mark protested. "I was only trying to make sure which one you meant. The others might have been confused, and you have to admit you were wrong about the software specifications." Zach didn't argue or raise his voice. "Forcing the issue at a meeting is unacceptable. Are you clear on that?" was all he said. Mark was clear. Zach had delivered his message—"I am the manager of this unit, and I expect to be treated with respect at all times"—both physically, by keeping Mark waiting, and verbally. No cajoling, no outrage, no arguments. Zach's behavior matched his words, and did not escalate the tension between him and Mark.

Some other subtle but increasingly pointed methods of dealing with insubordination follow. We recommend these only when you've tried the above disciplinary techniques without success, and are sure you *are* dealing with insubordination.

In each case, you actions will speak louder than any words. Under no circumstances should you carry these out in a retaliatory way (which will reflect badly on your professionalism and judgment), nor should you admit your covert reasons for doing the following, even if directly challenged. And under no circumstances should you threaten (or promise) such treatment without following through.

· *The cold shoulder:* Zach might call another meeting the next day and invite everyone except Mark . . . and for a while pay scant attention to Mark's contributions when he does attend meetings.

· *Rescinding privileges:* removing the insubordinate's "perks," from minor things like being able to keep plants on her desk, to taking away her company car. Managers who want to communicate an unmistakable "you're no longer wanted here" message have been known to remove even major resources such as secretaries ("Sorry, Mark, but I've decided that Mary and George need more secretarial help").

CORRECTING THE LOW-QUALITY, POOR-ATTITUDE WORKER: CAREER COUNSELING FOR "HOPELESS" CASES   You're probably wondering, Why should I even bother with hopeless cases? Because, like the mountain, they're there—and often as hard to move.

If your staff includes some disgruntled Duane who is a pleasant enough person but a minor disaster as a service rep, very possibly he shouldn't be in his position at all. He may have taken the job because he needed the money and nothing else was available, or because he was promoted to a level beyond his competency, or maybe he just didn't realize how temperamentally or technically unsuited he would be to the work.

His performance is consistently lacking in quality, quantity, or timeliness, and his attitude is either negative or disturbingly neutral. All the excellent suggestions you read above will be of no avail, because such an employee simply cannot, will not, or does not care to do the job to company standards. He's not malicious or vindictive; he's just thoroughly unmotivated.

In such cases, Duane needs career counseling more than he needs pep talks or correction. If you've already given the latter an honest try, it's time to straightforwardly suggest to Duane that another position (perhaps even another line of work) might suit him better. If you have specific ideas of where he might fit in better in the company, share them.

Reassure him that you're not bringing this up because you're about to terminate him, but that his performance and behavior tell you he's unhappy or unsuited to this job. If you present this in a calm, unthreatening way, there's a good chance. Duane will agree with your opinion. He may not be thrilled at the prospect of leaving, but many such employees have been known to welcome your offer to help them find another position (in this company or another) that they can handle.

Fire Somebody . . . ? ME?

Yes, you.

It's one of the hardest things you'll ever have to do, as a manager or as anything else. Even if you know you're justified, even if that worker was driving the entire unit crazy, firing a human being is never simple. Still, the fact is that you have little choice but to fire a subordinate when the difficulties he causes consistently outweigh the results he produces.

Though the very idea of dismissing someone is crushing to most managers, being fired should come as no shock to Sadie if you've been scrupulous in correcting, disciplining, and documenting her. Most situations are less than clear-cut, but after two disciplinary conferences, Sadie should have been told that one more screwup on her part would mean her job.

Still, Sadie isn't going to be exactly happy when you formally announce that the company no longer requires her services. You probably know your people well enough to predict whether they'll react with tears, anger, or pleas for one more chance; whatever their reaction, you must be completely sure in your own mind that the firing is justified and have the evidence to back up your decision.

As with discipline, your boss or a trusted co-worker can be an invaluable resource in guiding you. In fact, especially if you're dealing with a union member who may sue, you *must* check out your rights and legal responsibilities before doing anything else. This applies even if you've caught Sam red-handed, stealing checks from your desk. Suspend him, yes; but to rashly fire him on the spot says the wrong things about your judgment, even if Sam is guilty as sin.

THE TERMINATION INTERVIEW   Once you have the necessary documentation, there are a few things you can do to make the procedure a little less anxiety-provoking.

· Have all the necessary paperwork about insurance coverage, educational or other benefits, unused vacation time, and severance pay clearly worked out in advance. Don't add insult to what Sadie will surely perceive as injury by requiring her to go through a mile of red tape just to get her wages. In any case, a terminated employee hanging around the office cannot but be a painful or disruptive influence on the rest of the staff.
· Friday late afternoon is the preferred time for the termination meeting; it gives Sadie a few days to adjust to the fact before she begins looking for another position. However, if Sadie will need to visit Personnel, don't make her wait the entire weekend.
· If you've decided Sadie should clear out her desk and return her keys, credit cards, and other company property that very day, be sure you provide adequate time for her to do so *and* to visit Personnel before she receives her final paycheck.
· Don't allow the remaining staff to worry and gossip among themselves with no official word from you. A firing, no matter how expected, causes most people undue concern for their own jobs. On Monday morning, call your people together (if your staff is very large, call several subordinates whom you trust and who have the respect of your other workers). Let them know whether or not Sadie's position will be filled right away. Emphasize that Sadie's dismissal in no way reflects on anyone else. If you can, invite them to suggest applicants for her position; in this way you reinforce the message that Sadie, not the staff, was the problem.

After you've taken care of Sadie, don't forget to take care of yourself. Plan to spend your evening doing something active to take your mind off the firing, and use some of the stress-management exercises in chapter 11.

STEP-UP PLAN AND PLAN AGAIN

A Few Words about Hiring

Volumes have been written about how to choose, interview, and hire new staff, and a detailed discussion of hiring is beyond the scope of this book. However, much of what you've learned so far—

Defining goals,

Asking open-ended questions,

Listening to subordinates to learn about their areas of strength and aptitude,

Analyzing whether people are social, creative, or achievement-oriented, and

Matching the right worker to each task

—is exactly what managers use to conduct effective interviews. Even if you've never hired anyone before, you're better prepared than you think! Below are a few guidelines to make your search easier.

Before the Interview

- *Is the job description still valid?* If you have to place a want ad, have a full description of the job's duties, formal and informal, firmly in mind—and on paper, if necessary. (Delegate the job of writing the ad to one of your creative types, if you must.) Place it in the appropriate section of the classifieds, which is sometimes trickier than it sounds. Keep the full job description at hand as you read resumés.
- *What formal skills and qualifications must the candidate have?* These too should be spelled out clearly. Don't rule out resumés that lack one or two items; on-the-job training or concurrent courses are options for a likely interviewee.
- *What informal qualifications must the candidate have?* Must she be a generalist? Specialist? Strong in technical skills? Good with people? Utterly reliable? Not mind traveling? Willing to work all day alone in a windowless room? If you don't know exactly what you're looking for, forget about finding it. Resumés may not tell you these things, so you'll have to ask directly.

During the Interview

- After the pleasantries, explain what it was about her resumé that made you choose the candidate for an interview. Then tell her about the job and the formal and informal work requirements.
- Invite the candidate to tell you what she liked best and least about her last job. If appropriate, ask her what part of this job she would find most interesting to do.
- Invite her questions about the job and company, and answer them.
- Thank her for her time and tell her when you expect to make a decision. Then let her know when you said you would.

After the Interview

What overall impression did the candidate make on you? Professional, knowledgeable, punctual, pleasing personality? Any annoying habits? Can you envision yourself and your staff working well with her? Pay attention to your gut reactions; think them through in terms of the solid information you have, and use them to formulate more questions.

If you liked certain candidates enough to merit a second interview, you have another decision to make: Should you have their potential co-workers meet them? Seeing to the "personality fit" makes sense in certain jobs where a small, cohesive staff works closely together. If possible, and especially if you're hiring for a professional position, we recommend allowing two or three staff members to meet (if not interview) the candidates, perhaps at lunch. Your staff will appreciate your respecting their judgment, and group cohesiveness will be less disrupted if they feel they've had a say in the decision.

Planning Again for Advocacy

And speaking of your existing staff, what if your advocacy efforts on their behalf didn't turn out as you had hoped? Don't let disappointment or anger keep you from going to your boss again. You can still turn today's setbacks into tomorrow's victories by being tenacious and willing to compromise. Maybe Carlotta's sabbatical was refused this term, but you went back, put in another word for her, and nailed down the dean's assurance that she's first in line next time. Maybe you couldn't get Wilbur the raise he deserved this year, but your campaign makes him a prime candidate as soon as the budget loosens up. Depending on whether Wilbur knew you were pulling for him, you may want to give him your personal reassurance that despite budget constraints, you'll continue to fight for his increase. In the meantime, arrange for him to get some extra time off, a better office, or some other reward that will make his life a little easier. Your genuine concern and action will not go unappreciated.

Now that your people are busy running the unit like a well-tuned Rolls, you can turn your attention to another topic close to every manager's heart: money.

Using the Budget to Get More

ESTERBROOK hated the budget. "If there is anything that I hate about being a manager," he would say to himself, "it's the damn budget." When budget submission time rolled around, Esterbrook would do what he had to do. He would compile his unit's production statistics for the year and would estimate how much his unit would produce in the next year. He would figure out the previous year's personnel costs and calculate next year's by adding in planned pay raises and by accounting for any staffing or production changes.

Because he hated budgeting, however, Esterbrook didn't try to understand it. Because he didn't understand the budget, he didn't realize how it could get him more responsibility, resources, and renown in the company. And so Esterbrook was jealous of Feniman. Feniman was Esterbrook's peer and an up-and-coming young woman in the company. Esterbrook was jealous of her because he worked hard year-round "in the trenches" as he put it, yet Feniman—who seemed to flurry into activity mainly on budgeting issues—kept getting more to do *and* more staff and money to do it with.

Feniman, for her part, saw little point in telling Esterbrook that the budget was not just codes, titles, and numbers, but the very center of annual decision making by company executives. Or that by pitching her budget requests—always larger than his, by the way—to the issues that concerned the executives in a particular year, she was able to get more and more resources each year. Esterbrook needn't know, she thought, because he was an unimaginative, pompous, and self-righteous fellow who was as likely to try to prohibit her practices as he was to emulate them.

So Esterbrook went on hating the budget and Feniman kept on exploiting it—contrasting behavior that continued even when Feniman became a general manager and Esterbrook remained at his same old post.

In most companies there are more Esterbrooks than Fenimans. The budget does have a frightening lot of numbers in it, and those numbers

173

often come on a printout that is hard to pick up, let alone look at or figure out. Yet the more you understand about your unit's budget, and the more you understand about the budget as it applies to other parts of the organization, the more power you have to make things go your way.

This chapter is about budgeting—boring details and all. But it is also about power and the ability to manipulate the organization to your (and your unit's) ends—which usually makes the job of managing easier and makes your advancement more rapid.

What the Budget Is

The budget is an annual, itemized list of your unit's equipment, people, and materials and their cost. It looks like this.

006 . . . . . Printing Division . . . . . XYZ Company

Budget for 1985

Line Code	Item	Qty.	Item Cost	Total Line Item Cost
02-552252	Senior clerk	2	$15,000	$30,000
03-129878	Bond paper	100	50	500
04-446238	Typewriter	1	900	900
00-000003			Total unit costs	$31,400

Sometimes the budget will also include allocation of overhead—those things that your unit uses but that are paid for from other sources. Overhead items can include rent, utilities, and the costs of centrally provided services such as legal counseling and personnel administration. So your budget might look like the one above but with a few additional items.

006 . . . . . Printing Division . . . . . XYZ Company

Budget for 1985

DIRECT COSTS

Line Code	Item	Qty.	Item Cost	Total Line Item Cost
02-552252	Senior clerk	2	$15,000	$30,000
03-129878	Bond paper	100	50	500
04-446238	Typewriter	1	900	900
00-000001			Total direct costs	$31,400

INDIRECT COSTS

Line Code	Item	Qty.	Item Cost	Total Line Item Cost
05-202021	Rental		$30,000	$30,000
06-444222	Personnel service		5,000	5,000
00-000002			Total indirect costs	$35,000
00-000003			Total unit costs	$66,400

The budget that you see for your unit may also have another element: sales (if your unit deals directly with the outside world), or output to other departments (if your unit provides only internal services such as auditing), or some other measure of just how much your unit is producing. So you may have a section of your unit's budget that looks like this.

006 . . . . . Printing Division . . . . . XYZ Company

Income for 1985 (Estimated)

SALES (OR INTERNAL TRANSFERS)

Line Code	Item	Line Item Total
07-235433	Customer brochures—sales	$50,000
08-654213	Printing for company units	25,000
09-000002	Total unit income	$75,000

Which can of course lead to a final logical section that compares the costs of your unit with the income your unit generates.

006 . . . . . Printing Division . . . . . XYZ Company

COST CENTER PROFIT OR (LOSS) 1985

Line Code	Item	Total
09-000002	Total unit income	$75,000
00-000003	Total unit costs	66,400
00-100000	Unit profit	$ 8,600

Boring, isn't it? Only if you are Esterbrook. If you are Feniman, or like her, you see all sorts of things. You see that the bottom line, unit profit, is an easy way for *your* bosses to see how the various units under their command are doing.

You see that increasing unit income can make your bosses happy—so happy that they might be willing to increase your budget *now* if you can make at least a plausible argument that you will more than make up for the increased expense with future sales. ("Listen," said Feniman one day to her division manager, "when Lillian the programmer was floating in my unit last year before the computer system was fully on-line, I used her on sales for two months and what she brought in more than paid her salary. But now she's gone and so is that extra money. Why don't you give me a permanent extra salesperson in next year's budget?" Feniman's boss said, "Write up a request. I probably can get it approved." He did, and Feniman had another worker for her promotion campaign.)

If you're like Feniman you also see that some of your budgeted costs—such as overhead—depend on formulas (unit share = unit employees/total employees) that you might be able to change in order to get a more favorable bottom line for your unit. ("President Durkee," Feniman said one day, "my unit is charged for 20 percent of the rent here [based on employees as a percentage of total staff] but we only use 10 percent of the space in the building. I've got the blueprints and calculations right here." Voilà! Feniman's rent costs go down, her profits go up, and so does her stock with the bosses.)

Why the Budget Is Important

The budget isn't just something that wily managers like Feniman can use to skyrocket their careers. The budget is also a fundamental part of the operation of *any* organization. Knowing the budget is all but mandatory for managers.

Why? Well, what would you think of the manager who couldn't tell you how many people were working in his unit? This happened to New York City during the budget crisis of 1975, and city executives became a laughingstock as a result. And what would you think of the manager who couldn't begin to tell you the charges involved for having her printing unit produce a brochure for your unit? Not much, we suspect. And your bosses would think even less of a boss so out of touch with her unit's operations.

The budget provides you, the manager, with basic information about your unit's operation. Number of people, job titles, staffing for each job title, salaries for each job; equipment, materials, and rental costs.

The budget also provides raw material you can use to make better sense of your operations. Even if your budget figures come in annual lump-sum "line-item" form—the way we gave them to you on pages 174–75—no law says they have to stay that way. Expenditures can be broken down by month instead of by year so you can see how you're coming along in spending your annual amount. A month-by-month budget looks something like this.

Monthly Personnel Budget

Annual Amount	July Estimated	July Actual	Difference (+ or −)	August Estimated	August Actual
240,000	24,500	26,000	(− 1,500)	24,500	23,000

With this information, you can rein in fast spending operations early—and prevent embarrassing shortfalls. You can speed up slow spending operations, and thus help guard against failure to achieve results that you may have promised to your bosses. (This was part of Esterbrook's problem. He tried with all his might to deal with the budget only once a year, which is why he was caught off guard by such things as "funds unspent at the close of the budget year." If Esterbrook wasn't able to do anything with these funds, his bosses sure were: *They deleted a like amount from his next year's budget*—"He sure didn't need it this year, did he!"—and gave it to the ubiquitous Feniman, who always made sure she spent all of the budget she worked so hard to get.)

The budget is the single most important avenue for getting more funds. Top executives make "budget decisions." The main way top managers get a handle on all the diverse operations in their organization is to reduce those operations to budget terms: resources put into an operation, products put out by an operation, and—the bottom line—whether or not the operation pays its own way and by how much.

If you want to get top management's ear—and their recognition and their money—you'll need to speak their language. That language is the language of the budget. Consider this program the Berlitz of budgeting. Learn the language of this chapter and your travels to the upper reaches of your organization may come about sooner than you expected.

STEP-UP SET YOUR GOALS

Your overall goal for your sixth month on the job (or sooner, if budget deadlines loom) is to become familiar with your unit's budget so that you can argue persuasively for budget changes that will increase your unit's productivity.

Your specific goals are:

· To obtain (or, if necessary, create) a budget for your unit
· To develop, using only the funds in your existing budget, an alternative plan for doing your department's work
· To develop a budget request for the next fiscal year in which you show how the new people, the new equipment, or the new space will help realize some important company goal

When you reach these goals, you'll be able not only to manage the unit but to rearrange and expand it. You will have achieved a level of understanding and flexibility that will stand you in good stead as you move up through the organization.

STEP-UP   TALLY YOUR RESOURCES

The budget is, of course, a list of resources. But we are not talking here about the resources that are *in* the budget; we're talking about the resources that help you find out about and expand your budget.

Remember Feniman and how she reduced the space costs charged to her unit by securing a blueprint of the building? The blueprint was a budgeting resource, and so was the company's budget procedure manual, which detailed the existing "per person" basis for charging rental costs to units.

Remember that budgets are an organization's attempts to impose logic and comprehensibility on its operations. The numbers, the dollar values, the computer-generated budget reports, all of these comprise a process that applies facts and logic to the distribution of funds among organizational units. So, in tallying your resources your search is for facts: for documentation, for dollar figures, and for predictions about future events (such as next year's sales) that have some basis in here-and-now reality.

Here's what to look for:

· Your unit's budget
· Salary ranges for the positions occupied by your staff
· Lists (budget and other) of equipment in your unit
· Data on the space occupied by your unit

Getting or Making a Budget

Getting a copy of your unit's budget is sometimes harder than it sounds. Some companies do not provide detailed budgets to units. Unit managers simply make out position and equipment requests for the following year. Thus your office's files may have only a "budget" that looks like this.

1985 Request

Unit manager	1
Administrative assistant	1
Chief clerk	1
Clerical assistant	4
Customer interviewers	6
Claims examiners	4
Secretary	1
Typist	4
Total	22

You may then have to compare this list request to 1985 payroll records to see how much of the request was granted. If you can avoid it, of course, you don't want to "build the budget by hand," so go to *your* boss first. Ask for whatever budget data he has on your unit. He is likely to have a more detailed version of the following budget:

Customer Complaint Unit—1985 Budget Request

PERSONNEL SERVICES REQUEST

Position Code	Position Title	Number of Positions	Salary Range	Position Total
076	Unit manager	1	45,000	45,000
055	Admin. assist.	1	25,000	25,000
012	Chief clerk	1	24,000	24,000
032	Clerical assist.	4	11,000–14,000	48,000
085	Customer interviewer	6	14,000–22,000	100,000
019	Claims examiner	4	15,000–25,000	80,000
078	Secretary	1	22,000	22,000
046	Typist	4	10,000–13,500	43,500
	Total requested positions	22	Total requested funds	387,500

You can see this budget is more of a resource than the position request immediately above. The position code (or object code or line code, etc., depending on your company) is for the benefit of the computer that likes to use such numbers to store and retrieve information. The position titles are self-explanatory, as are the number of positions. The salary-range column can provide useful ammunition in your battle for more budget funds. If your four typists average under $11,000 per year—as is the case above (see last line)—and the top typist makes $13,500, then the remaining three typists get only $10,000 each. Listen to Feniman on this one.

"You know, Mr. Masekela, I have four crack typists, but because only one has more than a year's seniority—and she has four—three of them are making $3,500 less than she is. For the same work! Now, I think we have to do something for them before they up and quit. They don't need to make quite as much as Maddy, who is senior, but I think that $12,000 a year would be fair and would prevent any problems."

"Write it up" is what most bosses would say in response to Feniman's argument, and that alone is a major step toward getting the $6,000 that Feniman went after. What did Feniman do? She used the budget as a resource to argue *using facts* that her people needed more. And that is what your budget is—a source of factual information that can be used in a variety of ways to support claims for salary changes, personnel changes, and other changes that provide more and better resources for your unit.

So by hook or by crook, get a copy of your budget and, if possible, those of other units in your division—although your boss may be more hesitant about providing a divisionwide budget than about providing your unit's budget. Divisionwide budgets show the boss's distribution of funds among units, and some bosses would prefer to keep such information quiet rather than deal with argument and protests on the order of "We do just as much as the mousetrap division, and they have four more people than we do." Not that such arguments are improper or fail to get dealt with when made. It's just that you should be alert for your boss's reluctance to provide divisionwide budget information, and be prepared to get comparative budget information from other sources—for instance, your own ability to observe directly who's working where, your informal conversations with others, and reports (such as production, person hours, per-person sales) that together can convey a reasonably accurate picture of other units' resources.

Getting a Personnel List

The budget above provides the beginning of a personnel list. Let's look at a line we've seen before.

Position Code	Position Title	Number of Positions	Salary Range	Position Total
046	Typist	4	$10,000–13,500	$43,500

In making her argument for a higher salary for the lower-paid typists, Joan Feniman added more information about the individual typists.

Individual Position	Employee	Salary	Years with Company	Performance Rating
Typist 1	Maddy Smoot	$13,500	4	Excellent
Typist 2	Joe Cowan	$10,000	1	Excellent
Typist 3	Myna Byrd	$10,000	1	Excellent
Typist 4	René Odom	$10,000	1	Excellent

Feniman's argument had been about the relationship of salaries within the unit. But suppose she had found out that the average salary of typists throughout the company was $15,000. If you can't hear her, we can. (*"Mr. Masekela*, I have four typists breaking their backs in my unit, and I just found out they're practically the lowest-paid typists in the company. I found out because one of them told me and she was none too happy about it and in fact talked about leaving. We'd better do something about this right away. It's unfair and demoralizing, and the last thing we want to do is lose four crack typists.")

Follow Feniman's lead: Find out what the salary range is for various positions *throughout* the organization. Often this is available from the overall budget for the company; if not, the personnel office or payroll office may have salary-range information. Because the salary range (e.g., office managers: $25,000–40,000) gives information about salaries in general, not about a particular person's salary, it's usually less confidential. Nonetheless, it can be used to argue for salary increases on behalf of individuals, as Feniman did above. To see how easy it is, just practice the following speech: "Mr. Guion, I'm as good an office manager as you have, but my salary is in the bottom third of the office-manager range. I hope you can see your way clear to moving me to the top third."

When you look for salary-range information, be straightforward. "I'd like to see how supervising stenos stack up across the organization." Or "Do we have information about salary ranges for each position in the organization? I'd like to see how the range in my unit compares." If you're told that the information cannot be had, back off. Enough data for making budget arguments exists without engaging in a do-or-die battle over any one piece.

Other helpful information about personnel includes information on retirement dates. A high-salary person about to retire may give you a chance to argue for *two* junior replacements. You'll have more people power, and when it comes time to raise their salaries toward the retired person's level, the company will be committed to the two slots. Information on personnel positions that are available on *other* than a full-time permanent basis can also be useful. Part-timers cost less in terms of both salary and benefits. Your company may be willing to give you only half a loaf when you ask for a whole, but *you* have to know that half-loaves are available. Also, if your company hires temporary personnel from agencies, you may be able to make a bid for sixty days' worth of help.

Getting a Supply, Service, and Equipment List

If your unit has a detailed budget, supplies are probably listed. There may be one item, such as office supplies, that covers all supplies, or you may have several separate items:

1985 Budget

SUPPLIES

Object Code	Object	Quantity	Unit Cost	Total Cost
023	Publications	n/a	n/a	$5,000
031	Copy supplies	n/a	n/a	$8,000
025	Gen. off. supp.	n/a	n/a	$4,000

Service expenses may also be listed in your budget, or in your division's budget, and may look like this:

1985 Budget

SERVICES

Object Code	Object	Quantity	Unit Cost	Total Cost
077	Advertising	n/a	n/a	$16,000
078	Travel	n/a	n/a	$20,000
079	Legal service	n/a	n/a	$15,000

Entries like this mean that you have the funds in the last column set aside for the indicated services during the fiscal year.

Finally, equipment expenses may be listed as maintenance and/or as capital expenditures:

1985 Budget

MAINTENANCE EXPENSE

Object Code	Object	Quantity	Unit Cost	Total Cost
055	Copier maint.	n/a	n/a	$2,000
056	IBM equip. serv.	n/a	n/a	$4,000

Entries like these simply mean that you will have maintenance contracts that cost, respectively, $2,000 and $4,000, or that these amounts have been set aside for maintaining the specified equipment during the budget year.

1985 Budget

CAPITAL EXPENSE

Object Code	Object	Quantity	Unit Cost	Total Cost
088	Copy machine	1	$15,000	$15,000
089	Typewriters	5	1,000	5,000

Capital expense entries simply mean that your budget allows for the purchase and installation of the indicated machines during the budget year. Often your office will have equipment that's no longer carried on the budget. This *does not* mean that this equipment is useless for budgeting purposes. Old equipment exists so that you can ask for new equipment that performs more efficiently, breaks less often, and makes your company technologically trendy. It doesn't hurt for a manager to have the following list.

Equipment Inventory

Description	Age (Yrs.)	Condition (Good/Poor)	Better Product Available (Y/N)	New Request Planned (Y/N)
IBM Typewr.	9	Poor	Yes	Yes
IBM Typewr.	7	Poor	Yes	Yes
IBM Typewr.	4	Good	Yes	No
Steel Desk	12	Poor	Yes	Yes

Knowing all this helps you understand both your budget and your office better. Most important, a detailed knowledge of your service, supply, and equipment budget helps you be a better budget *strategist*. Listen to Feniman again.

"Mr. Masekela, we have a lot of clunker machines in our unit—that's why our maintenance expenses are so high. If you let me put in for $4,000 worth of word-processing computers in next year's budget, I'll bet you I can save at least that much in maintenance fees—the new machines will be under warranty—and in office temporary expense because the new word processors will cut document retyping by half." "Write it up," says Masekela, a man of few words and fewer dimensions.

Getting Information about Space

Feniman went to the company architect, or more precisely, to the architect's blueprints kept by the company's physical plant manager, in order to show that her unit used only 10 percent of the building's space but was being charged for 20 percent of the rent. The smart manager always collects information about space and his or her unit's use of it. The most tense and unsettling organizational situations involve disputes over the use of space. Budgeting aside for the moment, always be ready to complete the following statement: "My unit needs every inch of the space it now has and more because _____."

And your reasons should be very precise:

· "We have several areas where two people are sharing rooms designed for one."

· "The traffic flow through the claims and clerical area is a mess because desks have to be put in corridors designed for clear passage—which is, by the way, a fire hazard."

· "Our productivity in processing paperwork has gone down 10 percent in the last year and can be expected to go down another 10 percent this year if we don't get a file room that removes our mass of files from the work section. Either do that or computerize so that the files are kept on disks instead of in bulky paper files."

As the last example shows, space arguments are also budget arguments, not only for more space but for more modern equipment, or for materials that make the existing space more livable (such as dividers, soundproofing, or new lighting). Indeed, all of the various types of information resources that you tap can be mixed and matched with one another in a variety of ways: How you do it is limited only by your ability to construct strong and imaginative arguments for more funds.

STEP-UP ENHANCE YOUR RESOURCES

If you haven't gotten the idea after seven chapters, here it is: Enhancing your resources means making friends, making contacts—and using the friends and contacts you make. In the budgeting process, friends and contacts can get you information fast, explain its meaning, and clue you in to company developments you can take advantage of in asking for more budget funds.

In the budget process, your resource enhancers are

Your boss(es)
Staff office(r)s for budget, personnel, etc.
People of your rank who work for company decision makers
Company and industry reports

Budgeting and Your Boss

Your boss has the first vote you need when you ask for additional funds. Even if your proposal sits well with company higher-ups—let's even say they started thinking along similar lines on their own—your boss will certainly be asked what he thinks. If your boss votes thumbs down (because he hasn't been cultivated by you), you can lose your shot at more funds. Even if the higher-ups overrule your boss's veto of your proposal, he may retain a sour taste for that twit (you) who went behind his back to implement something "we just don't need." (You should understand that such opinions can hurt you badly *whether or not they are based on fact.*)

Your relationship with your boss is a continuing thing that affects all aspects of your management role. The budget should be only one of many things that bring you into close contact with your boss. In using your boss to enhance your budget, you should be drawing upon an already established relationship. A strong relationship with your boss is important because so much of the information that helps your budget strategy is best obtained informally. Indeed, the process may be so informal that only *you* know that relevant information has been exchanged. To show you what we mean, let's get back to Feniman, who is fishing for some acceptable way to ask for more money next year. The setting is her boss's office. The time is 6:00 P.M. Everybody has gone home except Feniman and her boss, who are sitting around shooting the breeze.

"You know," says Feniman, "I see that Horace over in purchasing has installed an IBM PC system with a data-base management program in order to keep track of orders and requisitions. I wonder if even that will work with the bunch of nitwits that he has under him. I've thought once or twice about a similar computer system over here—we have better people, but I'm not sure our work calls for all that technology."

"Well, Feniman, Horace's people ain't no better than the man who picked them," replies Masekela, who was primed to the task of cutting apart Horace, an old rival. "But the data-base management system isn't a bad idea over there. If it works Horace may even get another promotion before he retires in fifteen years. I don't think the system would work here, though; our work on troubleshooting problems is just too varied."

"Scratch that idea," said Feniman to herself. And she went on to other things, having quietly made and obtained an opinion on a potential project from a boss who was hardly aware of what was happening. The computerization proposal would not be in next year's budget, but several other proposals would be—because of their *positive* reception in similar off-the-cuff conversations.

What Feniman was doing is known as "floating a trial balloon." If the balloon falls, it's no big loss—it was just an idea. If the balloon rises on your boss's upbeat response—"You know, I think it would be just great if we had a computerized data-base management system in this office"— you can be off and running by saying "So do *I!* I'll be glad to work up a budget for the new system so that we can propose it to the powers that be."

The Budget and the Fact Holders

The facts crucial to the budgeting arguments you make are held by various units throughout the company: personnel, buildings and grounds, payroll, data processing. The people in these offices are the "fact holders." Your success in using the budget to get more depends in large measure on your relationship with these fact holders. Budgeting arguments succeed or fail on their accuracy. If you ask for more funds using an inaccurate statement, your request (and quite likely future requests) can be blown out of the water. Nothing is more chilling than to be confronted with "Byers, you say that your secretaries make less than any other secretaries around here. Well, I've talked to Whalen in personnel, and guess what? Your secretaries earn more than 60 percent of all the other secretaries in the company." End of request, and often the end of your willingness to ask for more for quite some time.

Timeliness also affects budgeting arguments. Believe it or not, many opportunities for increased funds occur because the chairman of the board read an article in *Newsweek* this morning about something such as pay comparability—women making the same money as men with similar but not identical jobs. Well, until next week's *Newsweek* comes out (or something else comes up), pay comparability is the budgeting hook of the week (and maybe even for the month or year, in your company). If you move fast, you might make a killing. But to move fast, you need to be on good terms with the fact holders. Let's see how our budgeting champion, Feniman, does it.

"Les, how are things over there in personnel? I keep hearing that you're the only one being considered for personnel director when old Lorraine retires next year. They couldn't do better.

"Look, Les. On this pay-comparability issue that the chairman is so hot on. I've got six women in my unit—secretaries, clerks, and receptionists—who spend all week digging papers out of files, and according to what I've read on pay comparability, that isn't any different than digging dirt out of ditches. Can I find out the average wage we pay our laborers and the average wage we pay our secretaries and clerks? Can I get this information without getting you in trouble? Yes? Good. Do you think I could come over sometime today to compute those averages? You're sure it won't inconvenience you? Great. I'll see you at two."

Now Feniman is well on her way to getting a few thousand extra dollars for her largely female staff. She is moving along because she is getting accurate information quickly. This information supports arguments that Feniman can memo around in a day, before the chairman gets bored with the issue. "Why not?" said the division manager, who wanted to give Feniman something for her efforts. "Give her people thousand-dollar raises, she's the only one with a lot of clerks. We can call this a readjustment rather than an equalization and stay away from the comparability issue. Then we can wait and see what the comparability committee that the chairman will appoint next week has to say—that should give us at least a year's breathing space."

Feniman got in under the wire because she moved fast and presented a topical, fact-supported rationale for more funds. She was timely and accurate. And she would have been neither had she not spent time cultivating the assistant director of personnel. Had she been a hermit like Esterbrook she would have received the same answer he did when he called the personnel department about anything, budget-related or otherwise. Namely, "The assistant director is not available now, Mr. Esterbrook. Can I help you? Well, I think we have those statistics but I'm not sure. I'll have to look later on. Can I have your extension so that I can call you back?"

By all means be a Feniman rather than an Esterbrook. Keep in touch with the junior executives (or even the directors) of the organization's staff offices. Be their friend as well as their colleague. Obtain information from them, but never use them in ways that compromise their positions.

The Budget and the Higher-ups

Feniman used her personnel-office contacts to get statistics that allowed her to argue for a program likely to win front-office support. Those contacts—and others, including those in the executive suite—can provide more than statistics. You also get glimpses of front-office thinking about the direction the company should take.

Are top executives considering cost cutting throughout the organization? It's better that you know this a month in advance than find out about it from a memo that gives you five days to produce a 10 percent budget cut. With a month's notice you may be able to pad your budget request with extra fat so that when the cuts come your unit's resources actually remain pretty much the same. With a month's notice you may be able to develop convincing arguments that your unit's budget should remain unchanged. You may also be able to soften up top management for these arguments by seeding the organization with "success stories" about your unit in the month before cost cutting is announced.

As we saw with the pay-comparability issue, quick access to top management's thinking is very useful when you're shopping for *additional* funds. Does the new company president make a big point of operating at her own computer work station, thus bypassing several secretarial and clerical steps in the process of communicating with other executives? Yes? Well, don't bother requesting two new secretaries and a new clerk in your next budget. You should, on the other hand, request some snazzy new computer work stations for your office, a programmer or two, and some training funds so that your unit can "follow the example set by our resourceful president."

Dishonest? Slimy? Not at all. Fads do occur in organizations, and the executives often set the trend. No law says you shouldn't take advantage of current fashion. Indeed, you have seven or seventy or seven hundred people working for you who have every right to expect that you seize opportunities on their behalf. If you miss the fashion parade in your organization, some of them, and maybe even you, may be out of a job.

The best kind of executive contacts to cultivate are people who are more or less peers: people who started in the company when you did; people who have worked with you; people who went to the same school you did; people whose salary level and title are roughly equivalent to yours. Find that staff assistant to the president whom you know, and go to lunch with her. Tell her about what's going on at your level, and ask leading questions about what's going on at hers. Tell her that you find the president fascinating—and you probably do, at least insofar as you are fascinated by how the president's thinking can affect your success. Your interest—and your picking up the lunch check—should elicit some stories about the boss that contain clues you can use in shaping a budget strategy.

Contacts with front-office staff also come in handy when you're implementing budget strategies. It never hurts to have your proposal introduced informally to the top executive by his or her assistant. Often this can be accomplished by simply filling in your front-office contact on any *new* budget proposals that your bosses have approved. Listen again to Feniman, who first gives her contact something useful to him and then provides information that the contact can use to Feniman's benefit.

"Len? Feniman. I just came out of a meeting with my divisional manager. That reorganization plan that you were worried about seems to have been dropped. Also, the computer work-station proposal for my unit has been made a part of the division's budget request. I know how enthusiastic the president is about this sort of thing and just thought I'd let you know. A word from upstairs would sure keep my boss hot on the proposal."

So by all means establish relationships with executive-suite staffers. Cultivate them. Be informed by them. Inform them in turn. Help them if you can. And when the time comes, ask for *their* help.

The Budget and the Brochure

In chapter 2, we told you to hide and forget annual reports, company newsletters, and things of that ilk. That was then. This is now. Information that was simply an impediment when you were a new manager needing to learn quickly about your unit's operations is now relevant to you as an experienced manager trying to guide your unit to bigger and better shares of the organization's resources. Find those annual reports, company brochures, and employee newsletters. You're going to pan for kernels of information that may turn out to be golden nuggets of resources for you and your unit.

The annual report—We've never seen an annual report for any organization that doesn't make some statement about core activities that make the organization successful, initiatives the organization is particularly proud of, and new directions the organization will take next year.

Read the annual report and find out about these core components, shining achievements, and new directions. Then write a list of twenty (yes, 20) new things your unit could do that relate directly to these core activities, outstanding achievements, and planned initiatives. "Trial-balloon" the ideas to your manager and to your upper-echelon contacts. When budgeting time comes around, several of your ideas should support requests for more funds, people, and things.

Brochures—Brochures are like mini annual reports. They highlight some activity that enjoys top-management support. Read these brochures much as you read the annual report—with an eye toward how you can develop activities for your unit that support (if the brochure describes a companywide activity) or copy (if it is a brochure from another unit) the activity.

Company newsletter—Chock-full of information that you can use in arguing for a bigger and better budget. Has the claims unit had their office redecorated? So they have. There they are on page 3, smiling in front of the floor-to-ceiling mural. Has the security department received $50,000 worth of computer equipment? Yes indeed. There's old Sergeant O'Conner on page 5, grinning crazily in front of a computer console he doesn't know the first thing about.

What to do? Ask Feniman. She even has a fill-in-the-blanks memo to her boss stored in her computer.

I've noticed that the _____ unit has received new _____. This is their second new _____ in _____ years. My unit has not had new _____ for _____ years, and I want you to consider such a request for my unit in next year's budget.

Feniman won't mind if you steal her memo. Neither will your employees.

STEP-UP PLAN YOUR ACTION

Your action goals with respect to the budget are:

· Obtaining (or creating) a budget for your unit
· Finding out how to do more with existing funds
· Making a proposal for new resources to pursue new activities

Another way of putting this is that you are going to find out what you have, figure out a way of getting more out of what you have, and figure out a way of getting more, period.

Getting Budget Information

One thing about the budget: It exists. Maybe not for your unit specifically, but certainly for your department, division, or company as a whole. And even if a budget exists only for parts of the organization that are larger than your unit, the information that will allow you to create a budget for your unit is available.

Ask the secretary or your assistant or anyone else who has been in your office for several years, "Where are the budget files kept around here?" and see what they show you. In most cases your search will end as it begins: You'll be led to budgeting sheets that resemble those we showed you at the beginning of the chapter.

If the search of your office is unsuccessful, go to your boss. "Is there a detailed budget for my office? If not here, where? Do you mind if I go get it, or if I draw one up myself? I just want to get a handle on my operations and I think a budget is the best way to go about it." If your boss says no to all of this, you may be in some horror movie. The boss is either a paranoid or is funding his home improvements out of company money. In either case, you should stop here and go on to the next chapter—although you might read the rest of this chapter in case your boss dies or gets arrested.

If your boss refers you to the budget office, go and make the same pitch there that you made to your boss; make some friends as well. Not only can the budget office give you a copy of your unit's budget, it may be able to provide you with a variety of budget reports in different formats (e.g., a five-year summary report, an expense-only report, an income-only report, a five-year growth-rate report). The budgeting function in some organizations is so computerized that the number of different reports is limited only by the imagination of the requester (i.e., you). Not only that, the budget officer may be ecstatic that someone is actually interested in her whole repertoire of budget reports.

Two reports are most useful. One is the *line-item budget*, which lists each item of expenditure in your unit (personnel, usually by position; supplies, usually in broad categories; services, usually by type; and equipment). Like most household budgets, the line-item budget lumps all like items together regardless of the activity to which the items are dedicated. Just as the household budget rarely breaks down utility expense into amounts for cooking, reading, and studying, the line-item budget does not break down personnel expense into amounts spent on customer contacts, bookkeeping, and report writing. In a business setting, however, it *is* important to know how many resources, and how much money, are being devoted to particular activities. The bank manager who does not know which employees are being assigned to which activities has little basis for making decisions about staffing, or about the importance and profitability of various activities.

Creating a Budget

The second budget report that relates resources to particular activities is variously known as the *program budget*, *activity budget*, or *cost-center budget*. There may not in fact be such a budget in your company, but that doesn't mean you can't create one. As we have stressed several times, the name of the budget game is organizing facts into logical arguments for more funds. Creating an activity budget is one way of organizing your budget information so that arguments for (and even against) more funds become obvious. The following program budgets were created for a local bank branch.

Program: Teller-Window Banking

EXPENDITURES		INCOME BY CATEGORY	
Object of Expenditure	*Annual Costs*	*Income Category*	*Annual Income*
Personnel	$200,000	Savings accts.	$ 75,000
Space	75,000	Check. accts.	250,000
Equipment	15,000	Traveler's chks.	25,000
Computer support	50,000	Cashier's chks.	10,000
Total Costs:	$340,000	Total Income:	$360,000
		Net program income (loss):	$ 20,000

Program: Cash-Machine Banking

EXPENDITURES		INCOME BY CATEGORY	
Object of Expenditure	*Annual Costs*	*Income Category*	*Annual Income*
Personnel	$ 25,000	Savings accts.	$100,000
Space	25,000	Check. accts.	250,000
Equipment	50,000	Traveler's chks.	25,000
Computer support	100,000	Cashier's chks.	00,000
Total Costs:	$200,000	Total Income:	$375,000
		Net program income (loss):	$175,000

You can see right away how the program budget aids decision making. One program for servicing customers—cash-machine banking—needs fewer people and much less space (although computer support costs are higher) and brings in more income (because it's open twenty-four hours a day). The other program for servicing customers—teller banking—costs more and brings in less. (And you wondered why those cash machines were springing up on every corner, sometimes without even a bank attached.)

If your company does not have a formal budgeting or cost-center budgeting system, try to rough one out for your unit anyway. At the very minimum, it will provide *you* with useful information about your unit. Then, since only you know about the program breakdown you have done, you can choose when and where to show your bosses particular comparisons that lend support to your requests for new budget resources.

Program budget reports, whether they are your own or come from on high, often dictate action. The type of report illustrated above certainly does—and has. If your program budgets are prepared by people outside your unit—the budget office or auditing office—be ready to respond when one program is shown to be superior to another. What the executives want to hear is "I see no big problems in shifting over to the more effective service delivery or production method," not "I don't know. People will resist. Maybe we shouldn't change so fast."

In short, be ready to act as program budget comparisons suggest you act, and be ready to make additional requests that maintain or enhance your budget position. What do we mean? Let's make Feniman the manager of the bank branch where program budget information strongly supports a shift to cash-machine banking.

"Mr. Hudson, I just can't wait to get four more cash machines out in the lobby. The biggest morale problem we have is tellers who are abused by ornery nickel and dime depositors who have waited in line too long. I want to shift the freed-up tellers over to the business/preferred-customer window. As you know, there's a lot of competition up here for the big-account/big-profit customers who *do* need to be serviced by individual tellers. With my expanded "Preferred-Customer Window"—it's in my next budget request—I think we can guarantee keeping our present customers and siphon off customers from the other banks as word spreads about our quick service."

Now, Feniman *is* quick. And so are you. A simple rule for doing well in the budget process is to respond to new circumstances as opportunities to ask for more, rather than as threats to be avoided and resisted.

Asking for More

Which brings us to your third budgeting goal: making a request for additional resources so that your unit can do something new or do more of something it is already doing. Feniman's expanded "Preferred-Customer Window" is a good example of a request for additional resources, although she is proposing to get the resources from another function that is being reduced.

Feniman's request is a good one, for the following reasons:

1. It's timely. (Some tellers will be freed up by the new cash machines. Banks are fiercely competing for new business these days.)

2. It promises a big return. (The tellers are being shifted to big-account/ big-profit customers, and you can be sure that Feniman has used her contacts in the account analysis office to get the numbers that back up her statement.)

3. It is made just as she is being cooperative when she need not have been. (If your bosses expect you to say "Not on your life" and you say "Certainly," *that* is the time to say "But I'd really like to have your approval on the new XYZ system." Gratitude is sometimes as important as logic in getting what you want.)

4. The request can be supported by many, rather than a few, arguments. (Although "big account/big profit" is a compelling argument, it's always good to have backups in case decision makers waver. For instance, "If we let the tellers go, morale in the branch will go through the floor and we'll alienate more customers." And "Do you really want to fire all of those black, Hispanic, and women tellers while all the lily-white computer operators and account representatives stay? We'll be in EEO litigation until the 1990s.")

These, then, are your guidelines for developing a budget request for new or added activities in your department.

· Relate your request to a "hot" issue in your company
· Make a request that promises a high return in profit or in new customers or both
· Make a request that can be justified by many arguments
· Present your budget request (if at all possible) in an "I've helped you, now you help me" situation

These four elements are crucial to effective budget requests. Several additional elements also help transform your budget *request* into living, breathing bodies and whirring, clacking technology.

Appeals to equity are also effective in budget arguments. Top management is sensitive to the divisiveness that is created when groups in the organization feel cheated. Indeed, a change that may be called for by the bottom line may be delayed or only half-begun because of management's worry that people will feel unfairly treated. If you see another unit get something that your unit could also use profitably, by all means let management know that you think it unfair that you don't have it too. You not only stand a chance of getting what you want, but you protect yourself when you argue that "Whatever your reasons for giving the computers to Howard's unit first, I just want your assurance that you won't compare my unit's output with Howard's now that he's working with high technology and we're still clanking away on 10-key adding machines."

Another thing that is very effective in budget presentations is *the chart*. The program budgets above are charts—information presented in easy-to-see and easy-to-understand formats. Bar graphs are even better.

Profit from Various Service-Delivery Methods

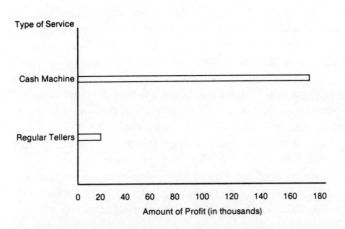

Pie charts are also effective. The point is that the more graphically and simply you can present the information, the more likely it is that decision makers will understand and react positively to your proposal.

STEP-UP USE AND ABUSE YOUR PLAN

When you make a budget proposal, *you are not alone*—particularly if you have a lot of good managers in your organization. You are not the only one bright enough and energetic enough to develop a sound proposal calling for a 10 percent increase in the funds for your unit. Suppose every other manager makes a request as good as yours. Suppose further that top management decides to spend no more than 5 percent in new-project "risk" money for the coming year. What's the result? That's right. Some people won't get any of what they asked for and most will get only some of what they asked for.

Here it is in chart form:

Manager Making Request	Percentage Increase Requested	Percentage Increase Granted	Rank in Getting More
Wong	10	5	2
Theodoropolous	10	4	3
Esterbrook	3	2	4
Feniman	15	6	1

There's Feniman again. And Esterbrook. But before we get to them, let's make a general observation: *Everybody* has gotten his or her requested budget increase cut to some extent. Realize that some of the new funds you request will be denied. This is *not* because your request is garbage. This is *not* because your bosses hate you. This is *not* because your bosses are stupid idiots who can't see how cost-effective your proposal is. It's simply that in most organizations the amount of money available for new projects is less than the total money requested for new projects. By definition, *this means some people will have some or all of their requests denied, no matter how deserving they are.*

If you remember this, you will be more effective. You will be like Feniman, who plays the game with a happy-warrior attitude—she sets her sights high and argues hard but doesn't gripe when she ends up with less than she asked for. Esterbrook, on the other hand, is just the opposite. He asks for a little because he "doesn't like those stupid bargaining games." He expects to get every cent he asks for because "I've figured it out scientifically." And he drips bitterness when his bosses *dare* strike a cent from what he requests. If you were a top manager making tough budget decisions year after year, who would you rather deal with: Esterbrook or Feniman? And who would you feel better about giving money to?

Notice something else about Feniman. Of all the managers, she asked for the most—and got the most. Generally, those who ask for more—within reasonable limits—get more, even if their request is whittled down in the process. Score yourself on the final result, not on the whittling.

Budgeting is a scramble for limited funds that features factual arguments, fads of the moment, and one more thing: outright power plays by units that did not think up your proposal but are perfectly happy to claim the right to carry it out and, thank you very much, get the money you asked for to do it. As you shepherd a budget request through the organization, consider the other units that may claim your proposal. It's good self-defense to prepare counterarguments in advance, and even broach these arguments to decision makers before anyone else does. For example:

"You know, Mr. Hudson, I can see the cash-machine division [CMD] downtown making a bid for one of our floor tellers. But that's a backroom operation, and our tellers are experienced customer-contact people. Besides, you need technicians down there—I think transferring tellers to the CMD wouldn't serve the tellers or the CMD. That's why I think that the best new use of the tellers will be on the enhanced business-service windows—they know customers, they know branch operations, and they are already a part of this branch's team."

Having made this argument in advance, you're better prepared to fight back when and if the cash-machine division does try to claim your people. You're familiar with the argument and so are some of the key decision makers.

No matter how well you fight, of course, another unit may successfully take over a proposal of yours. Don't become embittered; let the proposal go but make it plain that you'd like some compensation down the road, or even now if you have another proposal on the fire that decision makers have been lukewarm about.

STEP-UP PLAN AND PLAN AGAIN

Budgeting is the epitome of plan-and-plan-again. This year's proposal is vetoed—but decision makers encourage you to submit it again next year, when market conditions will be more favorable. Or your requested budget increases are denied wholesale as the company posts a record third-quarter loss; instead you are asked on extremely short notice to *cut* 10 percent from your current budget.

If you're not ready to plan and plan again in the budget process, you're unlikely to get much out of it. Some simple plan-and-plan-again strategies include:

· Getting next year's *permission* with this year's denial. Try never to give away something for nothing. If something is cut from this year's budget, get a commitment that the item will be considered in next year's budget.

· *Scaling down* proposals in response to bossly comments. Try to go into budget negotiations with preset fall-back positions and a bottom line. If your boss says four new business tellers are too many, be ready to explain how "It'll be hard, but I can see myself operating with three."

· *Getting feedback* on proposals that didn't fare well. Budgeting is an annual affair. When you come back next year you'd like to do better, so go to your boss about a month after the budget has been decided and say "I didn't do as well as I wanted with the budget. Feniman, for instance, did a lot better. Any hints about how I might do better next year?" Then listen and learn.

· *Cutting* (if, heaven forbid, you have to) *things* to save people. Go to the equipment budget, the supply budget, the maintenance budget or whatever, but do not cut people unless absolutely necessary. If you *must* let some staff go, try to do it as painlessly as possible (e.g., early retirements, voluntary furloughs, no maternity leave replacements). Believe it or not, the reasons for this are practical rather than humanitarian. If things turn around, wouldn't you rather have an experienced work team in place than a year's supply of copy paper, three new but empty computer work stations, and a decimated, demoralized work group?

If you learn to participate effectively in budget making, you gain some measure of recognition in the company. This helps qualify you for the next stage in your managerial career—making yourself an asset to top management. Moving upward and onward is the concern of the next chapter and the rest of the book. You'll be well on your way if you can use this chapter to fund activities that will be visible and pleasing to your superiors—and you may even get a raise.

Once you're comfortable with basic management skills, it's time to step into the larger world of your organization, your industry, and your profession.

In "Stepping Up," you'll learn how computers can help you stand out in the managerial ranks. You'll gain prominence by playing a role in your company's decision-making committees and building a network in professional organizations outside your company. Finally, you'll learn to reduce stress as you manage the most important thing of all: your health and well-being.

Part Three

Stepping Up:

Strategies to Move You Ahead

Better Management Through Computers

"WHO IS THIS MAN?" asked the chief administrative judge of the state court system. "I want to see the person who wrote this and I want to find out if he wants to come to work in the capital."

The judge had in his hands a set of computer-based procedures and reports that provided the kind of management overview that he had pursued in vain through ten years, one heart attack, and countless sleepless nights.

"Look. Look. A list of trial attorneys—ranked by the number of postponements they have requested over the last three years. And district attorneys—look at the top of the list—Assistant D. A. Melvin Krudz had twenty-seven cases dismissed because of police or prosecutor errors, and—look over here—he also leads all D. A.'s in number of postponements requested.

"But here's the best. Judge Seymour Sleepmor. On Mondays and Fridays he schedules half as many cases as any other judge in that court and then—*just look at this*—then he postpones 90 percent of the Monday and Friday cases he does schedule. This bum works three days a week, and not a whole lot then, either."

His clerks had never seen the judge so gleeful. Or so redundant:

"Who is this man? Who is this man? Who knows this John Cafano who did this report? He's made my day. Damn, he's made my year."

"Judge, he's the same guy who developed the employee-automobile data base for tracking down and keeping a record of people who park in spots reserved for judges."

"You mean"—the judge was now sounding awestruck—"the thing you used just this morning to get that twit Reynolds to move his car out of *my* space?"

"Yup. That's Cafano's tracking system. It's been picked up by most of the judicial districts, and the judges and clerks are as pleased as Punch.

And that's not all. Cafano says he's working up a time and leave control system for court personnel. Says it saves him a day a week already."

"This man Cafano," said the state's chief administrative judge in reverential tones, "must be a computer programming genius from way back."

John Cafano was nothing of the sort. In fact, he had never touched a computer in his life until just one year ago. A retired firefighter, he had begun a second career as the administrative coordinator of a judicial district in a downstate suburban county. John began his new job in February and spent six months learning the ropes. When things were somewhat under control, he took a closer look at the big gray box that had been sitting forlornly on a table in a corner since he arrived. Even though he wasn't an expert, John could tell it was a computer (the IBM label helped). He asked his assistant about it.

"Well, McMiniver, the old coordinator, wasn't very high-tech. So he put it over there and when any of us fooled around with it, he would ask why we hadn't completed some assignment if we had so much time to waste on the machine. We got the message, and the machine got cobwebs."

"I," said John to himself, "am going to see what this machine is about." So John began playing with the computer and the software that came with it. In two hours one night after work, John learned enough word processing to computerize his memo writing. In three hours one quiet afternoon, he learned enough about a very simple filing program to construct his now-famous parking-space protection program for judges. Graduating to a more complicated information management program, John started maintaining the performance records of judges and private attorneys and prosecutors. That took a week to set up.

John did acquire a reputation as a computer wizard, but he is the first to set the record straight—at least for friends like us. "They should only know how easy it is. I can't believe how much I've learned. And I can't believe how much time I've saved already so that I can learn more. The best thing I ever did was knock the cobwebs off that machine."

Have you ever heard of a "window of opportunity"? The phrase means that you may be able to take advantage of something only *once*, and then only during a certain time. The window appears and opens, the opportunity is there; the window closes and disappears, and the opportunity is gone.

For today's manager, the microcomputer window of opportunity is *right now*. Five years ago hardly an office in the country had a microcomputer. Five years from now most managers in the country will be working with a microcomputer in some way. Today, people who, like John Cafano, can effectively apply microcomputers to management are considered geniuses worthy of all sorts of rewards. Five years from now the same skills may rate no more than a satisfactory evaluation from your superiors.

Even for those who are blasé about the label "genius" and about raises and promotions, using microcomputers in most management settings makes sense for a variety of reasons.

1. Computers take the clerking out of managing. Whether you realize it or not, a great part of your day is spent doing clerical work: proofreading and correcting memos and reports, searching through files or Rolodexes or the piles of paper on your desk in order to get some piece of information, and the like. With a computer, the manager's clerical time can be drastically reduced—first edits become final versions without your ever having to decipher your writing for a typist. Electronically stored documents or telephone numbers appear before your eyes seconds after you want them. The computer will even check for spelling errors.

2. Computers make you and your staff more self-reliant. Are you sick of working your way up the waiting list for the typist pool? Tired of waiting for your production statistics to be computed by the central office staff? The computer is for you. Especially for the manager who types, the computer provides the ability to get much of what you want *when you want it* without having to rely on others.

3. Computers generate information needed by managers. Did you ever wonder who was your most punctual employee? Least punctual employee? Have you ever wondered who has taken the most sick days? The least? Or have you ever prepared vacation schedules and wanted to compare employees' requests with expected workloads *and* the seniority of the requesters? The computer can give you all of this and more. It aids your decisions by making important information easy to get (providing, of course, you do the ground work by setting up the reporting format and putting in the data).

4. The computer gives you expertise and authority. Unless you are surrounded by computer programmers, being the first on the block to have a computer work station invests you with the kind of mystique once associated with Einstein. Merely being able to use the computer brings *ooohs* and *aaahs* from the uninitiated, a response that the manager can help along by doing a trick or two from time to time. (Our favorite is to write, review, edit, and print a short document needed by an employee as soon as the request is made and *while the employee is watching*. Ten minutes

later, document in hand, the employee goes among the staff preaching the marvels of the machine—and of us.)

Make no mistake about it. The microcomputer is a new ball game. The microcomputer goes on *your* desk and not in some faraway office staffed by intellectual-looking nerds programming in COBOL, PASCAL, and other alien languages. The microcomputer talks to you—and you talk to it—in English. And the microcomputer comes with software that allows *you* to tell the machine what *you* want so *your* office can run better. The bottom line is that microcomputers bring tremendous powers of calculation, organization, and analysis to the workaday manager. If you fight to get them and work hard at using them, microcomputers will increase the productivity of your unit, enhance your control over operations, and make you a leading candidate for advancement in your organization.

STEP-UP   SET YOUR GOALS

What are your computer-competency goals?

In a nutshell: Get your hands on a microcomputer and learn how to use it. (If you're already looking at your office's microcomputer as you read this, some of the goals below won't apply to you. Skip those, of course, and get to work on the goal of making the computer one of your biggest management assets.) Your computer goals for your first year as manager are:

- To learn how microcomputers operate, especially in office settings— that is, to become "computer literate"
- To make a budget request or an equipment request for a microcomputer for your office
- To request software that allows the computer to perform word processing, file management and spreadsheet analysis
- To learn and apply the computer's word-processing, file-management, and spreadsheet-analysis capabilities to the work of your office

In short, you are going to learn about computers, get a computer, use it yourself, and then put it into operation in your office.

STEP-UP   TALLY YOUR RESOURCES

Educating Yourself

If computers are a mystery to you, the first thing to do is read about computers in general. Go to a large bookstore and find the computer books section. There, you're likely to see a large and utterly bewildering display of computer literature. Here are some pointers for picking out a book that will help rather than terrify you.

DO NOT buy a book that was published more than two years ago. The way things move in computers, several of the microcomputer brands of 1983 no longer exist and several new machines have taken their place. In addition, IBM's microcomputer design has gone from being one of many to a virtual standard. Unless you have a very recent book, the computer world you are reading about may no longer exist.

DO NOT buy a book that is about a particular *microcomputer*, for example, *The User's Guide to the Pomegranate 122*. The Pomegranate 122 may be incapable of business applications. Even if it is applicable, user's guides are generally full of enough technical material to paralyze all but the most fanatic owner—"Did you know that your Pomegranate 122 can dump a screenful of text onto your printer *upside-down*? Just type 'UP-DOWN DUMP.BAS' after completing all of the dump instructions on pages 18 and 19 of your manual. Each character will be printed upside down! Or, if you wish, you can simply print the screen right side up and then turn the paper over."

DO NOT buy a book with programming instructions. You can determine this by leafing through the book. If more than five pages are filled with esoterica like this,

```
10 PRINT USING 400
20 FOR J = 1 TO 4
30 READ N$, I, E
```

put the book back. You do not need to know a programming language in order to use the computer at work.

DO NOT buy a general book about computers, that is, one that tells you about the history of computers, the world's largest (smallest, fastest) computer, and everything from mainframe computers to hand-held computers. What you want to learn about is microcomputers. (The microcomputer is also being adapted as a remote terminal on older computer systems—central records continues to receive *its* data while the local office manager gets to use the machine however *she* wants.)

DO buy a book that covers the use of microcomputers in office settings. Such a book should have a chapter (or at the least a ten-page section) on each of the following applications: word processing, data-base management, spreadsheets, and integrated business management programs.

DO buy a book that is written in English, rather than computer jargon.

Check out the introduction and see if the author wrote the book for people without a computer background. Skim some of the text. Did the author succeed in making the subject understandable to newcomers?

When you find a readable book on microcomputer applications for business, buy it. Then buy two current computer magazines, such as *PC* and *PC World*. The magazines—because they cover all classes of computer users—will feature much of the stuff we warned you away from in your book purchase. There will be programming instructions, and articles about "PC TurboBoost Cards," and a lot of terminology that will mean very little to uninitiated you. But because the magazine also caters to business microcomputer users, you will find articles like "PC Tutors Managers," "Project Management with the PC," and "A Spelling Checker with a Mind of Its Own." These are the articles for you to read.

Taking Inventory

If other offices have microcomputers but your office does not, conduct an inventory. One of your goals is to submit a request for a computer, and, as you learned in the budget chapter, the more arguments you can make, the better your chances are.

What other departments have microcomputers? Most? Then your department is entitled. Do any departments with microcomputers do work similar to your department? Yes? Then you should have one too. While you're counting, take an inventory of your department's office machines. List them. Find out how old they are. Calculate last year's maintenance cost for each machine. Find out the replacement cost for each machine. Use a chart like the one below.

Office Equipment Inventory

Machine	Age	Annual Maintenance Cost	Replacement Cost
Selectric typewriter	4 years	$295.00	$998.00
SCM calculator	3 years	75.00	200.00

Hold this information in reserve for the budget argument that goes like this: "Why replace the old with the old when for just a little more we can get state-of-the-art office equipment that's more efficient, does a greater variety of things, and upgrades our employees' skills?"

Call several major computer companies and ask them to send you information about the use of their microcomputers in business settings. They may want to send a sales representative to deliver the stuff, but tell them the mail will do for now. You can always talk to a salesperson after you've read the material. The material you receive may contain information about document production time, mass mailing features, and other microcomputer capabilities. Again, you can use this information in arguing for your office's microcomputer.

The material you get from computer manufacturers may contain unfamiliar terms. "The CompuFab 42, in conjunction with its MEGA-WRITER word-processing software, provides all of the mailmerge capabilities your firm will ever need." When you read things like this it is time to go to the book you bought. It should give a lucid explanation of terms like *mail merging*—which is the ability of the computer to type letter after letter and automatically address each letter to a different person on a large mailing list.

Remember your goals. You want to be computer literate, and you want to develop arguments for having a computer in your office. You do not want to become the world's foremost authority on computers, and you do not want to make oracular statements about how the company's success depends on computerization. If you want to know when enough is enough, listen to yourself closely and throttle your education and your mouth when you begin to sound like this: "Well, J.G., give me microcomputers and I can LAN into the mainframe at 9600 baud with bisync protocols to download and input data. With some EPROM chips, an 8087, user patches, a compiler, and a plotter, I can do just about anything." We know the person who said this. We don't know what his boss—who was essentially speechless—thought. We do know that no microcomputer was forthcoming and that the boss has since been known to mutter about "technological crap" when anyone broaches the subject of microcomputers.

After you've read the book, the magazines, and the brochures, you're ready to talk to people. You've read enough to know which questions to ask, not enough to know all the answers. You're seeing other people to learn more, *not* to show them how much you already know.

STEP-UP   ENHANCE YOUR RESOURCES

Unless you are reading this across a time warp, you should have no trouble finding people to talk to who have a microcomputer. As a kid's toy or as an upper-middle-class status symbol, the computer seems to have invaded half the households in the country. Some colleges are requiring *every* student to have a microcomputer. Generous discounts for computer purchases have been offered to entire professions (e.g., teachers). Many companies buy their microcomputers by the dozen. So you have a world of contacts to choose from: your co-workers, computer salespeople, your neighbors, even your kids or your sister's kids.

Scouting the Neighborhood

Friends, neighbors, and children are good bets when you're ready to talk to a computer user. Your social world is a reassuring setting for your first computer experience. Your first time at a computer keyboard is a little like your first day behind the wheel of a car: You have only the vaguest idea what to do, the damn thing is expensive, and the likelihood of crashing is high. Better to do it in front of friends than in front of work competitors.

Ask about the kind of work the person does on the machine. If you're talking to your nephew, the "work" may be playing Space Invaders on his Commodore or ATARI. Play. Even when you're dodging alien missiles, your use of the keyboard resembles what you will be doing when you edit memos on the computer screen. In word processing, just as in fighting intergalactic invaders, the cursor moves about in response to your keyboard commands. If your friend has word-processing software, ask for a demonstration. And then ask to try your hand(s) at some simple editing. If you're like us, this first experience will leave your mouth agape and your head racing with visions of countless saved work hours.

Scouting the Office

Most organizations have microcomputers, perhaps not in every office, but somewhere. Your job is to discover the computers' whereabouts and the names of people who work in those offices. Call your contacts and ask for a friendly demonstration. Play it straight: Say you've heard a lot about the machine and want to see it go through its paces with an eye toward getting one for your office.

Looking at a computer that is up and running at your job is something more than looking at a computer in your neighbor's house. You are looking not at the Joystick 155 but at a microcomputer being used in a business setting, by your peer, in *your* organization. In other words, the benefits the computer provides to your fellow manager can probably be realized in your office, too. Ask for at least thirty minutes of your co-worker's time and tell him that you would like to see *all* the ways his office uses the computer. (An end-of-the-day slot is a good time for this, especially on an evening when the other manager doesn't have to rush home. Work demands on the machine should be pretty low and nothing should distract your friend from showing off the computer—perhaps even on into the night.)

Ask about specific applications used by the office you are visiting. Do they use word processing? Data entry? If so, how? Could they show you an example on the computer? Your questions need not show the slightest understanding of the computer. Listen:

"Tell me," Sally said. "What is this thing other than a fancy-schmantzy typewriter?"

"Good grief!" said Megabyte, the assistant manager of purchasing. "If this is a typewriter, then a Lincoln Continental is a tricycle. You want to see seven different designs for our purchase orders in less than two minutes? Watch!" And Megabyte began to make the purchase order lines and boxes dance around on the screen. Then she personalized ten lengthy letters in as many minutes by copying the document ten times and changing the second and last sentence each time. Then . . .

Ask next about record keeping. Is the computer used to store data about the office's work? What work? What kind of data? How is the data used? Could you see some typical data entries and the method for getting at particular items of information?

"Well," chortled Megabyte, "there it is, the vendors' 'Hall of Shame.' "

VENDOR	AVERAGE TIME FROM ORDER TO DELIVERY
Snodgrass Paper	17 weeks
Megalith Office Furniture	16 weeks
Punchless Staple Co.	15 weeks

"We're getting rid of them." Megabyte nodded toward the screen—which had been scrolling through *all* of the year's purchase orders only moments before she had called up the "Hall of Shame." "How about vendor by zip code?" asked Megabyte.

Ask your colleague to show you a spreadsheet if one is in use. The office may be using one to keep time and leave records—spreadsheets are just dandy for automatically deducting leave days and other time off from employee allotments. And the spreadsheet can do lots of other calculations for the manager, such as cost estimates, inventory valuations, and tax liability. The spreadsheet is a general-purpose tool for figuring out anything you tell it to.

"Yeah, the big bosses come to us a lot." Megabyte was crowing but Sally, who had heard the song before, didn't let it interrupt her education. "Why, only last week they wanted to know what the effect of a 2 percent increase in interest rates would have on our planned credit purchases. Well, I just changed this multiplier from a 1.10 to a 1.12 and voilà! In seconds I got the increased equipment costs and the increased supply costs for each month of a thirty-six-month payout period. Wanna see what a 4 percent increase would mean?"

After asking about word processing, and spreadsheet and data-base applications, ask your colleague what else her office's computer does. Ask yourself the following questions about anything you see.

- "What goes on in my office that's similar to the things that have been computerized in this office?"
- "How can I adapt the things I'm being shown to the operations of my office?"

The answers to these questions become the opening salvo in your bid to get a microcomputer into your office.

Scouting Out Formal Training

In addition to neighbors and colleagues, other parties may be downright eager to teach you about microcomputers. Some companies have begun microcomputer training for their managers. The purpose is to introduce managers to a multipurpose technology—the microcomputer and its software—that can achieve significant savings for the company when fully utilized throughout the management ranks. If your company has training like this, *run*, do not walk, to the nearest registration desk, particularly if class seats are limited.

Another party that is often quite eager to teach you about computers is the computer manufacturer. In large cities, IBM conducts introductory courses featuring hands-on demonstrations of their computer products. So do some retailers. One major target of these minicourses are managers who, once converted, can agitate on behalf of microcomputer purchases by their companies. Call up IBM in your town, and ask if they have hands-on demonstrations. If they do, go. You are likely to be treated to the microcomputer equivalent of fireworks on the Fourth of July as the computer is put through a variety of tricks.

You've read, and you've looked, and maybe you have even touched. By now you should know enough to make a bid for a microcomputer. Or, if one is already lying around, you should be champing at the bit to be off and running.

STEP-UP   PLAN YOUR ACTION

Requesting a New Computer

Computerless offices do exist. Even if there is a terminal or two, your office is not in the microcomputer age unless that terminal has a disk drive or two and an absolute minimum of 64K in memory. (You're in the microcomputer fast lane if your micro has a hard disk and 256K or more memory.)

A note here on technical stuff: You don't need to know it to run the machine. You do need to know a bit so that your bosses feel secure in giving you a machine and so some ambitious peer doesn't one-up you at some meeting.

Memory

A microcomputer's "K" defines the amount of instructions that the machine can hold and carry out at one time. A "K" equals 1,000 Kilobytes (over 1,000 letters or numbers). The holding and carrying-out area is called the processor (and sometimes the "working memory"). Working memory is 64K, or 128K or 256K—all the way up to 640K and beyond. The terminology you will usually see in sales and promotional material is 64K RAM (random access memory).

Disk Drives

A part of the machine also holds instructions and files until the working memory needs them. These are the disk drives and, in some machines, the hard disk. Disk drives and hard disks will receive and hold large amounts of instructions *(software)* and documents until the user requests that something be sent to the working memory. Disk drives handle information storage ranging from 180K to over 1,000K. Hard disks store ten, twenty, thirty, and even forty thousand K of software and files. The terminology you will usually see in sales and promotional material is "Two 360K double-sided, double-density (DS,DD) disk drives" or "One 360K drive with a 10-megabyte hard disk."

Software Programs

Software is simply a set of instructions that tells the microcomputer how it is supposed to act. The computer can be used as a word processor, or a calculator, or a video game, but it has to be told to behave like one, and the software does this. Some of the software used in business requires 256K or more of working memory to handle the instructions and the operations required by the instructions.

Enough detail.

You can go after a microcomputer in several ways. Budget requests are one way; another way is to ask your divisional manager for the microcomputer that you've spotted lying around unused in the department on the next floor. A third approach is to ask a computer dealer to "seed" your office with a loaner micro. (With seeding, the dealer hopes that installing the first computer on a six-month loan basis will lead to the purchase of several computers by your organization.) Whatever approach you take, you have to *justify* having a computer in your office. Use the memo below as a rough model for budget requests for microcomputers.

MEMORANDUM

To: Vair E. Big, Vice President for Administration

From: Y. O. Ewe, Manager, Administrative Services

Subject: Microcomputer Requests

COST SUMMARY

Hardware Request:	3 Microcomputers, 256K, 1 360K Disk Drive, 10-Megabyte Hard Disk (@ $3,000 per unit)	$ 9,000
	1 Letter-quality printer	1,000
	1 Dot matrix printer	1,000
	Hardware total:	11,000

Software Request:	Accounting package (1)	800
	Integrated business package (3)	1300
	Word-processing software (3)	900
	Software total:	3,000
	Total request:	$14,000

PERFORMANCE SUMMARY

	Present Equipment (Actual)	New Equipment (In Other Depts.)
Performance Measures:		
Typing time per page	8 minutes	6 minutes
Typist error rate	1% of copy	¼% of copy
Work backlog	2 weeks	1–2 days
Service capabilities:	Typing	Typing
	Standard mailing	Standard mailing
	Copying	Copying
		Mass mailing
		Graphics
		File management
		Printing

NARRATIVE

The reasons for the microcomputer purchase are straightforward: We can do more, and we can do it for less. We can use the saved employee time to clear up backlogs and begin new projects.

The new equipment costs are about twice as high as our current equipment—about $6,000 each three-year replacement cycle, or $2,000 per year. Work reductions of 20–40% (typing and retyping time), 50% (filing and retrieval time), and 30% (cost-calculation time) compensate almost tenfold for this additional equipment cost. The cost of this equipment, moreover, has been dropping year by year and should continue to do so.

This equipment also provides us with capabilities that previously required hiring outside contractors (mass mailings) or technical specialists (graphics).

The request *you* make will have specific facts and figures from your office. Fellow managers who already have microcomputers are a good source for these; if you have no peers with microcomputers, computer sales personnel should be able to provide them, as can computer magazines and office-management journals.

If you make a budget request, don't worry about having your savings figured out to the penny. Approval by higher-ups is likely if rough but honest estimates show big overall savings. The combination of big potential savings and the microcomputer's status as the CB radio of the 1980s gives your request a world of momentum. Don't lose that momentum by procrastinating over details or by exaggerating already large savings—you won't get what you never ask for, and being caught in a lie can kill the best of proposals.

Finally, remember that budget making involves negotiating. Trade down from three to two, or from a 256K system to a 128K system, or from a hard-disk system to a floppy-disk system. Just end up with a computer. You can use it next year to write up a request for another computer, or to ask for all the extras you missed out on this year.

Making the Most Of Existing Computers

Computers that are not used to their fullest abound in organizations. John, the court clerk we talked about at the beginning of this chapter, seized an underutilized computer and soon had it doing tricks that were noticed by the top court executives.

Here are the signs of an underutilized microcomputer:

The computer arrived three weeks ago (three months in one agency we know about) and hasn't been taken out of the box yet (the *unused* computer).

The computer sits in a corner and people walk over to it from time to time to get out or enter one or two pieces of information (the *underused* computer).

The staff has christened the microcomputer with a single functional name like "word processor" or "number cruncher" (the *single-barreled* computer).

The computer is only on when the "operator" is there (the *personal* computer).

The Unused Computer

With an *unused* computer, the manager may not have to strike any deals. If your office's computer is still in the box, your strategy is simple. Take the computer out of the box and put it on *your* desk. (Check it out with your superiors first, but don't leave them a lot of room to slip and slide. Unless "Absolutely not" is the reply, *any* answer to queries such as "Okay if I get that computer in there up and running?" should be taken as permission. The answer to "Do you know how to work it?" is "I was working with a micro just last week," which, if you enhanced your resources as we told you to, is true.)

The Underused Computer

The *underused* computer should be approached more carefully. Since it is used occasionally by the staff in your office, do not bring it to your desk. If you do, you are likely to have somebody coming nervously over to your desk every twenty minutes to call up a file, and you don't need that.

To get time on an underused computer, modify hours of access. Create the "manager's hour" at the end of the day (from 3:00 P.M. on gives you time during and after work). During the manager's hour you should educate yourself and then begin to use the computer for your work. Look also for effort-saving methods that your employees can use on the computer. Showing your staff the computer's benefits makes them more open to the new technology—and justifies, in their eyes, your work time spent fiddling.

The Single-Barreled Computer

Back in the old days (before 1983), almost all office computer terminals performed a single task (and many still do). For instance, an office terminal might only send and receive information from the company's computerized central records. In other words, the keyboard and screen in the office were "dumb." When not connected to a large computer in some faraway office, the terminal could do little more than light up. It's no wonder managers paid little attention when computers were single-talent machines and most of those talents were clerical.

All that has changed. The microcomputer is "smart"; indeed, it's downright brilliant. The microcomputer outperforms most room-size computers of a generation ago. The micro can word-process, maintain books of account, generate purchase orders, analyze sales, produce graphs, and schedule projects.

Microcomputers may be "smart," but many of the companies and managers using them are still "dumb." It is not unusual to go into an office and see a high-powered microcomputer being used only for word processing or only as a viewing screen for files. This is like using a Cuisinart as nothing but a Kool-Aid mixer.

What do you do if your office's microcomputer is being used for only a single function? You get all the software you can from anywhere you can. Your peers, your purchasing office, your EDP unit, and other sources are likely to have software that will make a multitalented star out of your heretofore one-dimensional unit. Then, as with an underutilized unit, schedule the machine so that traditional functions get done while new functions are being tried and put to use.

The Personal Computer

The truly "personal" computer is one that has been claimed—lock, stock, and barrel—by a single person in your office.

The microcomputer can become a personal possession in several ways. The machine may have been assigned to the person—she may be the office bookkeeper who received, as did all of the company's office bookkeepers, a microcomputer with accounting software. Or a single machine may simply have been taken over by someone when the computer arrived in the office.

Whatever the original story, a computer assigned to a possessive individual can be trouble.

"I," said Sysgen, "was an engineering student. We worked on computers all the time. I can handle that thing."

"That thing" was a newly arrived, high-powered microcomputer with a bundle of software. Sysgen was talking to his manager, who was scared to death of computers and who was perfectly happy to have the machine at Sysgen's desk. After a year, the computer was not the office's machine. Nor was it the manager's. The machine belonged to Sysgen. When he left for lunch or for the day, he draped the computer with a dust cover his daughter had made at school. It said Computer Asleep: Do Not Disturb. "This is not your area" was Sysgen's less precious response to anyone who dared touch the machine in his presence. So no one went near the computer. And the old manager did little for those who complained. "Sysgen is the expert," he would say. "Thank God the machine isn't in a place where people might come in and ask me questions," he would add—to himself.

When the old manager left, his replacement, who was unafraid of computers, had a hell of a time getting "Sysgen's" machine into more general use. "*I* do all the computer work around here," was Sysgen's first line of defense—which held for nearly a month.

Sysgen's second line of defense was a thing of beauty. When the manager forced him to teach the machine's functions to others, he developed "lessons" that would test the abilities of NASA computer scientists. Then he told his frustrated (and even tearful) students that they didn't have the "right stuff." Even the manager felt like a moron until a colleague showed him a remarkably simple but effective procedure for organizing files. The procedure operated off the very same software that had given him two hours of agony the day before under Sysgen's tutelage. As a result, the computer was moved from Sysgen's desk—but not before Sysgen dropped and broke the keyboard (on the very day the move was announced), said that "the inmates were now running the asylum," and told the manager that he was looking for another job.

Liberating a "personal" computer can be difficult. If someone feels that the computer is "hers" or "his," it will matter little that the company has title to the machine, that the machine is assigned to the office rather than the person, and that you, the boss, are ordering wider access. Sense of possession can be a stronger force than all of these combined.

So move cautiously. Come to the "owner" more as a student than a manager. This approach is less threatening and at the same time allows you to gauge just how possessive the individual is. If you encounter no resistance, fine. Thank and praise, and learn more.

If you encounter strong resistance, start emphasizing who the machine belongs to and who you are. "I don't like to get official, Irving. It's a pain, and it isn't the way people should work together. However, this is the office's machine, and if I think it should be used one way and not another, my decision stands. And I'll need your cooperation, preferably without having to order it."

We hope you won't have to order compliance. But if the situation calls for disciplinary measures, reread the sections on employee discipline in chapter 7. And get the computer *before* you get the employee if at all possible—damaged computers are hard to use.

Putting the Computer to Work

In tallying and enhancing your resources, you became familiar with three types of business software: word-processing software, spreadsheets, and file-management software. So, as your on-the-job computer education begins, your goal is to use this software effectively (and ultimately have your employees do the same).

Some software, such as Symphony, Framework, and Open Access, provides all three functions and is known as *integrated* software. If any such packages are popular with *your* organization, ask for a copy. If your office already has a microcomputer but it performs only one of the functions (say, word processing), your budget request (or supplies request, as the case may be) should be for software that performs the other two functions.

Managing Your Teachers

Unless your company enrolls you in "Computers for Managers" from twelve to two on Mondays and Wednesdays in the conference room, your learning time may be your own and your teachers may well be your employees. For an existing computer, you may have to strike a deal with the primary user. Even your training on a new computer may include employees who know computers and/or who will be major users of the new machine.

If a computer is in your office, you already know the primary operator (he or she should have been the first workplace person you consulted when you tried to figure out what computers could do). Now ask for lessons. Most employees will be cooperative, but be careful of the owner of the *personal* computer.

As you ask for training, keep two things in mind: Your employee is helping you, and your employee is doing an extra job. Compensate the employee in some way. Get her time off, give her some favorite assignment, or relieve the employee of an equal amount of work while she trains you—even if *you* have to do the work yourself. This is what Mary Starrett did when she had her subordinate, a records clerk, teach her how to use the computer.

"Mel, we've talked about how I could use the computer to do some statistical analysis of patient flow, medication errors, and mortality rates. Well, I'd like you to teach me over the next several weeks, but I know that's a real imposition with all you've got to do. So, from now until December first, I'll do all of your report cover memos. They come through me anyway, and if I do them from scratch, you'll have enough time to teach me without staying after five. When I've learned all I need to know, we will go back to the old system for those reports." This worked because Mel felt Mary valued him, knew his workload, and was respectful of his work schedule. Mary had a double dose of extra work—her learning and Mel's reports. But nothing is wrong with that. Managers *should* be the first to help out with the office's extra burdens, particularly if the extra burden was the manager's idea in the first place.

Helpful employees can be rewarded in other ways. One manager we know learned word processing on her secretary's microcomputer and made a point from then on to draft memos directly into the computer. This saved secretarial time (no scrawl to decipher, one less typing step), which the manager filled by giving the secretary more responsible and interesting tasks. Be ready to lighten the workload of fellow managers who give you computer time and instruction. Taking on a greater part of some joint task, assuming responsibility for some unpleasant job, and standing ready to answer *any* call for help: All of these are ways to pay for (and to help ensure the quality of) a computer education provided by peers.

One final training note: *Learn how to type.* Typing is indispensable for getting the most out of the computer. Once you have a machine, programs exist, such as Typing Tutor, that make learning how to type even easier than shooting down alien spaceships.

STEP-UP   USE AND ABUSE YOUR PLAN

Believe it or not, even in this computer-crazy age your request for a computer may be denied. Or, even though you *are* the boss, your attempt to get at a computer already in your office may fail.

What do you do if your budget request *is* dead for a year? Or if the company accountant really *did* convince top management that your office terminal was for accounting purposes only? Or if the madman who uses the computer for half the day and locks it up for the rest of the day is the board chairman's brother-in-law?

You keep on keeping on. Additional sources of computers include other parts of your company, sellers of computers, and the ultimate fallback, your own pocketbook.

Going After a Cheap (Free) and/or (Slightly) Used Computer

Some computer dealers offer free "loaners," betting that the "loaner" will become a purchase, or several purchases, before the loan period expires. Some organizations buy a dozen or so computers at once, sometimes on the assumption that more computers mean greater efficiency.

What does this mean to you? First, can you imagine *any* boss saying no to "I'd like to get a free, no-obligation BMI computer for six months to see if it helps my office run better"? Second, as an organization moves whole (or half) hog into computers, some offices won't be ready to put the computer to use right away. That, however, will not stop them from asking for a computer, and then having somebody write "USE ME" in the dust that accumulates on the machine. This is the machine to go after.

Claiming Another Office's Machine

First, document the low level of use. (Computers that are still in the original cartons are the best.) Then go to the manager who oversees the dormant machine. Tell her how much your office could use it and feel her out on the possibility of sharing it. If she agrees, fine; your foot is in the door. With hard work, you can probably learn and produce enough to claim the whole machine, especially if the other department continues to use it very little. If you and your office use it heavily, acquisition of a brand-new machine for your unit can be justified—"I just hate to keep using Iona's computer, Mr. Big."

If your peer is resistant, you'll hear: "Oh! We use that machine all the time. You see it in the box? No! Can't be. Why don't you come by tomorrow, and you'll see all we do on it." Stay late that night and watch your colleague trying to set up the machine. Then wait. One of two things will happen: The machine will be put into full-scale use in the other office, which scratches your takeover bid, or the computer will continue to sit idle—this time on a desk instead of in a carton.

Document any continued idleness. Then, if you're willing to put up with the other manager's disliking you, make a three-stage bid to your bosses for the idle machine. (Having made a budget request for a new machine in the past strengthens your bid—even if the bid was denied.)

Stage 1: "Gee, it bothers me a bit. I'm still hacking away with Selectric typewriters and Marsha has a PC that she hardly ever uses." This sensitizes your bosses to the issues and allows *them* to verify that the machine is idle.

Stage 2: "Instead of waiting for new equipment, isn't it possible for us to get Marsha's underused machine? She can have it back when we get our own." This gives you a sense of whether your bosses are willing to tackle Marsha. If they say no, drop the subject.

Stage 3 follows, by a day or two, any positive response from your bosses to the possibility of reassigning the machine to you. "I think we could really benefit from Marsha's machine. I'd like to send you a memo making that request formally. How about it?" A yes and it's yours. Even if the answer is no, you've made your bosses look more favorably on your office's request for a new computer.

Getting a Loaner from a Dealer

Your office may not qualify for a loaner if your company uses a competing brand of equipment, and loaners may have gone out of style by the time you read this. But free is cheap. For a few hours' work, the worst you can do is learn about computer dealers and their products.

Call the local office of the major computer manufacturers. You'll either talk directly to an employee of the manufacturer, or to an independent retailer who is an authorized dealer for the manufacturer.

Be ready to describe your office, your company, the number (roughly) and make of computers in your company, and how those computers are used. The manufacturer, quite understandably, wants to know the potential market in your company before it lends out its expensive machines for half a year. If there is a loaner program, ask how to qualify. If you need a proposal, write it up. If you need the approval of one of your superiors, go after it. (Bosses will sign off happily on most things that cost nothing.) If you have to meet a representative of the manufacturer, go, and be enthusiastic. The manufacturers want a convert who will sing the praises of the machine to the company. If you look excited asking for the machine, the manufacturer may see you as someone who will be equally enthusiastic in selling it to others.

If you're given a loaner, get right to work: You have a lot to learn and time is short.

Buying Your Own Computer

You are the ultimate beneficiary of your computer knowledge. Knowing computerized business applications makes you attractive to employers, and gives you an edge over computer illiterate peers in the race for promotion. Computers are also fun. This means that if all else fails, if the company you work for still uses abacuses, if the computer manufacturer won't lend you a dime (let alone a computer), if your computerized friends won't let you in the door, consider buying a computer *yourself*.

The expense of computers decreases monthly. Machines that cost $4,000 in 1983 are $2,500 in 1985, and falling. IBM's competitors (IBM-compatibles) can feature rock-bottom prices, especially as they struggle to compete. Machines without an MS-DOS operating system (which is what IBM uses) can sell for $1,000 or less. And these inexpensive machines often come "bundled" with software that provides word processing, file management, and spreadsheet analysis. The software you get with these machines may be all you ever get (software companies write fewer new programs for computers that aren't Apple- or IBM-compatible), but it may also be all you ever need.

The computer skills gained and time saved are comparable whether your machine is off-brand (which in business microcomputers is nearly everything except IBM) or a top-of-the-line model. And if you bought your own machine because your company is too stingy, or stupid, you'll also benefit from the "first kid on the block" syndrome. (Both the authors, who started with Kaypro IIs, were among the first in their business and professional circles to have their own computers. Colleagues began regarding us with a pleasant combination of interest, envy, and awe.)

So check out your personal budget. (You checked out computer prices while angling for a company-bought computer.) If you have the wherewithal, or if it's a choice between a $1,200 VCR or a $250 VCR and a $950 computer, go for your own computer. You'll begin making yourself a higher-priced manager, even if your *next* employer is the one to figure this out.

STEP-UP PLAN AND PLAN AGAIN

Every manager should be exposed to computers and what they can do—if not this year, then next; if not at work, then at home; if not in this company, then in another one.

If your budget request for a computer doesn't make it this year, submit another one next year. Keep reading your computer magazines and keep talking to computerized managers so that next year's arguments are more forceful. If the manager who nixed your bid to share her department's computer leaves, ask the new manager. He may be more enlightened. If the first computer company you asked for a loaner said no, ask another. The business computer market is lucrative, and a manufacturer who now shuns loaners may adopt the approach in the future. Finally, if your company is still lodged in the Stone Age with Neanderthal managers who think that a spreadsheet is a dual-purpose bed covering, and who poke fun at the computer you bought with your own money, start planning to take a walk.

Where? To a company that properly appreciates people willing to master skills that make managers more effective and companies more efficient.

Happy computing.

10

Networking Inside and Outside Your Company

SALOME LASALLE was head of commissary operations for her publishing house, an old-fashioned concern that subsidized all employee lunches and pampered its executives with white-coated table service. "Keeps them close to work, close to each other, and grateful," was how I. G. Hoover (founding father and still-active publisher) justified the low-cost lunches.

When old I.G. decided to join the computer revolution, the word went out to each department that requests for microcomputers would be entertained. LaSalle wasn't shy. She asked for and received an IBM PC. So did marketing, editorial, and production.

LaSalle quickly got the commissary computer up and running with some help after-hours from her eleven-year-old son, Todd (whose two-year-old $200 computer had made him something of a programming genius). Three weeks after its arrival, the commissary computer was generating daily menus and sixty-day menu plans, computerized food and supply orders based on the sixty-day plan, and instant reports of up-to-the-minute figures on customers, costs, inventory, sales, and more.

Other managers had been as ambitious as LaSalle, and so "the problem" arose. The company's auditing department—a perennial power—complained about all the different reporting formats used by various departments. The director of electronic data processing (EDP) echoed auditing's complaint. The EDP director also made a bid to be in charge of *all* computerization because "only professionals can cure the chaos that results when amateurs select their own hardware and software."

So a committee was formed to study the issue: the chief auditor, the EDP director, LaSalle, and several other department heads. Alfred Wiseman, the executive assistant publisher, chaired it. The committee met fifteen times over nine months, and no member fared better in the eyes of top management than LaSalle. In fact, the executive assistant publisher regaled I.G. with stories about her.

"You should have seen her when Hamster from electronic data processing went on and on about the extensive education you need to program computers and analyze systems. . . . Well, LaSalle just shot right back and said, 'Mr. Hamster, my eleven-year-old son taught me enough programming for the commissary's needs in two weeks, evenings only—and my menus come out with the writing where it's supposed to be, which is more than I can say about some of your paychecks.'

"The committee liked that one, and Hamster hardly said a word for the next three meetings. Seriously, though, LaSalle was the one who touched base with all the other operating departments so they could argue against Hamster's takeover attempt. She suggested and helped plan the parallel reporting system so that each department keeps its present reporting format while a second report is automatically generated in the format that auditing wants.

"Obviously, I.G., I liked what I saw of her. She gets the job done, and she proved she could lead the other department heads on the microcomputer issue. Since we've decided to keep microcomputer development in the departments, I think LaSalle would be a natural to head an interdepartmental network for computer applications. I think we ought to organize it right away."

I.G. agreed, and Sal stepped up a notch in salary and position.

Some Concrete Reasons Why Serving on Committees Helps Your Career

· No matter how good a manager you are, your reputation depends on other people. The more you're known as a hotshot, especially in high places, the more assured you are of good reviews and steady career progress. (Salome, for example, is known to old I.G. as a spunky leader. This alone is enough to remove most obstacles from Salome's career path—even though I.G. has never met her personally.)

· High visibility protects the competent manager. If someone (like your boss) sours on you, having fans in high places makes your critic a minority of one. If you've kept a low profile, however, your critic—no matter how inaccurate she may be—may be a *majority* of one. (Suppose Salome's immediate boss complained about her to the executive assistant publisher—how far do you think his complaints would get?)

· Top management cares about how departments relate. High-level attention is given to coordinating the activities of several departments. The assignment of a task to one department and not another is a top management chore. To learn *how* these decisions are made, you need to get closer to *where* they are made. (This means taking on assignments relating to interdepartmental issues, as Salome did.)

Professional associations can provide you with winning ideas and winning contacts. Many management innovations circulate first in professional associations or informal networks of managers in your field. If you want to be the first to learn about new techniques for managing your operations, develop and maintain professional contacts outside your unit and your organization. (Salome's ideas for computerized menu management came directly from a monthly trade journal for food and beverage managers. She even called the manager of the commissary featured in the magazine to discuss specific techniques.)

Your department's fate often depends on other parts of the company (the electronic data processing department, personnel, or legal affairs). Your department may be entitled to representation at those decision centers, *if it asks. You* may get to be the representative, *if you ask.* (Salome's first step toward becoming a major voice in companywide computer policy was her asking to be on the committee in the first place. "The commissary can be affected by what's decided, and I think it deserves a voice," Salome said as she nominated herself. "I think you're right," said the executive assistant publisher as he seconded her nomination.)

Work organizations are *political places*: places where individuals and alliances of individuals clash over policy, where power often dictates the outcome, and where memories of who was on what side can have an impact years after a particular struggle. You must know who is allied with whom and who has what power, and learn the preferences of powerful individuals in your company. This knowledge—best gained by getting close to decision-making centers—can keep you off the losing side in policy struggles. (Salome was always aware of how the executive assistant publisher was reacting to her. The more he smiled at her and frowned at Hamster, the bolder she became.)

STEP-UP SET YOUR GOALS

After six months as a manager, achieving your personal goals and your unit's goals depends increasingly on your ability to operate in settings outside your unit. You want to establish working contacts with policy-making bodies in your organization and maintain professional contact with similar managers in other organizations.

Your networking goals are:

To identify in three weeks the committees, task forces, or other units in your company that deal with important organizationwide issues such as computerization, reorganization, or budget management.

- To secure within two months a committee membership, a special assignment, or other appointment that allows you to work *outside of your unit* on an issue that affects your unit.
- To identify at least three professional organizations that relate to your work, and to join one of them within the month.
- To go to *every* informational, educational, and ceremonial event in the company over the next three months.

By "going abroad" and attending company functions, committee meetings, and professional meetings, you'll see and be seen, and learn what's going on and who's going where. You become a cosmopolitan instead of a local yokel from department X.

STEP-UP   TALLY YOUR RESOURCES

Your tally should survey the territory both inside and outside your organization for relevant committees, offices, and professional groups.

Internal Resources

Begin your tally by making a list of all the "decisions from above" that have affected your unit's operations in the last several months. Indicate what departments, individuals, or committees were responsible for these decisions. Below are three common examples; add your own to the list:

DECISION/ACTION	UNIT(S) RESPONSIBLE
1. Overtime limited or eliminated	Personnel office/budget
2. Office space reallocation	Divisionwide management (joint committee)
3. New statistical reports required	Electronic data processing
4. _____	_____
5. _____	_____
6. _____	_____

The important information here is in the second column, which shows the offices and committees that told you how to run your shop. Whether or not you liked what you were told, the point is that these units or committees have the power to direct your department. This makes them prime targets for your attempts to get involved in higher-level decision making. Participating in these committees will gain you more control over your own operations.

You may have found it hard to complete the list. Perhaps (and this is not unusual) you've been managing an established operation in a placid organization. Overhead decisions have changed nothing since you were made manager. Nevertheless, set your sights upward and outward—if only to cultivate the people and knowledge that can lead to promotion.

Where to Look

Your search for committees and offices that count begins in the office of the corporate secretary, the administrative director, or wherever your firm keeps a record of formally established groups. Ask for a list of existing committees. If no list exists, get a verbal rundown of the committees your contact knows about.

Some committees, such as planning and budget groups, are eternal because these functions are essential activities of the firm. Individual departments may have their own such committees to facilitate across-the-board reviews.

Policymaking committees are often attached to staff offices that support the operating departments:

Personnel offices may have an equal employment opportunity committee, chaired by the personnel director

The administrative service department may have a space allocation committee, chaired by the director of administration

Finance may have an audit standards review committee, chaired by the comptroller

Such committees usually include representatives from throughout the organization; your contacts in each department know your prospects of being nominated. Even if you're not eligible to join, your department may be invited to send someone else, which will win points with your boss.

For excitement and exposure, the places to be are "ad hoc" committees that spring up in response to some "problem." Salome LaSalle's committee was just such an ad hoc committee. Several operating departments had different computer systems and two overhead departments (auditing and data processing) were in a dither. The committee on which Salome made such a good showing was formed in response to "the problem."

Problem committees are for you if your unit is affected by the problem. That makes you a prime candidate for membership. When the problem involves disputes between your unit and another (as is frequently the case), one or two higher management representatives will likely be on the committee and can see you show your stuff. If the committee solves the problem, you'll be labeled a winner. Even if the committee fails, you gain exposure and win credit for your willingness to tackle a tough job.

Sometimes ad hoc committees arise informally when the managers of several departments meet regularly to resolve issues of common concern. Whether they're formally or informally created, ad hoc committees are a good launching pad for managers looking for promotions.

External Resources: Professional and Trade Organizations

Being cosmopolitan means looking outward as well as upward. You're eligible to join several professional or trade organizations because of your managerial status, specific job responsibilities, and your company's product.

For instance, as the personnel director of a small nonprofit hospital, you can join:

The American Society for Personnel Administration
The American Society for Public Administration (if it's a semi-public facility)
The American Society of Hospital Personnel Administrators

Every field has several professional organizations formed to meet the needs of its managers.

Professional Associations: The Short List

Here is a list of associations that cater to managers. Some cater to women managers, some to managers in particular businesses or professions, others to workers in government and nonprofit institutions. Wherever you manage, one or more of these associations almost certainly has a place for you.

Administrative Management
Society
Maryland Road
Willow Grove, Pennsylvania
19090

American Academy of Medical
Health Administrators
840 North Lake Shore Drive
Chicago, Illinois 60611

American Accounting Association
5117 Bessie Drive
Sarasota, Florida 33581

American Advertising Federation
1400 K Street N.W.
Washington, D.C. 20005

American Business Women's
Association
9100 Ward Parkway
Kansas City, Missouri 64114

American College of Hospital
Administrators
840 North Lake Shore Drive
Chicago, Illinois 60611

American Compensation
Association
P.O. Box 1176
Scottsdale, Arizona 85252

American Management
Association
135 West 50th Street
New York, New York 10020

American Marketing Association
250 South Wacker Drive
Chicago, Illinois 60606

American Planning Association
1776 Massachusetts Avenue
Washington, D.C. 20036

American Society for Hospital
Personnel Administration
30555 Southfield Road
Southfield, Michigan 48076

American Society for Personnel
Administration
606 North Washington Street
Alexandria, Virginia 22314

American Society for Public
Administration
1120 G Street, N.W.
Washington, D.C. 20005

American Society for Training
and Development
600 Maryland Avenue S.W.
Washington, D.C. 20006

American Society of Professional
and Executive Women
1511 Walnut Street
Philadelphia, Pennsylvania 19102

Association for Systems
Management
24587 Bagley Road
Cleveland, Ohio 44138

Bank Administration Institute
60 Gould Center
2550 Golf Road
Rolling Meadows, Illinois 60008

Bank Marketing Association
309 West Washington Street
Chicago, Illinois 60606

Data Processing Management
Association
505 Buse Highway
Park Ridge, Illinois 60068

Healthcare Financial Management
Association
1900 Spring Road
Oak Brook, Illinois 60521

International Food Service
Executive's Association
111 East Wacker Drive
Chicago, Illinois 60601

International Personnel
  Management Association
1850 K Street N.W.
Washington, D.C. 20006

Sales and Marketing Executives
  International
330 West 42nd Street
New York, New York 10031

National Association of
  Purchasing Managers
P.O. Box 418
496 Kinder Karmack Road
Oradell, New Jersey 07649

Women in Management
P.O. Box 11268
Chicago, Illinois 60611

That should get you started. To explore on your own, go to a library (call first) that has the *Encyclopedia of Associations*, which is published annually by Cole Research. The *Encyclopedia* has a 200-page directory of business and professional associations. The encyclopedia has information about membership (all of the associations above have at least 1,000 members, and most have well over that figure), about the services offered, and about the issues the association focuses on.

If you spot one or more associations that seem right for you, send a note asking for membership information. You'll receive glossy materials describing the organization in detail. You'll have a good idea of what's out there before you start nosing about the company to see what associations your superiors and peers have joined.

Some Magazines for You to Read

There is no shortage of management and business magazines. You can pick up several, such as *Fortune* or *BusinessWeek*, at the newsstand. Or you may want to subscribe to one of the publications listed below.

The Bureaucrat (Public Sector)
P.O. Box 347
Arlington, Virginia 22210

BusinessWeek
1221 Avenue of the Americas
New York, New York 10020

Fortune
541 North Fairbank Court
Chicago, Illinois 60611

Personnel
American Management
  Association
Trudeau Road
Saranac Lake, New York 12983

Personnel Administration
American Society for Personnel
  Administration
606 North Washington Street
Alexandria, Virginia 22314

*Hospital and Health Services
   Administration*
Foundation of the American
   College of Hospital
   Administrators
P.O. Box 98088
Chicago, Illinois 60693

Management Review
American Management
   Association
Trudeau Road
Saranac Lake, New York 12983

Monthly Labor Review
Department of Labor
Washington, D.C. 20212

National Safety News
National Safety Council
Chicago, Illinois 60611

*Office Administration and
   Automation*
Geyer-McAllister Publishers
51 Madison Avenue
New York, New York 10010

Personnel Journal
A. C. Croft, Inc.
245 Fischer Avenue
Costa Mesa, California 92626

Public Administration Review
   (Public Sector)
1120 G Street N.W.
Washington, D.C. 20036

Supervision
National Research Bureau
424 North Third Street
Burlington, Iowa 52601

Supervisory Management
American Management
   Association
Trudeau Road
Saranac Lake, New York 12983

Training and Development Journal
American Society for Training
   and Development
600 Maryland Avenue S.W.
Washington, D.C. 20025

Like our list of associations, this is just a sampler. If you want to take a closer look at these publications, go to the library (preferably one in a college with a business or public administration program). On the shelves where these journals are located you will find a host of others. Subscribe to those that interest you and address your current or future needs. The address for subscriptions is usually on the first page or two.

You now have a reading list, a roster of professional organizations, and in-house committees on which you might serve. Before you decide to join, however, enhance your resources: call on your colleagues for advice and opinions.

STEP-UP   ENHANCE YOUR RESOURCES

Your first "upward" committee assignment is crucial. Your superiors will inevitably view it as a test of your ability to move on to bigger and better things. Do well, and more high-visibility assignments will follow. Perform poorly, and your superiors are likely to say "Well, she's a good print manager, but she's over her head in committee work."

Evaluating Your Best Opportunities

Obviously, just knowing the names of committees and task forces isn't enough. LaSalle couldn't have known from the name alone that the Interdepartmental Task Force for Microcomputer Utilization Review would decide the company's computer policy for the next decade (and catapult her into prominence besides), but her instincts for protecting her unit and her work led her to seek membership.

If you want to know where the action is among dozens of committees and task forces in your organization, you'll have to ask around. You need to know which committees haven't met for two years; which are the chairperson's dictatorships; which are required as a matter of form but do little of substance; which, because of issues considered or the heavyweights doing the considering, are likely to have a major impact on the company (and, if you can get aboard, on your career). All this is very current, changeable information, so continue your research until you're ready to make your bid.

If Your Boss Is Helpful

If your boss has encouraged your development and seems at ease with the notion that you'll someday move on, be direct. Make it plain that you would like an assignment to a committee or interdepartmental project in an area of real importance to top management.

Your boss may welcome the opportunity to delegate one of her present committee assignments—either because she's bored with it, or because she, too, is setting her sights on something higher. She may be on a task force whose job is getting bigger than expected, so the members are looking to form working subcommittees—staffed in part by members' subordinates, such as yourself.

Use this opportunity to ask your boss about her committee experiences. Whether or not your discussions with a supportive boss yield a committee membership, at least you'll get an overview of the company's committee structure and politics. You'll also glean strategies for positioning yourself for a choice assignment (or for ducking dead-end assignments).

If Your Boss Holds You Back

If your boss seems less than overjoyed about your ambitions, be more circumspect—but get the same information. Ask him how decisions are made regarding personnel procedures or the divisional budget. Say you feel a bit disenfranchised, then listen closely to see if your boss expresses the same feelings. If he does, the door is open for a "We don't have a voice" session in which you can ask plenty of questions about just who *does* have a say. You might even work with your boss on a strategy for getting a piece of the decision-making action by getting on an existing committee or helping to form a new one (making sure there is a role for you, of course).

What if your boss is aghast at your aspirations? To "I wonder what serving on one of those committees is really like," he replies, "Why in the world would you ever *want* to be on one? That's not your role around here anyway. It's my job to be on any committees that include other departments." It's time for you to stop talking. And time to think about getting out from under a boss whose idea of employee development is to chain the crew to the oars.

Talking to Your Peers

Whether or not your boss tells you anything, your colleagues in other departments can be a valuable resource for your move upward. Other managers on your level may already be members of committees, or may be doing work on behalf of their boss's committees. Your peers can tell you what committees are considering issues important for your unit, and whether your bid to join a particular committee would be seriously considered. Your colleagues can also give you *inside* information on various committees. At any given time in any organization, some committees are dormant, some are in a state of siege, and some are functioning smoothly; some executives are fallen angels, and some are rising stars. Informed opinions help you make these distinctions and select a better committee.

When you talk with other managers, you may even sense a need for a committee that does not exist yet. Float the idea to the managers of starting a committee on your own. In many companies, user's groups have sprung up for managers with computers, and women-in-management groups have been created to provide support for women executives operating in what is still a man's world. If your discussions with fellow managers indicate a need that a committee could address, by all means create such a group—with or without top management's support. Management's blessing is helpful, of course, but on some issues (such as male-female equity or work stress) management would just as soon avoid giving an endorsement. Even without their go-ahead, membership is not without benefits. A real problem is being addressed, you gain a new measure of prominence, and the group is a valuable information network and a potentially powerful voice to boot. (Do not, however, expect these benefits if you organize a "Top Management Is Ruining Our Profit Sharing" committee.)

Evaluating Professional Associations

What professional or trade association(s) does your boss belong to? If the only thing he's ever joined is the bowling team, ask him to identify some of *his* bosses who belong to a professional association. When he does, tell him you'd like to talk to them before you decide which group to join. Unless gurgling noises emerge from your boss's throat when you say this, consider yourself free to see the superiors he named to discuss their professional organizations.

Your organization's chain of command is easy to break regarding this matter, and that alone says plenty about why you should join a professional group. Very simply, the executive vice president (whom no one dares go near at work) becomes the very approachable Louise MacDonald when she hosts the local American Management Association's holiday party. She even becomes approachable at work if the issue is recruiting you as a new member. (You may enjoy the same access *after* you join if you decide to work on association matters dear to Vice President MacDonald's heart.)

If your survey shows most of your superiors belong to a certain association, obviously that's the one you should join—if you're eligible. Survey your peers with a slightly different purpose: Ask them what that particular group has done for *them*. Are the meetings informative and relevant to their concerns? Are a lot of executives from your company— and from other companies—often at the meetings? Does the association provide contacts that can lead to better jobs in other companies? If your peers answer no to these questions, it's still smart to join the association that your bosses revere. Your peers, however, may have discovered another group that meets *their* professional and career planning needs. If this is the case, nothing other than money stops you from joining two professional organizations.

Association memberships, if not an automatic "perk" with your job, are expensive. Annual fees of $100 or more are not unusual. But consider the fee a bona fide career investment (even the IRS allows you to deduct the expense in most cases). The investment will be repaid several times over if VP MacDonald recommends you for a promotion or if someone you met at an association seminar smooths your way to a better job at another company.

STEP-UP PLAN YOUR ACTION

Joining an In-House Committee

Select your committee by using a three-stage evaluation:

1. Will I be able to get on the committee?
2. Will the committee give me more clout and visibility?
3. Who can get me on the committee?

Will I Be Able to Get On the Committee?

You stand a good chance of joining any committee on which your peers already serve, or one whose work directly affects your unit. Committees of managers set up to advise staff offices (EEO committees, safety committees) are also likely targets. Committees that are *not* likely to accept you include those whose members are one or more levels above your supervisor, those whose tasks do not affect your unit, or on which another manager from your area already serves (although you can certainly bid for membership if your unit's current representative steps down).

Will the Committee Give Me More Clout and Visibility?

Rank your eligible committees on these criteria:

Committee visibility (that is, are key executives on the committee?)
Importance to management's concerns (which bigwigs supported the committee's creation?)
Likelihood of a successful committee product (is the committee populated by outcasts and troublemakers, or is it stepping on the toes of powerful organizational units?)
Relevance of this committee's work to your unit

Use the following chart, ranking the committees on a scale of 1 (irrelevant to my work, members almost invisible, management doesn't give a damn, and nobody will listen anyhow) to 3 (committee very relevant to my work, all the big bosses will see me, the issue is top management's baby, and whatever the committee decides will fly). Total your score in the last column. We've done the first entry as an example.

Committee Name	Relevance to My Work	Visibility for Me	Support from Top	Likelihood of Success	Total
Personnel	2	2	2	2	8

Do your best to join the high-scoring committee, making the second-highest your alternative. After all, your first choice may turn out to be a bomb, or after a few months you may feel ready to handle two committee memberships.

Who Can Get Me On the Committee?

Three people are important in securing your committee assignment: your boss, someone influential with the committee leaders, and you.

Your boss is important because his nomination almost assures your appointment. If your boss won't support you, you'll have to either trim your sails or maneuver around his opposition while blocking any possible retribution (risky business, which we don't recommend). If your boss is favorably inclined, ask first for his advice and then for his support. He'll appreciate your respect of his knowledge, and he'll be a zealous advocate when you announce your candidacy. If your boss is uneasy with your upward aspirations, a strong endorsement from on high (a committee member, that is) may stave off bossly opposition. Even if your boss is supportive, your candidacy is furthered if a committee insider assures him that you'll be an asset.

If you can enlist the support of the committee's chairperson, your membership is all but assured. Company executives of equal or greater rank than the members, and peers who influence committee decisions, can also deliver powerful endorsements for you—the more the better.

You, of course, must present the argument that your unit deserves to be represented on the committee. You must convince your superiors that you are a potential asset to the committee's work.

Remember Salome's argument: "The commissary will be affected by this computer committee's decisions, and I've put a lot of work into computerization already. I know I can help create a solution that pacifies everyone and moves us forward."

This is exactly the line of reasoning that gets you committee assignments. It hardly need be said that only *you* can make sure your argument is logical and persuasive, and speaks to the committee's needs. Spend a week or so polishing your arguments for membership:

· "I just found out that my predecessor Forbisher was on the space allocation committee. Now I see why. Given the space disputes we've had over the last months because my unit had no input, it makes sense to give me Forbisher's seat. I won't have to spend so much time fighting for my people, and we'll all accomplish more."

· "As a woman manager who's responsible for carrying out personnel policy around here, I've got a double-barreled interest in the personnel department's EEO compliance committee. Ed's about to step down as our department's rep on the committee, and I'd like to have the spot."

Once you've perfected your argument, see your boss. Spend at least one conversation floating the idea of doing some work on a higher, more interdepartmental level. If your boss is supportive, talk about specific committees and campaign strategies. If he's not supportive, you *may* want to consider working around him. By now you know your boss well enough to sense whether his nonsupport means he doesn't want you horning in on his territory or that he simply has better things to worry about than helping you. Even if he's too busy, let him know that the department needs, for instance, a representative on the division's EEO committee and that you'll be the rep if he can't.

Joining a Professional Association

Choosing a professional association is less complicated than choosing a committee. If there is the slightest connection between your work and the association's purposes, few associations will reject your dues or participation, and your company may automatically enroll everyone at your level. Unless you're not a physician and you're thinking of joining the American Medical Association, don't worry about your qualifications.

Rank the professional organizations you're considering on these criteria:

· Relevance to your work (Does it cover my level of management? My work and professional responsibilities?)
· Extent to which company executives are active members (Do my bosses belong? Go to association meetings? Sing its praises?)
· Satisfaction expressed by peers who are members (Do they say it has helped them at work or in your profession?)

Again, 1 is the lowest score (not very relevant, hardly a top manager in sight, peers found it useless) and 3 is the highest (very relevant, anybody who is *any*body belongs, peer members get a job offer a month).

Use the following chart and total your score in the last column. We have again filled in the first row as an example.

Professional Associations

Name	Relevance to My Work	Bosses Active	Peers Pleased	Total
American Marketing Assn.	3	3	3	9

When you announce your impending enlistment—an action that may enhance your standing on the spot—ask your boss or peer if you must complete an application to join. This will probably result in your being invited to the organization's next scheduled event, where you'll be welcomed with open arms—and the opportunity to start making contacts immediately.

Your Organization's Social Activities

Even if you're not selected for a committee and join no professional organization, a third strategy does exist for smoothing your upward progress: Participate in the charitable, social, and ceremonial affairs of the company. Most companies raise funds for charitable groups, draw blood for hospitals, and conduct collections for everything from Snodgrass's retirement to Farthingham's facelift. While it is not the same credit that Salome LaSalle got for helping iron out her firm's computer difficulties, you can score points by being your department's blood captain, United Way coordinator, or retirement luncheon organizer.

These social and philanthropic activities make the organization look good. If you play a key role in them, you look good. In addition, retirement luncheons and blood-drive award ceremonies often attract top executives. These events mean direct conversations between higher-ups and managers like you. You, of course, realize that positive and lasting impressions can be made at an award ceremony as well as anywhere else. Indeed, it's wise to talk business, at least indirectly, on such occasions.

Contribute also to groups with whom you are not actively involved: Attend their lectures and ceremonies, if only briefly. Your contributions and attendance will likely be reciprocated. Most important, you're maximizing your exposure and solidifying your reputation as an active, involved person. Make no mistake: Top management takes note of people with such reputations.

STEP-UP   USE AND ABUSE YOUR PLAN

You took a committee job to learn, to help your unit, to get exposure, and to make a favorable impression on influential bosses; but how much a committee can further these ends isn't always predictable. Yesterday's sure shot can be today's dud, so keep a critical eye on the committee you've joined. Committees are fragile. If the problem addressed by the committee is resolved, the committee has little reason to exist—though it may stagger listlessly along nibbling at issues related to the original problem.

Fred Upencoming, for example, was ecstatic when he was appointed to the staff of the reorganization committee. At the time of his appointment, the committee was studying and deciding work allocations throughout the company. When Fred attended his first meeting (at which most major reorganization decisions were approved), he shook in his boots. Never before had he seen so many executives in one place at one time . . . and he hasn't seen them since. The big decisions had been made, the hotshots rarely came to the reorganization committee's subsequent meetings, and the committee ground to a halt a year later.

Even a committee with a strong mandate can bog down if a forceful chairperson leaves or two powerful committee members struggle for control, both of which happen frequently. The biggest events of Fred's year on the reorganization committee were the triumphant departure of Alexia DeRauen, the committee's original chair, and the simultaneous firing of Ross Brucard (the next chairperson) and Howard Smythe, who thought he, not his archenemy Brucard, should have gotten the job. DeRauen had so successfully led the reorganization effort that a rival company had lured her away with an executive vice presidency. Brucard and Smythe had fought so bitterly over what turned out to be the dregs of the reorganization effort (making manuals conform to the new titles) that they had become an embarrassment to the company.

Committees also have tenuous *official* existences. Unlike departments and staff offices, which have day-to-day business to conduct, the committee is the often unpopular dilettante of organizations. It arises suddenly, often on some executive's whim, and then ponders and decides issues which can mean life and death to the "working departments." Consequently, a real tension exists between committees and the more permanent departments, which frequently propose, sometimes successfully, that the committee be disbanded or that its work be given to another committee known to favor the departments. Fred Upencoming was never officially notified that the reorganization committee had been disbanded. The meetings simply stopped. But he knew something was up when Operations Manager Isaac Francis, who had often complained that the committee shouldn't meddle in the implementation of the reorganization, told him with a smirk, "I wouldn't hold my breath until your committee gets together again, Fred."

If you encounter any of the things Fred did, start looking for the exit. You don't want to be on a meaningless committee, get caught in cross fire between two factions, or (even worse) get drafted by the losing side. You can't risk being seen as a villain by the members of operating departments.

What are the signs of a dead-end committee?

Meetings go on for two hours without deciding anything
Chairpersons let everybody ramble meaninglessly to their heart's content
Committee members take you aside right away and tell you how horrible other committee members are
Disagreements erupt between the same individuals at meeting after meeting
Operating-department heads seem to be able to veto anything they don't like
After several meetings you haven't heard a single useful thing

Plenty of committees look like this from the inside; though outsiders consider them the center of the action. If you find that your first-choice committee is a disaster, try to get on another committee right away. Six months or so after you've joined committee number two, cite the pressures of your heavy extracurricular schedule as you resign from the first. (It helps if your new committee's work demands made you miss a meeting or two of the original committee.)

Quitting a Professional Organization

Leaving a professional organization that doesn't serve your needs is as easy as not renewing your membership when it expires. Some executive may question your absence from the organization's functions, although it is just as likely that no one will notice (you needn't send out announcements).

Before you sign up for a second year, evaluate how your association helps you develop in your present job and as a professional with career potential throughout your industry.

Have the journals and newsletters given you management advice or technical knowledge that you've applied on the job?

Have the meetings, presentations, and conferences addressed topics of current concern to you and your company?

Were the members you met interested in and well informed about happenings in your field?

Did you hear frequently about job openings in other companies?

Did you see your bosses (and your bosses' bosses) at the events held by the professional association?

If the answer to most of these is no, let your membership expire and waste no more time at the meetings.

Don't Be a Social Johnny/Janey One-Note

Variety is surely the spice of life in the social and philanthropic activities of your company. You simply don't want to be the department blood captain four years running. Sooner or later you'll be bored, people will cringe at your approach, and you'll find yourself nicknamed Dracula.

After blood, there is United Way, or the holiday party planning committee, or the bowling team. Plan to take part in several social and charitable activities over the next few years. You'll increase your companywide contacts and lengthen your resumé, both of which will pave a smoother road to the corner offices in your company.

STEP-UP PLAN AND PLAN AGAIN

If you end up on a useless committee or become a member of a professional group that doesn't serve your needs, you already have a contingency plan in place: Leave for a better one.

Sometimes getting off committees is harder than getting on, especially when the committee has just submitted a reorganization plan that the administrative director has roundly criticized. When a committee is embattled, pressures can develop for members to stand fast with one voice against the criticism. There are obvious dangers involved in standing on the parapets shouting epithets at the administrative director or other management heavyweights. The trick is to leave the committee without being labeled a traitor by your peers.

In such cases it's extremely helpful to have been active in a variety of tasks outside your primary managerial responsibilities. You can then reasonably claim that the press of *all* of your outside duties is beginning to affect your day-to-day managing. The committee you want to leave cannot refute your claim, though it may try to strong-arm you into staying. Therefore, you need to be careful of your overall work reputation as you depart from the group. If you have committee tasks to complete, complete them even if you have to work after the effective date of your resignation. The same holds for association responsibilities. Don't "cut and run." Deserting the proverbial sinking ship can hurt you far into the future— long after people have forgotten that the committee you left was a rat hole.

Minimize any resentment you feel, and keep your bridges intact. Even if the committee members were all squabbling sloths, say nice things as you leave. "I've learned a lot" is an old standby, and it's always true . . . even if what you learned was that the committee members are idiots. There's simply no sense in potshotting once you have the resignation you wanted. If you fire a departing broadside, some members who do not appreciate your low evaluation may see to it that you get yours down the road.

But don't give up or swear off after one bad experience. Your committee work is important groundwork for a future in upper management, and your next opportunity may be the chance you need to shine.

11

Stress Management

EVEN AS A ROOKIE, Gus had no doubt he would someday rise to a position of authority in the demanding field of criminology. Several times promoted, he became the best detective on the force—careful, cool, and reasonable even during the toughest, bloodiest criminal investigations. His colleagues envied the way Gus kept every detail under control. Gus loved his work and took it seriously. Citations for consistently high quality made him a senior agent by age thirty and a top administrator in a national law enforcement agency at age thirty-five. Calm and determined, Gus let nothing slip away from him.

Gus also knew that years in such high-pressure jobs had made him all work and no play. "I've worked so hard to get where I am," thought Gus, "it would be foolish to let the job ruin my health now." With his doctor's okay, he began jogging to control the inevitable effects of his stressful work. After a few months of daily exercise, Gus felt noticeably stronger and more energetic. "If jogging feels this good, running must feel even better," he thought. After a few months he was running ten miles a day and decided to train for a marathon. He applied the same attention, practice, and standards of quality to his sport as he did to his work.

His family and colleagues were there to cheer as Gus placed a respectable eighth in his first marathon. Exhausted but elated, Gus vowed, "Next time I'll be number one! I'm looking forward to the next marathon—I never felt better in my life." Several months later, Gus was five minutes late for work. His co-workers could hardly wait to needle him good-naturedly when he finally came in; Gus was *never* late for anything, and here at last was proof he was human after all.

But when he hadn't arrived half an hour later, amusement gave way to apprehension. Gus *always* called if something delayed him. He had never missed a meeting in his life. Had he been in an accident? Was one of his children suddenly taken ill?

Finally Gus's wife called to explain. The office was utterly shocked to learn that Gus—cool, collected Gus, the marathon runner—had suffered a heart attack at the age of thirty-seven.

Gus survived. Equally important, he changed his approach to work when he was well enough to return to his job. It had taken a coronary to make him realize that his carefully controlled, unrelenting perfectionism caused him more stress than organized crime—or his marathons—ever could.

Some Concrete Reasons Why You Must Manage Stress

1. First the bad news: Ten people die in this country every 2 minutes and 45 seconds. That means well over one hundred people will die before you finish reading this chapter—most of them, according to increasing evidence, from stress-related or stress-exacerbated illness.

2. *Right now you're a prime candidate* to suffer the effects of stress. You were recently promoted, and a promotion can be just as *physiologically* stressful as being demoted or fired. Unbelievable? But it's true. You're about to be—or already are—performing all kinds of new duties (i.e., everything you've read about in this book), you're busier than you were before, and you deal with new people who see you in a new role. Your leisure time has decreased or even disappeared. These conditions alone are enough to put you in a higher illness-risk category this year. (In "Tally Your Resources" you'll find out just how much your new position affects your health.)

3. Paradoxical though it seems, even success can have adverse effects on health (Judy Garland and John Belushi are flamboyant examples; the heart attacks of ordinary managers rarely make *People* magazine, but are well documented in every cardiology journal). The "too much too soon, out of control" syndrome affects everyone, far more than hard work alone.

4. A ten-year research study completed in 1983 stated: "People don't get sick from germs or risk factors like smoking, high blood pressure, or high cholesterol; what's killing them is the fact that we have been hit with 300 years of civilization in a few decades." Future shock is real; people begin to feel as if they're losing control of their lives and their society, and respond by getting literally sick.

Now the good news: Since 1980, research has increasingly shown that although stress itself is unavoidable, you can indeed learn to *handle* stress much more safely and effectively. You can turn negative stress (properly called "distress") into positive energy (or "eustress," from the Greek prefix *eu-*, meaning good, as in euphoria. Eustress is the excitement and raring-to-go energy you feel when you can't wait to tackle a new project). That is, the boss who looked like a threat can be perceived as a challenge; what looked at first like an overwhelming (and boring) project can be perceived in a positive light and handled as a stepping-stone to another promotion. Relabeling the stressors around you (bosses and projects, for instance), or controlling your reaction to unavoidable stressors (such as rush-hour traffic) through relaxation techniques, puts *you* in control.

In short, stress management is no luxury—it's as essential to your health as food and sleep. Your success *and your satisfaction* as a manager depend on it.

STEP-UP SET YOUR GOALS

Be an Overachiever and Live to Talk about It

We're going to ask you to do the hardest thing there is: change. And not just to increase how much exercise you get, which is difficult enough—but to change how you think about stress and how you react to it, thereby improving your health and well-being.

If you're thinking "I can't change how I think! No one can," we're happy to tell you that you're wrong. You can prove it yourself, and improve the quality, as well as the length, of your life in the bargain. (Yes, even with the dozens of other things you have to worry about because of your new job.) You're reading this book to gain confidence and control over your new duties. You can use this chapter to feel more in control of yourself and your entire life.

Your Stress-Management Goals

Beginning today (and for the rest of my life) I will:

- Get an annual physical examination
- Examine and rethink some of the mental rules and assumptions I have about work in general
- Practice new, healthier responses to stressful situations
- Give myself frequent encouragement, praise, and support, rather than berating myself if I make a mistake
- Get regular physical (aerobic) exercise
- Practice at least one relaxation technique daily (meditation, deep breathing, full-body relaxation, five-minute vacations, self-hypnosis)
- Use time-management techniques to provide extra time for exercise and relaxation (not just for more work!)
- Pay "selective inattention" to minor annoyances
- Spend time doing what I enjoy, both at work and in non-work-related activities

- Eat and drink sensibly, quit smoking, and limit my use of drugs or tranquilizers
- Laugh more often: See funny movies, spend time with a friend whose sense of humor I enjoy, listen to comedy records, have a pillow fight or ask my mate to tickle me. (Laughter itself has been increasingly recognized as a revitalizing and healing activity that actually reduces pain. Laughter releases endorphins, which are natural painkillers, and is a true form of *eustress*—that is, it releases more oxygen, increases your heart rate, dilates your pupils, and so forth—and it's good for you.)

Just in case you're thinking "Okay, these look like great goals and I'm sure they'll be good for me and I'll do some stress management just as soon as I've made sense of this job," think again. You need to handle your stress *now*, before the demands of the job take their invisible but very real toll on your health.

Perhaps relaxing and enjoying yourself sound antithetical to the work ethic and contrary to what we've been telling you for the past ten chapters. They're not. The whole point of this book is to put you in control of your job so that you can use your energy to get ahead and enjoy your work, not just stay afloat. Don't wait until you can barely cope before you protect yourself and your health.

In other words, don't be a victim of the "If I feel good, I must not be working hard enough" myth (a variation on the "The worse it tastes, the better it is for you" myth). If you feel bad, it's because you're not taking adequate care of yourself. Too much stress means deteriorating effectiveness—to yourself, your company, and your family.

Stress Defined: If It Isn't Nervous Tension, What Is It?

No, stress is not "nervous tension." Stress is your *body's reaction* to the demands made upon it—to the events around you, or to the thoughts in your mind—and nervous tension is only one possible response to stress. If you *think* something is stressful, your body will react in a particular way (sweating, shaking, laughing nervously, or shallow breathing, for example) when you encounter that situation. Your body may in fact react that way even when you just *think* about the stressful situation.

Research increasingly shows that modern living provides infinite potential for stress—as if you needed proof of that. Luckily, people can actually learn to ignore many of the problems around them and deal constructively with unavoidable stressors. An attitude of "I can handle this . . . I won't let it get to me," coupled with stress-reducing behavior, is the best insurance of health.

How Your Stress Reaction Works

Imagine you're walking alone down a dark street after midnight, when suddenly you think you hear footsteps behind you. In fact, you're *sure* you hear footsteps. No one who can help you is around.

Depending to some extent on your size, you probably feel something between alert concern and utter terror. Whatever your perception of the situation, here's what's happening in your body: As you feel alarm, epinephrine (formerly called adrenaline) is released. Heart rate and breathing increase, and blood concentrates in the brain and muscles for quick action. Your pupils dilate and your hearing becomes sharper. Your muscles tense, ready for "fight or flight." Your physical capacities are ready for peak performance. You choose flight. And you're able to run faster and farther than you ever thought possible from the stranger behind you, although you may need a stiff drink at home to calm down.

Now imagine that you're an experienced, physically fit plainclothes police officer in the same situation. Although all the same physiological changes happen in your body, your attitude is much different: This is exactly what you've been trained to handle, and you capture the mugger with little trouble. You're left feeling wide awake, to be sure, but this time it's eustress: energizing and positive.

Back to real life now. Stress lurks far more often for most of us in the wilds of the average office than in a dark alley. You can't literally fight with or flee from your boss or clients, no matter how upset you are with them. Your speedier heart rate still sends your blood pressure up, but you often have no physical opportunity to get it back down by releasing fight-or-flight tension naturally—and if you send it up ten times a day, pretty soon it just stays there. Similarly, tensed muscles that cannot run or fight turn their tension into backaches or migraines. This is why stress damages the health of so many managers who have "safe" desk jobs. (Police officers and emergency-room nurses, whose jobs are considered highly stressful, report that it's the inactivity and repetitiveness of paperwork that really drive them up the wall.)

Not that an office job can't be physically stressful. Your new managerial position may require you to speak to a mob of hostile citizens at a citywide meeting. But if you're confident that you can control the situation, basically enjoy and believe in what you're doing, and have experience handling such events, you'll feel tremendously alive and vital—where others would crumple under the pressure.

Again, few of us are called upon to face such dramatic situations. The stressors you're likely to encounter are more mundane (a stalled subway; Bud, your records clerk, cracking his gum as he waltzes in late for the third time this week; four more "top priority" projects on your desk Monday morning; Mr. Snively, your obnoxious, demanding client; your own perfectionism), but physiologically just as unhealthy for you. Though the basic physical stress reaction is the same for all humans, you can control and modify your personal response to stressors. Stress is your *reaction* to events around you, but your *response* can range from extreme anxiety to neutrality to eager excitement—depending on *how you judge* the event and *how you choose to respond* to it.

If, for example, you do a slow burn or fly into a rage when a subordinate is two minutes late for a routine meeting, you can learn to express your displeasure in ways that won't damage your health (or hers). Though you may never be the serene soul who functions calmly amid chaos, you'll live longer and be healthier.

In other words, it's all in your mind. If you *think* that missing out on the Paradise project is a tragedy, your body will agree with you—and respond by creating indigestion, ulcers, or other symptoms. But stress isn't "out there," ready to jump on your back and raise your blood pressure (though often your boss and a host of new responsibilities may appear that way). It's how you choose to respond to the demands made upon you—whether you take it easy or fly off the handle, get tense and anxious or use your nervous energy to take control—that affects your health and well-being.

The Laws of Conservation of Matter and Energy—and Stress

Ever wonder why articles and books on stress never talk about "stress elimination" but always "stress management"? It's simple—if you eliminated stress completely from your life, you'd be dead. You need *some* stress even to walk around and function at all (just ask anybody in solitary confinement). You need more stressors—in the form of challenges and solvable problems—to flourish and grow at any age. Too little stress (boredom, isolation) is as deadly as too much. It's only when the problems appear overwhelming and challenges start looking like threats (or stop coming at all) that your body translates stress into distress.

CHART 11A   How You Allow External Stressors to Affect Your
            Health

EXTERNAL STRESSORS
*(Unavoidable or
uncontrollable)*

Tight deadlines
Moving to new office
Boss yells at you
Major new project
Too much work
No interesting tasks
Hard-driving office
Subordinates fighting
Secretary quits
New assistant hired
The weather
New federal regulations
Busy season at work
Boring, routine work
Et cetera

1. YOUR GENERAL ATTITUDE TOWARD WORK

Distress-Prone	*Eustress-Prone*
I should be perfect	I take my time and do a good job
I must try harder	I enjoy a challenge
I'm the only one who has any brains around here	I like working with others
	I take things easy
I'd better hurry up!	I'm competent; I can handle it
I should please others	
Why even try?	
I only look out for Number One	

2. YOUR JUDGMENT OR PERCEPTION OF EXTERNAL STRESSORS

Distress-Prone	*Eustress-Prone*
This is terrible! (or overwhelming)	This is annoying but controllable
Nobody else has to put up with this crap	This doesn't really affect me
	This could be a good opportunity if I work it right

3. YOUR BEHAVIOR RESPONSE TO EXTERNAL STRESSORS

Distress-Prone	*Eustress-Prone*
Excessive use of coffee, liquor, drugs	Taking your time
Yelling, using sarcasm	Enjoying the challenge
Grinding your teeth	Setting or reordering your priorities
Working overtime	Delegating work
Tensed muscles	Asking for help
Insomnia	Learning new things
Headaches	Getting excited
Complaining	Deliberate relaxation
Making mistakes	Exercise
Being oversensitive	Selectively ignoring certain minor problems
Withdrawing	

Types of Stress

Stressors are rarely in short supply: daily events, people, or the nagging voice in your head provides plenty of triggers for physiological reaction. Types of stressors and examples of each include:

Internal stress:	Constant worry that "any day now they'll find out I don't know the job very well yet"
External stress:	Your boss warning you to shape up or ship out
Mental stress:	Having to do tedious computations, complicated tasks
Physical stress:	Having to listen to heavy drilling outside your window all day, or lift heavy equipment
Work-related stress:	The company is in the red, and your job security looks precarious
Personal stress:	Family problems, or a friend's illness

External and internal stressors can be further defined as follows:

Time stress:	External: tight work deadlines Internal: the "hurry-up" syndrome
Anticipatory stress:	External: bomb threats or changing federal regulations Internal: catastrophizing, imagining that "Mr. Big will hate my report"
Situational stress:	External: driving in a blizzard Internal: being in a small room when you suffer from claustrophobia
Encounter stress:	External: being disciplined by your boss Internal: experiencing shyness, or being forced to work with a client you dislike

Once triggered, your immediate reactions to stress alarm (muscles tightening, shallow breathing) are almost always unconscious. But if the epinephrine has no outlet in action—no chance for fight or flight—and if you experience the trigger frequently, stress reaction becomes *chronic*. According to Ronald Dushkin, M.D., the chronic stress response begins to click in habitually, even if the actual intensity of the stress is low or manageable. This is where stress really takes its toll on your health—and where you can learn to reprogram your reaction and response to it.

STEP-UP TALLY YOUR RESOURCES

This time you'll tally not only your resources but your weaknesses: your stress symptoms, what triggers them, your stress personality, and what you currently do to keep the effects of stress under control. Prepare to feel depressed or anxious after you've completed some of these self-assessments; you may not be thrilled with what you learn.

Then cheer up. *You have control.* Remind yourself that you can turn around whatever damage stress has caused you. You *can* modify your reaction to the stressors in your life, and feel happier as well as healthier. The truth may hurt at first—but knowledge is power.

Symptoms to Watch For

Imagine you're in a managers' meeting and have just completed a major project—slightly past deadline. It was rough going: The work was complicated and required every bit of your ingenuity. You've earned the relaxation you're looking forward to, and aren't paying enormous attention to the meeting. Suddenly, without warning, your boss asks you to make an impromptu presentation of the project, how you accomplished it, and how it will mesh with several other departments—to a tough vice president who's walking in the door.

How do you feel (your *emotions*)?

_____   _____   _____

What are the *physical reactions* you ordinarily have in such a situation?

_____   _____   _____

Maybe under emotions you wrote "nervous," "tongue-tied," "furious," or "scared"; your physical reactions might have included butterflies in the stomach, a shaky voice, sweaty palms, or a pounding heart.

If you weren't sure about your physical reactions, that's your first order of business. Pay attention and learn what your body is trying to tell you. Many people are not aware that they're experiencing stress, especially if the stressor is boredom or something equally undramatic. Here are some immediate and long-term signs of stress to look out for:

CHART 11B: Stress Symptoms and Signals

BEHAVIORAL	PHYSICAL	EMOTIONAL	PSYCHOLOGICAL
Overeating	Headaches	Anxiety	Diminished creativity
Smoking	Hypertension	Depression	Self-rejecting
Using liquor or drugs	Backache	Fear	thoughts (low self-
Procrastination	Digestive prob-	Loneliness	esteem)
Complaining	lems	Impatience	Insecurity
Irrational arguments	Heart disease	Boredom	Indecision
Short-temperedness	Fatigue		
Insomnia	Muscle tension		
	Shaky voice		
	Shaking hands		
	Cramps		
	Facial tics		
	Grinding teeth		

Remember, even if nothing in your life is particularly stressful at the moment, you may be suffering from these symptoms because of the chronic stress response mentioned earlier.

How Does Your Job Drive You Crazy?

Unless you are the sole owner and CEO of the company (a position that carries its own stressors, to be sure), you are controlled to some degree by others—perhaps others you've never met. The self-assessment below is designed to measure the amount of stress you feel from the procedures and people you must deal with.

The Work-Stress Inventory

In the space, note how often you experience the stressor in the item. As you read through these, think about how your body reacts to each condition.

FREQUENCY SCALE

1 = Never, 2 = Infrequently, 3 = Sometimes, 4 = Often, 5 = Always

_____ 1. I have differences of opinion with my boss(es).
_____ 2. My subordinates are unclear about what my job is.
_____ 3. My unit is often in conflict with other units we must work with.
_____ 4. I am not sure what's expected of me.
_____ 5. The demands of others for my time are in conflict.

_____ 6. Management expects me to interrupt my work for new priorities.

_____ 7. I lack confidence in management.

_____ 8. I hear comments about my work only when I make a mistake or miss a deadline.

_____ 9. I have little or no opportunity to help make decisions that affect me.

_____ 10. I have to be cautious about how much I say in meetings.

_____ 11. I have too much (or too little) work to do.

_____ 12. I have to accept upper management's decisions without being told their rationale.

_____ 13. My peers are trained in a field different from mine.

_____ 14. I must often go to other departments (offices) to get my job done.

_____ 15. I have unsettled conflicts with my subordinates (or co-workers).

_____ 16. I get little support from my subordinates.

_____ 17. It seems there's always a crisis; I can't work calmly, according to my plans.

_____ 18. The assignments I get have little meaning or interest for me.

_____ 19. I don't have the opportunity to use my knowledge or skills.

_____ 20. I receive too much (or too little) supervision.

_____ = Total

If you scored from 20 to 40, your work-stress level is basically manageable and probably doesn't affect your health or immunity to disease. If you scored from 41 to 80, you have plenty of room for improvement. Relaxation techniques and attempts to change how you interact with your co-workers will significantly reduce the distress you feel. A score of 81 to 100 means you have a serious need to change your environment, your attitude, and your behavior. Changing your environment—that is, quitting your job or transferring—is usually the most difficult to accomplish. Even if you feel like a mosquito in the sticky web of bureaucracy, you can do much to help yourself.

Update: Type A and Type B Personalities

The concept of the coronary-prone personality—the hard-driving, rushed, competitive Type A, as opposed to the more steady, relaxed, deliberate Type B—has gained credibility since it was first introduced by Drs. Ray Rosenman and Meyer Friedman in 1956. More recent research has shown some interesting twists to their original findings. Complete the questionnaire below to find out which type you are.

The Glazer Life-style Questionnaire

Each item below is composed of two sentences separated by a series of lines. Each pair represents two extremes of a certain behavior, and somewhere along the line is a description of your own behavior. For instance, on item 3 below, think for a moment of the least competitive person you know, and of the most competitive; then put a check mark where you think you belong between the two extremes.

1 2 3 4 5 6 7

1. I don't mind leaving things temporarily unfinished.   — — — — — — —   1. I have to get things finished once I start them.

2. I'm calm and unhurried about appointments.   — — — — — — —   2. I'm never late for appointments.

3. I'm not competitive.   — — — — — — —   3. I'm very competitive.

4. I listen well, and let others finish speaking.   — — — — — — —   4. I anticipate others—nod, interrupt, and finish their sentences for them.

5. I'm never really in a hurry, even when pressured.   — — — — — — —   5. I'm always in a hurry.

6. I'm calm when I have to wait.   — — — — — — —   6. Waiting makes me nervous.

7. I'm very easygoing.   — — — — — — —   7. I'm always going full speed ahead.

8. I take things one at a time.   — — — — — — —   8. I'm always doing two things at once, or thinking about what I have to do next.

	1 2 3 4 5 6 7	
9. I speak slowly and deliberately.	— — — — — — —	9. I speak forcefully and use lots of gestures.
10. If I'm satisfied with my own performance, I'm unconcerned with what others think.	— — — — — — —	10. I want recognition from others for a job well done.
11. I do things slowly.	— — — — — — —	11. I walk, eat, etc., quickly.
12. I work steadily.	— — — — — — —	12. I'm hard-driving.
13. I express my feelings openly.	— — — — — — —	13. I rarely let my feelings out.
14. I have many outside interests.	— — — — — — —	14. I have few outside interests.
15. I'm satisfied with my job.	— — — — — — —	15. I'm ambitious and want to get ahead quickly.
16. I never set my own deadlines.	— — — — — — —	16. I always set my own deadlines.
17. I don't take responsibility for things that aren't my problem.	— — — — — — —	17. I feel responsible for everything.
18. I judge my performance in terms of quality, not quantity.	— — — — — — —	18. I judge my performance in terms of how much I produce.
19. I tend to be casual about work.	— — — — — — —	19. I often work weekends or bring work home.

                              1   2   3   4   5   6   7

20. I'm not very   — — — — — — —   20. I'm very precise
     detail-oriented.   and detail-
                                                         oriented.

Add the number values above each check mark; the total is your score. If your total is between 20 and 29, you have nothing to fear from cardiac disease; you're a very relaxed B1. A score between 30 and 59 makes you a B2: still relaxed and able to handle stress. Between 60 and 79 is the AB category; you're a mix of A and B, and could slip into being a Type A if you're not careful about how you handle stress. Scoring from 80 to 109 means you're an A2: prone to cardiac disease. And 110 to 140 means you're at serious risk to suffer a heart attack, especially if you smoke.

Participants in our stress-management seminars have sometimes been shocked into taking better care of themselves when they saw what their scores meant. If you're similarly surprised, then this book will pay off for you in more ways than one.

If you're a relatively safe A2, however, you may already be thinking "But precise, hard-driving, competitive managers are exactly the ones who get to keep their jobs (let alone get promoted) around here." It's true that too many companies reward the very behavior that's killing their executives. The ironic fact is that this superefficient, churn-it-out type A behavior is often not even genuinely productive.

The Myth of the Super-Type-A Team

How can a Type A who constantly puts in unpaid overtime (and squeezes every drop of work from his people) *not* be productive? The fallacy of the supereffective Type A's was demonstrated several years ago when management experts Waino Suojanen of Georgia State University and Donald Hudson of the University of Miami realized that much of the Type A's sound and fury signified nothing more than spinning wheels. Type A's worked hard, all right—it's just that they spent much of their time manufacturing crises so that they could work hard solving them. What they produced had little effect on the company's bottom line, but they were so visible, running madly about with their electronic fire extinguishers, that upper management could not help but take notice. (Meanwhile, their subordinates were suffering even more stress, trying to manage—or avoid—the next pseudo-crisis.)

Such Type A's have been called "stress junkies." Stress junkies, who are often workaholics, get hooked on their own epinephrine; they unconsciously "build fires" just to experience their stress-response surge while they put them out. This is counterfeit eustress, however, not the real thing.

Control: Why Every Type A Does Not End Up in the Hospital

Like nicotine or drug addiction, stress addiction—even though it feels terrific at the time—does nothing for human health. Yet it's a fact that many obsessive Type A's never get sick or have heart trouble at all. How can this be?

This is where your attitude and perception come in. Researchers in the area of psychosomatic medicine believe a strong relationship exists between coronary disease and what they call *field-dependent* and *field-independent* frames of reference.

Field-dependent individuals look to the external environment—the boss, the size of their paycheck or office—to provide praise and approval; only then can FD people value and understand themselves.

Field-independent individuals evaluate themselves by internal or self-contained standards. To the FI person, other people's opinions count, but not as much as their own.

In other words, you get sick depending on whether you derive satisfaction primarily from within yourself or from others. Problems arise because field-*dependent* Type A's (hard-driving, competitive, impatient) are torn by constant conflict: They're trying to be both loved and aggressive at the same time. Though they may win "success" in terms of more money or responsibility, they always feel at the mercy of those who award the promotions. FD Type A's have higher cholesterol levels than field-*independent* Type A's, who are less concerned or psychologically dependent on others' approval. Field-independent Type A's are often "stress seekers" rather than stress junkies; they look for opportunities where their natural predisposition to hard work will really pay off, and often enjoy success as entrepreneurs. For them, stressors are a source of true eustress.

Type A's who believe success means position and money often lack the independent personality structure to support their climb to the top. These are the hypertense managers who blow their stacks (and their hearts) without even the inner satisfaction of a job well done.

"You Will Live the Way You Think"

Those are the words of Dr. Clayton Lafferty, CEO of Human Synergistics in Plymouth, Michigan. Lafferty describes three thinking styles or orientations that directly affect your behavior and health. Security orientations, like the field-dependent style above, tend to produce the most stress because those who need the most security often feel the least control.

Personal/Task Orientation: You're primarily concerned about using and developing your talents. You derive enjoyment through your work itself and from contact with others. The stronger your leaning toward this style, the less likely you'll be to complain about depression and nervous tension. It's similar to the creative-achievement style discussed in chapters 4 and 7.

Task/Security Orientation: Your major concern is to gain promotions and political security on the job by being competitive; you strive for power and perfection. Likely medical problems for people with this orientation are ulcers, high blood pressure, allergies, arthritis, acute dermatitis, hyperacidity, insomnia, excessive smoking, weight problems, and depression. They often include the power-control individuals discussed earlier.

People/Security Orientation: You seek the goodwill and approval of others at all levels, and operate on the job in conventional, accepted ways. This orientation is also a source of physical problems and depression, though to a lesser extent. Some social-affiliational individuals fit this description.

Of course, if a low-control Type A is deprived of his stressors, even to recuperate from a heart attack on a beach in Acapulco for three weeks, he may quickly feel as anxious as if he were thrown into solitary in Sing Sing. As you'll see in "Plan Your Action," relaxation doesn't necessarily mean doing nothing.

But don't you field-independent, personal-task Type A's get too smug. Surviving in the fast lane of the fast track (or just staying in the race at all) extracts some price from everyone's health. Fortunately, attempts to modify (not eliminate) stress-addicted behavior have proven extremely successful, both with medication and with relaxation techniques you'll learn below. A note of caution here: Treating only the symptoms of stress (elevated heart rate, headaches, backaches, stomach problems) with medication is not in itself bad, but beware—you may be ignoring the real issues because of a false sense of security. If the underlying problem is

A feeling of being distracted or unfocused
Constant fatigue

General dissatisfaction with life

The feeling that nothing you do really makes a difference

Frequent frustration

Emotions you cannot or will not express to significant people in your life

Feeling isolated from people or from work that holds real meaning for you

you can't rely on drugs and exercise alone to reduce stress or prevent damaging your resistance to disease.

Everyone feels extra-susceptible to colds when unusually tired or depressed, and for good reason: Distress reduces the immune system's efficiency. You're exposed to all kinds of potentially deadly bacteria and viruses in your lifetime, but ordinarily your immune system wipes them out—as long as it's in good working order.

Certain feelings, beliefs, and experiences, then, can literally make you sick. Fortunately, your body is a system of checks and balances: You can practice other responses and adopt other beliefs that will reduce distress and strengthen your immune system.

Who's In Charge Here?

The problems in the preceding list reflect feeling out of control of what's happening in your life. Because this feeling correlates most strongly with the ill effects of distress, assessing your feeling of control is important to the stress-management program you'll be planning for yourself.

Luck, Work, Brains, and Fate: The Locus of Control Scale

Read each item, then consider whether or not you believe it to be true (at least 51% of the time) in your own life. If it is, mark it *T*; if not, mark it *F*.

— 1. I was promoted more because of my skills than because I happened to be in the right place at the right time.

— 2. Most problems solve themselves or go away if you just don't fuss with them.

— 3. I'd rather be smart than lucky.

— 4. Usually it's useless for me to try to get my own way at home.

— 5. Whether people like me or not depends on how I act.

— 6. In school, I didn't try very hard because I felt like the other kids were smarter than I was anyway.

— 7. Mostly, people can get their way if they're persistent.

— 8. I have (or have had) a good-luck charm.

— 9. Parents ought to let children make most of their own decisions.

— 10. People get mad at me, but they rarely have a reason to.

— 11. Hard work is what makes for success.

— 12. When my morning goes well, I know the whole day will be good no matter what I do.

— 13. If I try, I can keep from catching whatever "bug" is going around the office.

— 14. Sometimes bad things happen and nothing can be done to stop it.

— 15. My parents helped me when I asked them to.

— 16. My boss blames me for things that aren't my fault.

— 17. I have a lot of choice in deciding whom to be friends with.

— 18. It was next to impossible to change my parents' minds about anything.

— 19. When a team wins, it's more because of their fans' cheering than luck.

— 20. Sometimes wishing can make it so.

How to score your assessment. First notice the odd-numbered items (1, 3, 5, etc.). Circle only your ODD-numbered FALSE answers.

Now notice the even-numbered items (2, 4, 6, etc.). Circle only the EVEN-numbered TRUE answers.

Note the total number of circled items (Odd Falses and Even Trues) here: Total ——

The assessment above, based on the work of psychologists Marshall Duke and Stephen Nowicki, Jr., measures how much you think your behavior influences the world around you.

A low score of 0 to 4 circled items means that you see life as a game of skill rather than of chance. You generally believe that you can control what happens to you, both good and bad. You often take the initiative both professionally and personally, and people see you as an energetic person who finishes what (s)he starts. You're aware of and sensitive to what's happening around you. You take responsibility for both your achievements and your mistakes.

An average score of 5 to 8 means you've answered some items in each direction; for you, a feeling of being in control may be situation-specific. At home, for example, you may be able to persuade your family to accept your ideas and do what you'd like them to; but at work you may feel that your superiors call the shots and determine your rewards no matter what your competence or skills.

A high score of 9 to 20 suggests that to you, luck is more important than skills. Women and minorities often score high on this test, at least partly because they see the world realistically: Often they *do* have fewer job options, lower pay, and less opportunity for advancement, regardless of their skills or accomplishments.

However, a high score here also can mean that you believe luck or superstition affects your life more strongly than you do. To repeat: the feeling or conviction that you lack control over what happens to you correlates highly with frequent distress symptoms, poor physical health, depression, anxiety, and low self-esteem (much the same as the field-dependent and security orientations described earlier).

What Makes You Feel Good?

Now that you know what drives you up the wall and some of the reasons why, let's look at the brighter side:

What do you do that you really enjoy?
What makes you feel good about yourself?
What activities make you feel competent, hold your interest, and provide you with a comfortable degree of challenge?

Whether your answer was sports, lovemaking, dinner out with a friend, writing symphonies, or dozing in a hammock, you owe it to yourself to be as serious about your mental and physical health as you are about your new job. You can reverse the effects of distress by increasing the eustress in your life.

The Eustress Tally

Place a check mark by each item that, in your honest and considered opinion, you believe to be true:

___ My good qualities outweigh my bad
___ I enjoy working in groups and generally get along well with people
___ I avoid eating junk foods and get enough vitamins
___ Even when things go badly, I have confidence that I'll work things out eventually
___ The work I do is basically fulfilling though sometimes difficult
___ I'm generally realistic; I face the music when necessary
___ My job allows me to use my skills and intelligence

— I take regular vacations
— I like most of the tasks and activities I'm responsible for
— I feel in control of my life experiences and events
— I have at least some influence over what happens to me both at work and at home
— Even when I'm really down or depressed, it rarely lasts longer than a few days
— I enjoy getting away from it all now and then
— I have a good sense of humor; I like to laugh
— I have at least one good friend I trust and care about
— I take advantage of the company's free physical examination and health benefits (or provide my own)
— I don't worry excessively about problems at work or at home
— I make it a point to take some time for solitude or mindless fun
— I can laugh at myself
— I know when I'm getting tired, and I take a break or quit
— When I'm down or anxious, I'm aware of the reasons I'm feeling that way
— I don't keep busy just for the sake of looking busy
— I tend to see change as a challenge instead of a threat
— I get regular exercise, on my own, on a team, or at a health club
— I don't overuse alcohol, cigarettes, or drugs, and no one else thinks I overuse them
— I usually am able to solve problems at home and at work the way I'd like
— I see my physician when a cough or cold lasts more than a week
— I'm pretty good about "leaving the job at the office" when I go home
— I have at least one major interest outside my job that I spend time on and enjoy
— I have at least one or two people in my life who care about me and give me unconditional support and understanding when I need them

It will come as no surprise that the more items you've checked, the higher your resistance to disease, and the more generally satisfying your life. Out of the thirty items, a score of 10 is minimum for maintaining good health, and scores of 15 to 20 still have plenty of room for improvement. If you scored under 15, "Enhance Your Resources" and "Plan Your Action" include ideas and techniques you can make part of your daily routine.

You can retake these assessments in six months or a year to see how much you've changed.

Unavoidable Acts of God (and Humans)

So far we've been focusing on your personality and mental outlook, since they are the most significant indicators of how stress will affect you. External events, however, will also affect your health this year. Following is The Social Readjustment Scale, developed by Drs. Holmes and Rahe of the University of Washington Medical School. It measures the relative amount of stress that significant events—welcome or tragic—hold for people.

The Social Readjustment Scale

Circle the value for each item that applied to you in the last 12 months.

100	1.	Death of spouse
73	2.	Divorce
65	3.	Marital separation
63	4.	Jail term
63	5.	Death of close family member
53	6.	Personal injury or illness
50	7.	Fired from work
47	8.	Got married
45	9.	Marital reconciliation
45	10.	Retirement
44	11.	Change in health of family member
40	12.	Pregnancy
39	13.	Sexual difficulties
39	14.	Gain of new family member
39	15.	Business adjustment
38	16.	Change in financial state
37	17.	Death of a close friend
36	18.	Change to a different line of work
35	19.	Change in number of arguments with spouse
31	20.	Getting a major mortgage or loan (for a house, business, etc.)
30	21.	Foreclosure of mortgage or loan
29	22.	Change in work responsibilities
29	23.	Son or daughter leaving home
29	24.	Trouble with in-laws
28	25.	Outstanding personal achievement
26	26.	Spouse beginning or quitting work

26   27. Starting or ending school
25   28. Change in living conditions
24   29. Revision of personal habits
23   30. Trouble with boss
20   31. Change in work hours or conditions
20   32. Change in residence
20   33. Change in schools
19   34. Change in recreation
19   35. Change in church activities
18   36. Change in social activities
17   37. Mortgage or loan for lesser purchase (car, TV, appliances)
16   38. Change in sleeping habits
15   39. Change in number of family get-togethers
15   40. Change in eating habits
13   41. Vacations
12   42. Christmas
11   43. Minor violations of the law

Scoring: If your score is below 150, you can feel pretty safe; you have only a 1 in 3 chance of a serious health change in the next two years. A score of between 150 and 300 means that your chances go down to 1 in 2, or 50-50. Over 300 points means you need to begin a stress-management program immediately; there's a 90 percent chance that within two years you'll experience a serious change in your health.

Reprinted with permission from *Journal of Psychosomatic Research*, Volume 11, by Dr. T. H. Holmes, "The Social Readjustment Rating Scale." Copyright 1967, Pergamon Press, Ltd.

You'll note that many of the items on this list can be seen as positive events as well as negative—pregnancy, promotion, change in financial state, son or daughter leaving home, outstanding personal achievement, and so forth. Several other items will apply to you simply because you were promoted recently.

Now that you have a good idea of your field independence, security orientation, and eustress/control tallies, you can judge more realistically whether the events above will cause you health problems—or be a source of newfound energy. Even if you're an easygoing Type B who's thrilled with your new managerial role, remember that adjusting to change is in itself stressful. Guard your good health by incorporating some of the following suggestions and techniques into your life.

ST🖭P-UP   🖭NHANCE YOUR RESOURCES

Enhancing your resources simply means building on the above: creating more eustress and more quality relaxation for yourself, capitalizing on your strengths, minimizing your weaknesses, changing your perception of current stressors, and modifying how you react to stressful situations.

Before You Do Anything Else

If you're over the age of twenty-five, it's important to have a physical examination regularly, especially before you begin a diet or exercise program. If you're over thirty, it's vital. Over forty—do the words *crucial* and *essential* get our point across? Too many eager joggers/dieters/parachutists inadvertently harm themselves and their health by changing their routine without consulting a professional.

"Professional" doesn't mean just physicians, of course. Counselors, psychotherapists, psychologists, qualified hypnotists, nutritionists, support groups (like SmokEnders and Overeaters Anonymous, as well as informal networks) and formal professional organizations (discussed in chapter 10) can be effective stress-reduction resources. In addition to their primary services, they can offer the invaluable: objective feedback about your current state of stress. If your family and friends can't or don't support you in your new role, it makes sense to consult qualified experts.

Experts include people you know who have been in your position, in your own organization or elsewhere. A trusted colleague can give you inside information on general coping strategies, which boss's bark is worse than his bite, and who's really Godzilla in disguise. (For a detailed discussion of how to approach and question a colleague, refer to chapter 4, "Your Superiors.")

Listen to Your Body

Current research supports the notion that simply becoming a manager should reduce your stress: If distress is triggered not by the pressures of decision making but rather by the feeling that those decisions are useless, then you supposedly have less distress since you have more power. Indeed, top managers, with all their pressures, suffer less stress-related illness than subordinates who have less control over their jobs.

Until you get to be CEO, however, learning to recognize and respond to the following signals can significantly reduce the negative effects of distress:

Cold hands, especially if one hand is colder than the other

Indigestion, diarrhea, too frequent urination

Susceptibility to every cold, virus, or "bug" that goes around (your immune system may be weakening)

Muscle spasms; soreness or tightness in your jaw, back of neck, shoulders, lower back

Shortness of breath

Headaches, feeling tired most of the time, sleeping too much or too little

Becoming suddenly accident-prone

Unplug the Stress Messages; Turn Up the Encouragement

Even more important than recognizing stress symptoms is believing that you have the right to reduce the stress in your life: to stop feeling guilty or driven about work, and to stop thinking you have to please your superiors (or family) before you can take care of your own needs.

Taibi Kahler, building on Eric Berne's principles of Transactional Analysis, identified five "drivers" that result in stress and interfere with mental health. They are common messages that you heard from your parents or teachers when you were a child—on purpose or inadvertently, from supportive or demanding adults. Carried over into adult life, they can sabotage your feeling of control and satisfaction. They are:

Be perfect! For perfectionists, life is constant frustration. Though intellectually they may know their obsessive behavior is useless, they feel powerless to relax and find satisfaction in what they do, because nothing is ever good enough.

Hurry up! Typical of low-control Type A's, such people feel compelled to do everything at top speed (driving to work, presenting reports, making love) even if they have adequate time. No matter how much they do, there's always more waiting.

Try harder! If at first they don't succeed, they try, try again—and again. No one ever told them to try something *different*, to abuse their plan or plan again. They attack the same problem the same unsuccessful way, which only causes more failure and wasted time.

Please others! These individuals put their needs last, yet don't always get the rewards or necessities they assume others will provide—and feel guilty asking for them. Frustration and low self-esteem result.

Be strong! An unrealistic sense of responsibility keeps these people working through illness and even exhaustion. They find it difficult to relax and delegate work, usually until they're too sick to get out of bed.

Almost everyone has one of these messages on a tape loop playing in the back of his or her head, especially when the pressure's on. The next time you hear it, and every time after that, unplug the tape—and reassure yourself instead:

> "It's okay to be satisfied with a good job—I don't have to be perfect to be good."
>
> "It's okay to take my time and enjoy what I'm doing."
>
> "It's okay to do something different, to try a new angle, or decide this problem isn't worth solving after all."
>
> "It's okay to ask clearly for everything I need, and to say a tactful no when I choose to, as others do."
>
> "It's okay to rest when I'm tired or stressed, and to expect others to carry their share of the load."

You're Entitled to Change Your Approach: A Selection of Stress-Management Techniques

BEHAVIOR REHEARSAL   Often people tend to recreate in adult life the same situations that gave them trouble when they were younger and less experienced. If, for example, you were shy or a poor leader as a teenager, you don't need to remember that old behavior and reproduce it now. Rather, choose someone whose leadership you admire, and act as if *you* were that person. Rehearse in your mind—better yet, aloud with a friend—the situations that make you feel uncomfortable. Actually try the new behavior on for size. (If at first you feel silly doing this, you'll know it's working.)

If you were the meanest foreman in the company, used to yelling at the crew to get your way, you no longer have to shout to get your point across to other managers. You don't have to change your personality, just your behavior—and only in certain circumstances. Most people think that if they change their attitude about themselves, their behavior will automatically follow. This, while often true, is very difficult. But changing your *behavior* first, especially emulating the actions of someone you admire, is much easier. Gradually, actions that felt alien at first will feel comfortably like "you," and your attitude and self-concept will change as well.

BE YOUR OWN P.R. PERSON   When introducing ideas or making requests, position what you say to be attractive and beneficial to your boss or client. A bank, for example, wanted to keep its low-balance customers from using tellers and encourage them to use the more cost-effective cash machines. To the managers' surprise, customers resented the change, saw it as a privilege that was being taken from them, and angrily refused to cooperate. Management's mistake? They neglected to position—that is, redefine—the change as a customer benefit ("They're available twenty-four hours a day! Less waiting, fewer mistakes! A computer you'll love!"), even more desirable than the status quo. You can position yourself this way too. The "everybody wins" approach encourages you to think well of your ideas; when you *act* as if your proposal will be accepted, as if people will of course treat you as you want them to, they will pick up on and respond to those self-confident cues.

YOUR OWN HEAD-START PROGRAM   Rather than ignoring or denying predictable crises, face situational stressors early and give yourself a head start on managing them—or planning again. Whenever you feel anticipatory anxiety coming on, force yourself to stop catastrophizing. Instead, substitute a *positive* self-fulfilling prophecy: "Dean Frankenstein went wild last year when the grants were due, and he's starting to do it again. I'll delegate the work tomorrow, keep him posted by memo, and avoid him when possible. I don't have to buy into his craziness to get the work in on time."

If time is already impossibly short, pull the plug on your if-only's and I-should-have's and immediately substitute action for self-castigation. It will reduce your anxiety better than anything else. At home, allow yourself time to feel angry or upset; then deliberately let go of the problem until you're back at work and can do more about it. If all hell is breaking loose in your company and little you can do will help, your job is to manage your inevitable chronic stress: Get adequate sleep, take extra physical care of yourself, and involve yourself in non-work-related activities to give your mind a rest.

EXERCISE: AEROBICS, CALISTHENICS, ET CETERA   You have no time for exercise? That's no excuse (see "Time Management," below). No facilities? The only "facilities" you really need are a pair of decent running shoes. Whether or not you're wearing them, you can take the stairs instead of the elevator, walk to work or park on the far side of the lot, play more ball with your girl (or boy or spouse or friend), join or start a neighborhood volleyball team, or jog. If your town has a Y or your company a fitness program, you're all set (your standing at work won't suffer if you're seen at the gym, either). Until you've experienced it, the energetic stamina aerobics provides is difficult to imagine. Your resistance goes up, and the new sense of control over how you feel is a big psychological plus.

STE℗-UP ℙLAN YOUR ACTION

Strategic Habit-Breaking

One of the most difficult things about breaking existing habits and starting new ones is that we're usually smack in the middle of the habit (or further) before we're even aware of it.

Whatever drives you craziest—impromptu speaking at meetings or presentations, sudden conflicts with co-workers or family, business travel, or getting through your busy season—you can plan for such encounters, use them to practice your new behavior, and enjoy calming down afterward.

- *Before* a stressful event, close your eyes and use your imagination. Visualize the setting and people involved. Watch the scenario unfold as it usually does; then replay it in your mind. This time, see yourself acting more forceful (positive, calm—whatever) about it. Visualize the other people responding accordingly. Don't worry about being strictly realistic; the important thing is to see yourself doing well. Run through this movie-in-your-mind several times until it seems familiar to you; in fact, develop it into a mini-series. The more you envision it, the less unnerving the real thing will be.
- *During* the stressful event, be nice to yourself. Don't let your inner voice undermine your assurance ("Oh, God, he'll never go for this idea—why did I ask for this meeting?"). Concentrate on reassuring yourself that you're changing, and that's what counts ("It was difficult for me to ask at all, and I did it. That's a big first step.").
- *After* the event, refuse to criticize yourself even if you did do poorly. Change the "Why-didn't-I-do-that!" to "Next-time-I'll-try-this." Then give yourself a genuine pat on the back for what you *did* do well ("I remembered all the points I wanted to make—I was smart to make notes beforehand."). Treat yourself to a reward just for having *tried* a new behavior. And give yourself a break: Enjoy the relief of getting through it alive before you start thinking about how you'll do next time.

Relaxation 101

Astonishing as it sounds, many people literally don't know what it feels like to be completely relaxed. These relaxation exercises can be used at any time, in (almost) any place, and will relieve many stress symptoms. They also feel extremely good. The more you do them, the more quickly you can replace the tension and stress in your body with relaxation.

DEEP BREATHING   This may be the only relaxation technique you'll ever need, even when you're in the middle of a nerve-racking meeting. Responding immediately to the signals noted above (cold hands, headaches, etc.) with deep breathing not only reduces the effects of stress, but puts you in psychological control as well. Few of us learn to take deep breaths regularly; we experience shallow breathing as "normal," but it's not. (Some people respond to stressors by scarcely breathing at all.)

Deep breathing means using your abdomen, not just your chest muscles. Learn to feel your stomach expand; take a deep breath right now and try to "break your belt." Don't hold your breath; let your diaphragm push out the air from your lungs naturally. Relax, let your shoulders drop, and take five more deep breaths right now. Focus on your stomach muscles as you inhale and on your diaphragm as you exhale. If you feel a little lightheaded at first, it's not that you're hyperventilating; you're just getting more oxygen than you're used to. Regular deep breathing, not just when you feel stress, will increase your stamina by strengthening your lungs and the amount of oxygen they can hold.

THE FIVE-MINUTE VACATION   You can discreetly do this at your desk anytime you need a mental break. If you ordinarily spend twenty minutes a day getting coffee or soft drinks (which do nothing to reduce your stress level), try a shorter coffee break and a few 5MVs:

- Sit comfortably (if you can't leave your desk, rest your chin or forehead in your hand, as if you're concentrating on papers before you).
- Take your phone off the hook or hold your calls.
- Take several deep breaths and let your eyes defocus or close, whichever you prefer.
- As you breathe deeply, use your imagination to reconstruct a scene from the most pleasant vacation you can remember. Use all your senses: feel the sun warm your face, hear the crash of the waves, smell the salt air and suntan oil, feel the sand under your feet, taste (and

feel) the cool drink in your hand, see the sunlight glint on the water.
· See the scene in real or fantasized detail: color, light, other people. Put yourself in the scene; breathe, relax, enjoy. If outside thoughts intrude, brush them away by recalling, "I'm at the beach (campsite, Disneyland) now" and breathing deeply again. Continue to live in your scene until you feel yourself relaxing; enjoy the calm for a few minutes, then leave the scene, slowly open your eyes, and (if you feel like it) stretch.

Five-minute vacations make a perfect reward at the end of an hour's boring work, and you'll see your productivity and calmness increase. If a tight deadline has you so tense you can hardly work, it's a perfect antidote. (Encourage your staff to take them too!)

CHANGE YOUR SCENERY   If you can get away from your desk or office when stress hits, do so—even for a few minutes. Take a jog around the floor or the block to drain that epinephrine (if you're nervous) and get your circulation going (if you feel like lead). As you run, pretend you're seeing everything for the first time (or concentrate on something delicious you're going to have for dinner)—otherwise your mind will remain stuck on the same problems and the stress reaction will continue.

ENCOURAGE YOURSELF   Is your inner voice nagging you that you foolishly let Mr. Rickles get the better of you again, and that trying to relax now is just a waste of time? Refuse to listen to such sabotage; acknowledge that you're upset or angry, then reassure yourself that relaxing is good for your health. *Then* you can replan how you'll handle Rickles next time.

TAKE OFF YOUR WATCH   Sacrilege? Heresy? Impossibility? No. Try it for a few weeks. "Hurry-sickness" is one of the prime traits of high-risk Type A's. If having no timepiece in the office would raise your anxiety instead of lower it, work up to it by forgetting your watch on weekends and evenings. We guarantee you'll survive.

OVERCOMING COMMUTER STRESS   You don't have to drive to drive yourself crazy; subways and buses now do it for you. This process will reduce the muscle tension, generalized anxiety, palpitations, dizziness, faintness, and nausea that often accompany commuting. You can't avoid the trip, but you can change your reaction to commuting and use it to enhance your health while you minimize negative effects.

- Face up to the hassle: Acknowledge that delays, crowding, and general unpleasantness are part of your life twice a day. Simple conscious acknowledgment helps minimize frustration and puts you in control.
- Center yourself: To stop your mind from racing and worrying, concentrate on counting five deep, slow breaths, with your eyes closed if possible. Raise your shoulders, drop them, and smile. Repeat.
- Body scan: Mentally scan your body from head to toe, noticing each area where muscles are tense or tight.
- Flex-relax: Start with your feet and work up. Concentrate on flexing your toes, holding the tension, and then letting it go. Relax your toes, and enjoy how they feel. Keep breathing deeply and regularly as you slowly repeat this process—flex and tighten, then relax—your leg, stomach, back, chest, shoulder, neck, and facial muscles.
- Sail away: After all your muscles have been tensed and relaxed, and you're settled on the bus, continue breathing deeply. Take another five-minute vacation, daydreaming or fantasizing about a relaxing setting. (You may have to force yourself at first, but you can do it.)

By the way, the body-scan, flex-relax, and sail-away activities work even better when you can quietly sit or lie down at home. Even sitting at work, you can tense your muscles by pushing your feet against the floor and arms against the chair.

Other hints: If you dread the rush-hour drive, try waiting an hour (not necessarily in your office) for the traffic to decrease. Play soothing music in the car (or on your headphones) or listen to books on tape; anything to take your mind off the frustration of the situation. If you can break the monotony by taking a different route to work, by all means do so.

Time Management

Time-management techniques are simply another form of planning, because managing your time really means managing yourself. In *How to Get Control of Your Time and Your Life*, time-management consultant Alan Lakein offers seven rules that virtually guarantee an hour saved per day—time for you to exercise, rest, or do whatever makes you feel good.

- *List your goals, then set your priorities.* Sound familiar? This time, however, you're doing it for your lifetime goals, both professional and personal. Then make another list for your five-year goals; and another for six-month goals. Everything you do should move you closer to accomplishing these objectives. If not, seriously consider whether you're not wasting precious time.

· *Make a to-do list every day* and set priorities here too. *A* means a must-do; *B*: important, but could wait; *C*: can be put off indefinitely.
· *Start with As, not Cs.* Sure it's easier to fill out this week's schedule (which you could do blindfolded) than tackle a major new project (where do you begin?). But the project is an *A* and the schedule a *C*. There's always *some* small task you can do to get started on a huge one. Figure it out, and do it first. The momentum will probably carry you along to accomplishing more than you thought you could.
· *"What is the best use of my time right now?"* is a priority-setting question to ask yourself frequently. (And sometimes the best answer is "Relax.") Whatever the answer, it should move you toward your unit's goals or your personal goals.
· *After sorting them, handle papers only once.* Reading and shuffling papers without taking action on them wastes thousands of people-hours. Don't pick it up unless you can do *something* to move it along if not get it off your desk for good.
· *Do it now*—right now, while you're thinking of it. Do not get coffee first, or water the plants, or pass Go, or collect $200. Instead, reward yourself after you've done it.
· *Follow the 80/20 rule.* Have you ever noticed the fascinating fact that 80 percent of your meals out are eaten in the same 20 percent of your favorite restaurants? And that 80 percent of the time you select from the same 20 percent of your favorite outfits? Similarly, 80 percent of your sales come from 20 percent of your customers (and these are certainly your "A" customers); 20 percent of your staff gives you 80 percent of your discipline problems, and a different 20 percent of your staff probably turns out 80 percent of the best work. In other words, concentrate your efforts on the 20 percent of people and procedures (and that includes exercise and relaxation) that, for you, produce the most and the best. You can gradually decrease time spent on the rest with little loss.

STEP-UP USE AND ABUSE YOUR PLAN

Practice, Practice, Practice!

The secrets of the universe and of the ages (and of this chapter) will do you no earthly good unless you *act* on them. Using your plan means practicing your chosen new patterns of behavior!

You say you can't remember to practice? You're too set in your ways?

Make routine work for you, not against you. Plan to do some time management, some deep breathing, some encouraging messages.

· Do them every time you encounter a particular stressor: before meetings, at 4:00 P.M., when you have to talk to certain colleagues or clients, when it's time to tackle a mound of paperwork. Soon these formerly dreaded stressors will look less forbidding because you know you can control your reaction to them.
· Have your secretary or a co-worker (or your spouse, kids, friends, wristwatch alarm, etc.) remind you several prearranged times a day to take five minutes for your health.
· Build it into your schedule. Let your subordinates know that you're convinced stress management is important. With your boss's okay, organize (or delegate) a brief, structured "stretch break" twice a day, if it's feasible in your workplace. Encourage (don't force) your staff to attend—and always attend yourself.

Take a few minutes now to go back through the relaxation exercises and coping strategies in the preceding sections. Jot down the ones that appeal to you in the spaces below. Think also about activities (strenuous or not) that make you laugh and/or feel competent: socializing, entertainment, sports, and so forth. Jot these down too.

Now circle three (and no more than three) activities that you want to incorporate into your daily routine.

_____   _____   _____

_____   _____   _____

_____   _____   _____

Then choose the *one* (yes, only one) technique that sounds easiest; the one you will have the least trouble doing regularly. Make a contract with yourself:

THE FIRST WEEK
· Do it at least once a day for the first week, if it's a brief activity that takes no more than twenty minutes.
· Do it at least twice during the week if it's a longer activity (playing volleyball, for example).

THE SECOND WEEK
· Add one more brief technique from your list. Again, promise yourself that you will do it once a day—then do it!

THE THIRD WEEK

· Add nothing new. Congratulate yourself for keeping to your plan, and don't get down on yourself if you've forgotten or missed some days. Reconfirm your commitment to reduce your stress, and Do It Now.

If you wish to practice your chosen techniques more often, by all means do so. But under no circumstances should you set yourself up to fail by promising to make major changes in your life all at once.

Whatever you've chosen to do to reduce the effects of stress in your life, be prepared to feel strange at first when you do it. That's normal. (In fact, the stranger you feel, the more you can congratulate yourself that you're replacing your old habits with new ones. Just like those sore muscles the day after you start exercising—the ache reminds you that you've done something good for yourself, and they don't hurt for long.)

Stick to your program for three weeks, no more. See how it feels to make time for people and activities that affect you positively. Then fine-tune your plan during the fourth week, junking what didn't work well and expanding upon the activities that made you feel good about yourself.

· Did jogging feel physically good, but bore you stiff? Try running with a partner, at a gym, or consider another workout technique. You won't stick with anything that provides only minimal satisfaction.

· Did you assume that since you spend your day talking to people about their problems, you automatically need time by yourself to unwind—only to find you were a miserable failure at trying to nap for half an hour after work? Maybe for you relaxation means more time with people—people who'll listen to you unload about *your* problems, or extroverted friends who can take you out of yourself so you can relax and forget about work.

STEP-UP PLAN AND PLAN AGAIN

Chances are good that after a month you'll feel noticeably better physically and mentally. If you're still worried about the time you're spending on reducing the distress in your life, think again about how you can use time-saving techniques. Once you're hooked on eustress, however, you won't want to stop. Feeling healthy feels too good!

Of course, the same stress-management program won't suit you for the rest of your life. Once you've resolved to make lower stress a top priority, don't hesitate to try something you've never done before. Exploring in itself provides a nice shot of eustress epinephrine.

If your original stress plan didn't work well, or didn't suit you, why? List the reasons (no matter how irrational they may sound) here:

1. _____

2. _____

3. _____

If you were still adjusting to the effects of the change itself, you may be sabotaging yourself by not going ahead with your plan for another week or two. It takes as much time to get used to relaxing as it does to readjust to more work, so give yourself every chance.

Addicts and Carriers

In some cases, you may need to examine and rethink your most basic priorities. If your program didn't seem to affect you (or if you managed to completely ignore doing it), you may be one of the folks discussed earlier in "Tally Your Resources": a stress addict. Do you suspect you're hooked on that epinephrine rush more than you thought? Do you enjoy being in overdrive so much that now—thanks to relaxing twice a day—you feel somehow lost without it?

Many managers do. Paradoxical as it sounds, once a person gets rid of the monkey on his back, he misses its company. If you feel like climbing the walls now that you're not madly rushing around, or if you've begun "relaxing with a vengeance" like Gus in the opening story, it's wise indeed to "plan again."

First, every time you hear those "you should be working harder" voices in your head, replace them with the following:

Relaxed people accomplish more because they're truly in control

Competent people take care of their health

I can do good work, relax, and enjoy it, all at the same time

It feels strange now, and that's normal. Soon I'll be used to my new routine

Still have excess type-A energy coursing through your nervous system? Instead of spending it on spurious crises or things you could delegate, channel it where it will do you some good. Reread your six-month goals list, and add to it if necessary. What is it *you* really want to do? What will make you feel good about yourself and in control of your work or your personal life?

Then translate those goals into tasks:

· I want to develop a new proposal that will utilize my capabilities and expand my knowledge

- I want to learn more about _____ on my own or in a class
- I want to complete the following personal project: _____
- I want to spend more time with these people: _____

If you're a stress addict, chances are you're a stress *carrier* as well. Stress carriers may *feel* little distress (or enjoy their epinephrine rushes), but their aggressive attitudes create serious stress problems for their subordinates. Remember that because they have less authority, your staff are even more susceptible to job stress than you are. Their distress means lower productivity, which in turn means problems for you as their manager. Encourage your people to take care of themselves, to give their work their best shot, but not to overdo it. That way everybody wins.

The human body is amazingly resilient. No matter what fiendish things you've been doing to yourself up to now, you *can* overcome years of physical distress by retraining how you think (substituting encouraging thoughts for self-critical ones), how you react (taking the time to plan your action rather than falling into old ruts), and how you treat yourself (by following a healthy exercise schedule).

You may still be wondering whether stress management really works, or if it's worth all the time and effort. It is. Whenever you doubt it, remember: Nobody ever complained on his deathbed, "I wish I'd spent more time on my business." Give yourself the time to relax and enjoy the success you've achieved.

Index

absences, employee's unexpected,
  100
achievement orientation:
  behavior associated with, 150–151
  boss's, 59, 62–63
  dangers in, 153–154
  leadership style and, 153–154
  personal/task orientation and, 257
  rewards geared to, 151–152
action plans, 4–5, 23–29
  in budget planning, 190–195
  for changes, 88–92
  for computer competency, 210–218
  in correcting subordinates, 160–65
  in delegating responsibility,
    118–120, 125–126
  in employee development, 141–160
  evaluation of, 28–29
  for gathering information on boss,
    67–74
  inquiry phase in, 26
  in learning new job, 22–29
  in networking, 234–235
  organization phase in, 23
  in people management, 43–49
  for performance evaluation,
    141–147
  priority list in, 28
  reading phase in, 23–25
  revisions in, see revised plans
  in STEP-UP program, 4
  in stress management, 268–272
  work avoidance and, 27–28

  see also plans, planning
activity budgets, 192–193
adrenaline, see epinephrine
advocacy, employee, see employee
  development; promotions, employee's affiliation, need for, see
  socialization orientation
annual reports, budget planning and,
  189–190
appointments, scheduling of, 38, 40
assertiveness training, 141
assignment schedules, 14
attitudes, personal:
  stress and, 247, 256
  subordinate's positional, 46–48

Berne, Eric, 265
biases, 50
body language, 65, 71
body scan (relaxation technique), 271
bosses of managers, 53–77
  achievement orientation of, 59,
    62–63
  action plan for gathering informa-
    tion on, 67–74
  in budget making, 179–180,
    185–186, 191, 194, 198
  committee assignment and,
    231–232, 235–236
  and communication with pre-
    decessor, 44–45
  control orientation of, 59, 62–63

277